I SHOULD CARE

(Photo: Universal Pictures)

I SHOULD CARE
The Sammy Cahn Story

BY

SAMMY CAHN

ARBOR HOUSE

New York

"I Should Care"

I should care, I should go around weeping
I should care, I should go without sleeping
Maybe I won't find someone as lovely as you,
But I should care,—and I do!

For all my beautiful friends,
but most of all for my beautiful Tita

ACKNOWLEDGMENTS

"All The Way"/Copyright © 1957 by Maraville Music Corporation/Used by permission

"Be My Love"/Copyright © 1949, 1950, 1951 by Metro-Goldwyn-Mayer, Inc./Used by permission

"Because You're Mine"/Copyright © 1951, 1952 by Metro-Goldwyn-Mayer, Inc./Used by permission

"Bei Mir Bist du Schön"/Copyright © 1933, 1937 by Harmes, Inc./Used by permission

"Call Me Irresponsible"/Copyright © 1962, 1963 by Paramount Music Corp./Used by permission

"The Christmas Waltz"/Copyright © 1954 by Sands Music Corp./Used by permission

"Come Fly With Me"/Copyright © 1958 by Maraville Music Corp./Used by permission

"Day By Day"/Copyright © 1945 by Barton Music Corp./Used by permission

"Ev'rybody Has The Right To Be Wrong"/Copyright © 1965 by Sammy Cahn & James Van Heusen/Used by permission

"Five Minutes More"/Copyright © 1946 by Morley Music Co., Inc./Used by permission

"Guess I'll Hang My Tears Out to Dry"/Copyright © 1944 by Chappell & Co., Inc./Used by permission

"High Hopes"/Copyright © 1959 by Sincap Productions, Inc.,1959 by Maraville Music Corp./Used by permission

"I Should Care"/Copyright © 1944 by Dorsey Brothers, Inc./Used by permission

"I, Yes Me! That's Who!"/Copyright © 1970 by Chappell & Co., Inc./Used by permission

"If You Should Leave"/Copyright © 1937 by Chappell & Co., Inc./Used by permission

"I'll Walk Alone"/Copyright © 1944 by Morley Music Co., Inc./Used by permission

"I'm A Musical, Magical Man"/Copyright © 1974 by Warner Bros./Used by permission

"I'm From B'postrophe"/Copyright © 1944 by Stratford Music Co., Inc./Used by permission

"It's Been A Long, Long Time"/Copyright © 1945 by Morley Music Co., Inc./Used by permission

"It's Magic"/Copyright © 1948 by M. Witmark & Sons, Inc./Used by permission

"I've Heard That Song Before"/Copyright © 1942 by Morley Music Co./Used by permission

"Look To Your Heart"/Copyright © 1955 by Barton Music Corp./Used by permission

"Love and Marriage"/Copyright © 1955 by Maraville Music Corp./Used by permission

"My Kind of Town"/Copyright © 1964 by Sergeant Music Co., Glorste Inc., Van Heusen Music Corp./Used by permission

"Please Be Kind"/Copyright © 1938 by Harms, Inc./Used by permission

"Pocket Full of Miracles"/Copyright © 1961 by Maraville Music Corp./Used by permission

"Rhythm Is Our Business"/Copyright © 1935 and renewed 1962 by Laursteed Music Co./Used by permission

"Saturday Night Is The Loneliest Night of The Week"/Copyright © 1944 by Barton Music Corp./Used by permission

"Say One For Me"/Copyright © 1958 by Feist, Inc./Used by permission

"The Second Time Around"/Copyright © 1960 by Twentieth Century Music Corp./Used by permission

"Stardust"/Copyright © 1928 by Hoagy Carmichael/Copyright © 1929 by Mills Music Co./Used by permission

"Swanee"/Copyright © 1919 by New World Music Corp., renewed 1952/Used by permission

"Teach Me Tonight"/Copyright © 1953, 1954 by Hub Music Co./Used by permission

"The Tender Trap"/Copyright © 1955 by Barton Music Corp./Used by permission

"Thoroughly Modern Millie"/Copyright © 1967 by Northern Music Co./Used by permission

"Three Coins In The Fountain"/Copyright © 1954 by Robbins Music Corp./Used by permission

"Time After Time"/Copyright © 1947 by Sands Music Corp./Used by permission

"Until The Real Thing Comes Along"/Copyright © 1936 by Chappell & Co./Used by permission

"Walking Happy"/Copyright © 1962 by Famous Music Corp. & Paramount Pictures Corp./Used by permission

"You're a Lucky Guy"/Copyright © 1939 by M. Witmark & Sons, Copyright © renewed 1966 by Laursteed Music Co., Van Heusen Music Corp., Shapiro, Bernstein & Co., Inc./Used by permission

Contents

PREFACE *"Look to Your Heart"* 9

CHAPTER 1 *"Shake Your Head From Side to Side"* 15

CHAPTER 2 *"Rhythm Is Our Business"* 33

CHAPTER 3 *"The Things We Did Last Summer"* 55

CHAPTER 4 *"Bei Mir Bist Du Schön"* 63

CHAPTER 5 *"I've Heard That Song Before"* 73

CHAPTER 6 *"It's Magic"* 95

CHAPTER 7 *"Guess I'll Hang My Tears Out to Dry"* 103

CHAPTER 8 *"Love and Marriage"* 119

CHAPTER 9 *"All the Way"* 129

CHAPTER 10 *"The Tender Trap"* 149

CHAPTER 11 *"Three Coins in the Fountain"* 173

CHAPTER 12 *"Please Be Kind"* 181

CHAPTER 13 *"Until the Real Thing Comes Along"* 191

CHAPTER 14 *"Come Fly With Me"* 207

CHAPTER 15 *"The Second Time Around"* 217

CHAPTER 16 *"Call Me Irresponsible"* 223

CHAPTER 17 *"I'll Walk Alone"* 243

CHAPTER 18 *"You're a Lucky Guy"* 255

Appendix ... *Makes Strong Men Whimper*

and Women Faint 273

Lyrics 277

Songography 309

Index 313

"Look to Your Heart"

Look to your heart
When there are words to say
And never leave your love unspoken

Speak your love
To those who seek your love
Look to your heart
Your heart will know, what to say
Look to your heart—today!

JULE STYNE, my long-time collaborator, on two occasions said to me, "Open with the closing"; I'm sitting here in my dressing room at the Golden Theatre, where *Words and Music—Sammy Cahn* on the life and times of Sammy Cahn—has improbably become a hit, and I guess what I'm doing now is opening with the closing.

Improbable? To me it hardly seemed even possible that anyone would be interested in my life story, but, as with so many things in my life, the impossible became possible, thanks to a few people and a lot of luck.

Arthur Pine, the literary agent, having seen to the putting together of an autobiography of my chum Phil Silvers, came to me and asked if I'd be interested. I said, "If anybody's interested, I guess I am," and I told him I could bring it off if I had the help of a professional writer—and one emerged in the person of Jerry Tallmer of *The New York Post*, whose work I'd long admired. The third and most crucial interested party turned out to be Donald Fine, the head of Arbor House, the firm whose imprint is on the spine of this book. From first to last Don Fine has been a dear, decent, and dependable taskmaster.

And now that I'm opening with the closing, and am living the most incredible "rub of the lamp," I want to mention the people I call "my Aladdins." If you rub a lamp, you get an Aladdin— at least I always have, going back to Jack Kapp, who opened the doors of the recording world to me via Decca Records, and Morris and Elsa Stoloff, who opened the doors to Columbia Pictures.

In my first venture onto the Broadway stage, my Aladdins must begin with Pat and Morris Uchitel. Morris Uchitel is a phenomenal Horatio Alger who started within a block of me on New York's Lower East Side; along with his brothers he went into the business of manufacturing that item without which no jacket can be made: coat fronts, which are the coarse inner lining and shoulder pad of the coat. Morris parlayed this mundane feature into a personal fortune that led to his greatest fortune, his wife Pat, a marvel among women.

Many years ago, as you will see in the pages that follow, I was trying to get Doris Day a part in the film *Romance on the High Seas*. Little did I know that Pat Uchitel, then Pat Brewster, was trying to land the same role through the good offices of Ray Heindorf, musical director of Warner Brothers. Actually, I never found this out until years later. I am not sure if Doris Day, who got the part, came up with as fine a prize in the end as Pat did with Morris Uchitel. For Pat's last birthday I managed to scrape up the only thing left of her screen test for *Romance on the High Seas*—the vocal track of Pat singing a Ray Heindorf song called "I'm in a Jam with Baby," which will

"*Words and Music.*"   (Photo: Martha Swope, New York)

"Words and Music." The cast.   (Photo: Martha Swope, New York

never quite rank in the catalogue with his classic "Some Sunday Morning."

Pat and Morris came into my dressing room after I opened in *Words and Music* and proclaimed the layout insufficiently splendid. I said, "Morris, I don't want you to do anything about the architecture or the decor of this dressing room. I may be out of here next week." Morris saw the logic of that statement. When producer Alex Cohen later assured me I would be in the theater through the following September and maybe November, eight months away, I allowed Pat and Morris, along with my lovely wife Tita, to take over the redecoration of the dressing room. They hired Harry Hinson & Co. to come up with a new wall pattern that's a sort of elegant spin-off from the original Shubert green, which must have been applied during the first run of Rudolf Friml's *Desert Song*. Along with Harry Hinson came John Rosselli, who wanted to empty his antique store on East 72nd Street—all the ashtrays here are his—as well as Lauren and Bobby Peltz; he's president of Flagstaff Foods, from which come all the wastebaskets. Benoit Dreyfus, an importer of rare jewelry and a friend, wanted to supply a gold star for the door. I said, "A gold star? They'll take away the star, the door, and the building." Seema and Ivan Boesky would not be dissuaded from chipping in. He's a Wall Street broker, and since she's the daughter of Ben Silberstein, owner of the Beverly Hills Hotel, I figured, well, it won't hurt them too much to go for the elephant coffee table that's now on display here. There's Warren and Josette Cowan, who keep sending cases of Cutty Sark, and Mrs. Harry Gould, from whom flows all the vodka, and Mel and Joseph Axler, who nightly provide me with one of their fine Beuche-Girod watches.

Special thanks to Dasha and Henry Epstein, who added a room to their Bedford, Mass., home so Tita and I would have a hideaway from the theater, and to Irving and Jackie Mansfield

(Jacqueline Susann), loyal friends who never let a day go by without checking in.

Last but far from least, Frances and Andrea Basile, who are, in the appropriate respective order, my mother-in-law and my sister-in-law: My mother-in-law spends her days knitting doilies and making pillows for me, and Andrea, being in fashion on that avenue which is two blocks west of Fifth—we *never* say Seventh Avenue—has been steering every buyer who comes to town to the Golden, to see the show or maybe the dressing room, whichever is the bigger attraction at this point.

Just before the deal for the show was closed I was told there were five "points" left, representing $5000 worth of investment in *Words and Music*. This presented me with a quandary. Morris Uchitel would have put up the entire sum if I'd asked, so I didn't ask. I gave a total of one point ($1000) to my four sisters, Sayde (Mrs. Sam Bernstein), Pearl (Mrs. Joe Zodi), Florence (Mrs. Jules Goldberg) and Evelyn (Mrs. Abe Greenberg) and their men. One point gone. Tita and my manager Ed Traubner took a point between them. Two points gone. Pat and Morris got one point. Three points gone. Bobby Peltz took one point. Four points gone. In desperation I passed along the last point to Benoit Dreyfus, Harry Hinton, and John Rosselli—and to the other love of my life, Helen Lee Caldwell, designer of children's clothes based on the characters in Milne's Pooh books.

Was I done? Was I safe? No. There were still Irma and Justin Bayer, not of the aspirins but of that material which is the backing for all needlepoint . . . I told Justin, "No way." How did I know he was a distant cousin of associate producer Harvey Granat? Justin came up with his own point.

Peace and love to you all.

CHAPTER 1

"Shake Your Head From Side to Side"

Anytime you're feeling low,
Wanna make your troubles go,
Shake your head from side to side . . .

As a kid I certainly wasn't a sissy, but I was very slight and wore glasses and always carried a violin case, so I wasn't exactly a *shtarker*, the big stud in the gang, the fella who can put his big fists on the cheeks of any of the *pishers* any time he wants—which makes him the *shtarker*. But the fellows all loved me because I was very mischievous. I was the kind of fella who would surreptitiously tie the window-shade cord to the briefcase of the teacher's favorite, knowing that at the first sound of the bell he would tear out of the room and pull down the window shade, hitting three students on the head and starting a riot. One of my favorite daydreams was to set off the fire alarm. Day in and day out I would stare at the little hammer hanging alongside the little window with the line: "BREAK IN CASE OF FIRE." One day, full of courage and anticipation, I lifted that hammer, and an amazing thing happened —a billion-to-one coincidence. All the bells in the building began to ring. I ran out of that building—P.S. 147—and didn't come back for two weeks.

When a fella had a date in those days and needed some money he would steal something he could sell right away to a junk dealer. I remember this one guy, a real *shtarker*. He came to see me one time and said: "I need a bathtub, I got a date." I knew he didn't need to bathe in it. I said: "I can't get you a bathtub." He said: "You'll steer for me." We went up to the fourth floor of this building to an empty apartment and he uncoupled this white bathtub from the plumbing. We're coming down past the second floor, I in front, steering, and he carrying the bathtub, when he suddenly shouted: "Watch out!" The bathtub slipped out of his hands. I went over the side, over the banister, and watched the bathtub crash down the stairs and through the door of an apartment. I never will forget this family seated around the kitchen table watching an uninvited bathtub come to dinner. Needless to say, no sale.

One summer I was on Grand Street with my buddy Frankie Miggs when this same big guy came up to us. He was in his underwear—the kind that looked like an old-fashioned bathing suit. He said to us: "Well, I'll see you guys. I've got to go over to the Gouverneur Hospital." We said: "What do you mean?" He said: "I got a busted arm." "You got a busted *arm?*" "Yeah, I was playing handball this morning at Cox's in Coney Island and I went for a shot and slipped and busted my arm. I went to the hospital but it was crowded and I got tired of waiting and said the hell with it and left." He'd been walking around all day with that broken arm. I guess if you're a *pisher* the pain must be incredible, but for a *shtarker?*

Frankie said: "Get dressed immediately." The *shtarker* said: "Why do I need to get dressed to go to Gouverneur Hospital?" Frankie said: "Just get dressed." A little while later, resplendent in his suit, shirt, and tie, the *shtarker* and Frankie headed for the Fifth Avenue bus, the *shtarker* protesting all the way: "What are we doing on the Fifth Avenue bus? This don't go to the Gouverneur Hospital." Frankie: "Just be quiet and sit

still." So here they are, heading uptown, away from Gouverneur Hospital, busted arm sitting on the aisle, Frankie alongside him. All the way uptown Frankie is whispering to busted
arm: "When I push you, I want you to fall in that aisle and let
out all the screams of pain you've been holding in all day."
There's a certain point the Fifth Avenue bus makes a sharp
turn, and when it did, that evening, the *horrible* screams of pain
that echoed in that bus caused all the windows on the street to
open, the horrified bus driver to almost go up on the sidewalk,
the passengers to quiver. And Frankie is yelling: "His arm is
broke! His arm is broke!" By the time the bus got uptown
there were already two lawyers from the bus company, and,
when it was finally ascertained that the arm was really broken,
they made a very handsome settlement on the spot.

Another time this same Frankie, during a baseball game in
the Jackson Street Playground, got hit on the jaw by a swinging bat. Resourceful Frankie did not head for Gouverneur
Hospital. As you may have guessed, he headed for home to
dress, looked up a friend who drove a taxi, got into the taxi,
and headed for the first ill-fated Rolls-Royce that might appear. When it did, Frankie took a deep breath and said to his
friend, "Now," and the cab driver did his best to make the cab
enter the Rolls-Royce through the side door.

I said I wore glasses; I've worn glasses all my life. They
served a double purpose. Naturally they helped me to see, but
even more important they were a direct source of financial
benefit. When I needed money I would take this little optometrist's screwdriver I had borrowed from an optometrist and
open up one screw. Out would pop the lens. I'd go to my
father and cry, "Ma'll kill me, I've got to get a new lens," and
he would give me money. I would immediately restore the
lens, and off I'd go to the movies. I could do this once a week
with him—with my mother, *never.* My mother had this extraordinary X-ray vision. I could enter a room and she would

look at me and say: "How'd you get that spot on the back of your pants?" And you know something: there would *be* a spot on the back of my pants. I could never even come to her and ask for money for an eyeglass lens. She would say: "Take it out of your pocket and put it back in your glasses."

I never thought of my father as gullible. He was just dear, trusting, and kind, and I was, as I say, "mischievous." He used to have a little Ceylon tea box that looked like a pirate's chest. My father would take the old twenty-dollar bills—they were yellow-orange—and fold them in three and hide them in that little box. And I'd dig into it. I'm sure he thought it was a magic box because he could never fill it. I knew it was a magic box because I could never empty it.

My father only beat me once or twice in my life—and he was a very bad beater. I mean he didn't know how: He was the sort of man whose whole reaction to anything in life was "Ts-ts-ts." When I showed him Boulder Dam he went: "Ts-ts-ts." The first time I took him to Broadway—"Ts-ts-ts." His name was Abraham Cohen. A man who never had a hard word or thought for anybody. We were once in the temple on that section of the Holy Days that's called Al Chait, when you have to pound your chest and pray: "Dear God, please do not punish me for this, and this, and this"—a ton of sins, all the sins you might commit. My father, who was *not* a humorous man—he never made a joke in his life—turned to me and said: "I don't know why I'm hitting myself. I haven't done anything."

I really can't abide all this hate-mother, hate-father jazz nowadays. My mother and father were people I more than loved; I respected them. I never spent one moment with my mother when she and I weren't at each other, but I loved her, I never hated her. My God, she could give Molly Goldberg crash courses in love, humor, and warmth.

Her maiden name was Alice Riss, and in Yiddish her first

I refuse to answer any questions. No prize will be given for a) finding me, or b) guessing who did the décor.

Here, in our early twenties at the Hotel Evans in Loch Sheldrake, the Catskills, are Ed Traubner (my business manager for over 45 years—on a handshake), Phil Silvers with hair, and me with the same amount of hair it seems I've always had.

Here we are again forty years later! Still chums!

name was Elka. To this day there's an "Elka" charitable or-
ganization in New York City, named for her. All my four
sisters have been president of it at one time or another. She
also founded a storefront temple. She was also a power in the
Democratic Party on the Lower East Side. I remember her
taking me to the Edward F. Ahearn Democratic Club on East
Broadway to fix a truancy rap. Right away I could see the
difference between Democrats and Republicans. The Democrats fixed the rap.

My parents were both originally from Galicia in Poland.
They'd come here around 1905, 1907—in Poland, it was po-
groms all the time. To be a Galitzianer was to be the lowest
kind of Jew. All other Jews suspected us because we were
supposed to be a little smarter. It seems to me all my life I've
been exposed to the "smart Jew" syndrome—by Jews and
Christians alike. And more than once I've been inclined to
say: "I have proof positive that the Jews are *not* the smartest
people in the world. My father wasn't smart." But my mother
—*there* was smart. All the cunning, all the humor—everything
that makes me what I am, if I'm anything—comes from her.

My father looked like a sweeter and more lovable version
of H. V. Kaltenborn, that fellow who announced the news—or
misannounced the news—that night, you'll remember, when
Dewey beat Truman.

My sisters are Sadye, Pearl, Florence, and Evelyn. I arrived
June 18, 1913, between Sadye and Pearl. When you're the
only son, there's no margin for error. If there are four
brothers, and one turns out to be an idiot, it's not such a great
tragedy. But I was such a bad boy, running away all the time,
sleeping on floors in the Broadway area. I could be home on a
five-cent subway fare, but I didn't go home. I remember when
I first started with music, picking out simple chords, my
mother would say, "What is he doing? What is he doing?"
When she finally saw I was not going to make the Big

Three—doctor, dentist, lawyer—she pulled off the great coup of getting me a job at the United Dressed Beef Corporation, about which more later. Our home was like a Jewish Lourdes, everybody coming to my mother and saying: "Elka, give me an *eytse*"—a little advice.

Paradox? Irony? Full-circle? I was born at 10 Cannon Street. Sixty years later I live on North Cañon Drive in Beverly Hills. I'm often asked if there's a plaque on the building where I was born. Not only did they *not* put a plaque on the wall at 10 Cannon Street, but they tore the building down and removed the street *and* the neighborhood. I think that's a pretty sobering thought.

My father had a little restaurant called Cohen's at the corner of Madison and Scammel streets. He would get up at four in the morning and walk three blocks to open the restaurant. His life was much like that of the ox that turns the wheel that draws the water. He was in charge of everything, with my mother and sisters helping now and again on holidays. There was a saloon next door for which my father provided steaks. My sister Sadye was a waitress, she being the oldest, and we all helped. In those days I had a lisp. I was often lifted to the bar of the saloon, my first experience with "on stage." I would get coins for singing: "I mith my Thwith, my Thwith mith mithes me, I mith the kith my Thwith mith gave to me." Right around the corner from my father's restaurant was Levy's Produce Store, run by the father of Lou Levy— Long-Shot Louie, the lindy hop dancer.

I don't remember ever being poor or hungry, I swear to it. First of all, we had the restaurant. That ruled out hunger. If it was cold I could sit near the coffee urn, and my father would bring over a bowl of hot soup. Which I'm addicted to, to this day—and to this day it has to be as hot as it can be. I'm always telling waiters: "Save yourself a trip back and forth. Tell the chef to make it *hot*." The waiter always says: "Don't I know how you want it?" Then he comes back with cold soup. Figures!

I do remember my mother taking the bedsprings once a week and burning them with kerosene to kill the lice. I remember being bitten, but not hungry. Later on in life I remember being hungry, when Lou Levy and I would go up to the Kellogg Cafeteria on 49th Street and have a cup of coffee and sit around until seven in the morning, which meant we could check into the Rex Hotel on 47th and Sixth—it's no longer there—and sleep all that day and the next.

My father had a brother Mike. My father almost went to ninety before he died about ten years ago; Mike went way past ninety. He rented out brownstones in the West 20's—a magic business, it never lost money. My brother-in-law Jules Goldberg, Florence's husband, is still in this business, and it still doesn't lose money. When I was in the process of my divorce, a dozen years ago, luckily my mother had already passed on and didn't have to be told. If she'd been alive it would have killed her. So I never told my father about the divorce, but one day his brother Mike called him—old Mike, then ninety-four, ninety-five, ninety-six—to say he'd just read in Winchell's column that Sammy *"hut zakh gi get,"* *get* being Yiddish for divorce. So my father asked me: "Sammy, *hut zakh gi get?* Mike told me." I said: "Pa, Mike is getting old." My father said: "What do you mean, old? Mike is not old. He's only ninety."

All my life everyone was after me to do something for this poor hard-working father of mine. After my first big hit, *"Bei Mir Bist Du Schön,"* I bought him and the family a house in Sheepshead Bay. So he sold the restaurant for $200 or $300. Well, it injured his health and his mental state. He didn't know what to do, to the day he died. I would gladly have undone all the good fortune just to bring back his little restaurant, his little stake, but there was no way you could do it.

The thing we believe the most beneficial is often the least beneficial. A funny thing: When Lou Levy took *his* father out of the grocery store it was completely different. It didn't injure his father's health or his mental state. He became a man who wore Lou Levy's clothes and went to burlesque shows. Well, I guess you win some and you lose some.

But it was all fun in my boyhood, even the going to school, except for the fact that I had no arithmetic ability at all. The only arithmetic I've ever learned was at the gin table—and I can only add from the other side of the table, upside-down.

I went to P.S. 147, on the corner of Scammel and Henry Streets, and to Seward Park Junior High, which is still on Grand Street, near Hester. They're after me all the time to come back as an eminent former student, but that would be the worst fraud. My record for truancy stands to this day. I would sign in at around 8 : 30 in the morning and by 9 : 15, after the first class, I'd be running down the street to the poolroom. The Seward Park Poolroom also had a gymnasium where some of the great fighters worked out—Sid Terris, Benny Leonard, Ruby Goldstein, Ben Jeby, all of whom were annihilated by Jimmy McLarnin. I was a rack-up boy. I'd rack up the balls at ten cents an hour, which the owner grudgingly gave me, but within *one* hour I'd steal enough from the re- freshment stand to go to the movies and vaudeville, which for me was my real school.

There used to be a little movie theater called the Windsor, at Grand and Clinton. It was going there that taught me there were other places in the world. The movies taught me every- thing. Years later I used to go to California on the *Super Chief*, with all its silver, crystal and impeccable service, and at one of the stops along the way I'd look out the window and see some fellow looking up at me blankly. I'd say to myself: How can he look at me and this train and not wonder where it's coming from and going to?

At Loew's Delancey I discovered vaudeville at the age of ten. I used to sit right behind the orchestra leader, Ruby Zwerling—later the conductor at Loew's State, the flagship theater of the chain—and read the music cues off his music and get to feel a sense of show business. It was there that for the first time I saw Milton Berle, in a flash act—four girls and a brash comedian. To this day when I see Milton Berle he'll slip a line in from forty years ago. I can always tell how old Milton is because I was ten at the time and he was fifteen. I saw all the great stars. I think a sense of vaudeville is very strong in anything I do, anything I write. They even call it "a vaudeville finish," and it comes through in many of my songs. Just sing the end of "All the Way" or "Three Coins in the Fountain"—"Make it mine! *Make it mine! MAKE IT MINE!"* If you let people know they should applaud, they *will* applaud. Maybe that's why so many singers love to sing my songs. But not the way *I* love to sing my songs. Come to think of it, if it weren't for the fact that I get to sing my songs, I'd go into some other business.

How I loved vaudeville, especially when I discovered the RKO 28th Street, a vaudeville house where every act that hoped to play the Palace auditioned: Harry Lauder, Bea Lillie, Smith and Dale—I saw them all.

I was also pretty glib at brazening out a lie. Once I was with a buddy at a movie house in the middle of the day—Loew's Delancey, as usual—and a woman friend of my mother suddenly said hello to me. There was *no* way of avoiding her; we were face to face. So I hello'd her back. She went off and I said to my buddy: "She'll be at my house in seven minutes." Sure enough, when I got home at three o'clock, supposedly after school, there she was. My mother said: "Why weren't you in school today?" I said I'd been in school. My mother said: "Mrs. Baron says she said hello to you in the movies." I looked right at Mrs. Baron and said: "*You* saw *me? I* said hello to *you?"* Know something? After a while she began to think maybe she hadn't.

Like I said, my mother got me a job at the United Dressed Beef Corporation, on the site of what is now the United Nations building. An interesting commentary: The United Nations is on the site where once stood a slaughterhouse. I was eighteen or nineteen years old, and I started as a messenger boy delivering meat orders. Then I was promoted to order boy, one of three or four boys who sat at phones beside a window, taking the meat orders. On the other side of the window was the head beef grader. And you can believe that, if anything went wrong, that window would fly up. Once on the phone I took an order for fifteen hinds and ribs. I said: "Fifty hinds and ribs?" The answer came, "Yes, fifteen hinds and ribs." "Let's check again—fifty hinds and ribs?" "Yes." Well, do you know what happens when you take fifty instead of fifteen hinds and ribs out of cold storage, and thirty-five have to be returned? I'll tell you what happens: In the heat the meat shrinks and the process of decay begins.

The window flew up. "What idiot took this order for fifty hinds and ribs?" "Me, sir," I said proudly. "You stupid little son-of-a-bitch, you'll sit on your ass by those phones until you learn to take an order correctly."

Eventually I was promoted again, to "candle boy." All meat at the United Dress was slaughtered kosher, on a Friday. The chuck and/or kosher sections would then go immediately to the Jewish butchers, because Jewish people—if orthodox—will not eat aged meat. The hinds and ribs go into the freezer to be sold to the *goyim* whenever. I'll never forget the first time I went to the killing floor and saw the steers and the sledgehammers. I was sick for three days. But the evidence of man's ability to adjust is such that within a week I was eating my lunch on the same killing floor. Not anything went to waste on that floor, not *anything*: hoofs, horns, skin, blood, pituitary glands.

Well, a candle boy went with the head grader into the freezer to grade hinds and ribs. When I say freezer I mean freezer. I must tell you how we dressed. We used to put on two pair of "longies"—long underwear, the kind with a drop flap in the back. Then two pair of long woolen socks, after first wrapping our legs in newspaper; then two pair of pants; two jackets; two sweaters; two sets of gloves; a heavy overcoat; then a big white coat like a doctor's coat; and, for the final touch, a straw hat. Why the straw hat? Because anything else was foolhardy. It was before they had today's hardhats; all the meat rode on rails, on hooks, and if one fell off and hit you in the head it was ouch-and-bile time if you weren't wearing a straw hat.

The candle boy had a clipboard and a searchlight and walked along with the grader. The finest meat—which may surprise you, as it did me—went to the chain stores, not the restaurants. I don't care what anybody tells you. The grader would walk down the row and could determine the quality of the meat by the feel of it. He'd run his hand under the rib, feel the grain, the marble, and say: "A&P" or "Gristede's" or whatever. The candle boy then wrote it down. And if the grader couldn't tell the quality by the feel he'd say "Candle boy," and the candle boy flashed his light. In the old days they'd actually had candles, hence the name, but we'd come a far piece.

Later a buyer from one of the chains would come in, and if he accepted this rail of beef he'd hand you his stamp, which was like a branding iron, very heavy, and you'd have to hit the hind part and the rib part with it. I was very thin and, I have to say, weak. You'd have to hit it, bang, bang, bang, up and down, and sometimes I couldn't. I had a buddy named Stanley

Ungehauer or Kowalski, just like in *A Streetcar Named Desire*, and if he saw I couldn't lift my arm he'd come running down the aisle and grab this iron out of my hand and complete the job. He was always doing this for me. He had a smile that warmed up the coldest, most frigid icebox, and whenever I hear Polish jokes I never laugh because I remember Stanley, who saved my life more than once.

All this time I was also the violinist with the Pals of Harmony, a little Dixieland band made up of my friend Frankie Miggs (real name, Migliano) and all these Italian boys. I'll never forget my first out-of-town gig. Frankie called to say we were playing at the Hotel Brigant in Atlantic City. It took us almost eight hours in a bus to get there—for me a great adventure, because I'd never traveled by car. We arrived at this little island off the coast of Atlantic City. I remember vividly my first inclination when we arrived at this exclusive hotel, on its own little island, which I discovered later was surrounded by Jew-eating alligators. I knew at once it was a place we shouldn't be. The Vienna String Quartet maybe, but not Frankie Miggs and His Pals of Harmony. One of the first things I saw was a sign saying RESTRICTED CLIENTELE, which translates into no Jews, Negroes, Catholics, or *anything* allowed. We were escorted to our accommodations, which even today seem to me lusher than most of the suites I stay in now. All the service was the finest silver with this emblem of a ship, a "brigant"—or brigantine—upon it. The maids in little white aprons and caps, the waiter in tails with silk britches—what the hell were *we* doing there?

So we called a meeting, the subject of discussion being: "What do we do with Sammy? I don't know if you guys have noticed it; he's Jewish." Someone said: "Ho, we'll pencil a mustache on him and call him Sam Valente." I've had a mustache ever since.

That two-week engagement at the Hotel Brigant in Atlantic

City lasted just one session where we played for tea. I wish I could describe the reaction of those rich guys when the first slide trombone ushered in a Dixieland rag. I have never liked Atlantic City then or since.

My mother was the agent for the band, the booker. I don't think she *ever* accepted my chosen life, but she would do what she could to nurture what I wanted to do. So Frankie Miggs, who was the drummer, got us all the Italian work, down below Grand Street, and my mother got us all the bar mitzvahs and Jewish weddings. If you were a friend of Elka and were having any kind of *simkhekh*—a happy event—you hired Sammy and his band or else you were in a lot of trouble for *eytses*. In fact, I first thought of joining the Pals when I saw my mother pay them $25 for playing at my own bar mitzvah.

One time the band needed some new uniforms, those little white navy-type jackets. For this I went to still another—and lifelong close—buddy, Edward Traubner. His father's business was the manufacture of white duck uniforms, and I figured I could get the band jackets wholesale.

(In his book *The Rat Pack* Richard Gehman called me "the king of wholesale," and I guess that's true. I think I'm a nut, and I also think I have spent more on wholesale than most people spend retail. I guess I inherit this from my mother. One day she came home from the market with two cans of deviled ham. "Ma," I said, "what're you doing with deviled ham?" She shrugged and said: "It was on sale." When the day comes that Sammy Cahn goes into the ground, he's even going to do that wholesale, because now I'm the son-in-law of Salvatore Basile of Brooklyn, proprietor of Basile's Mortuary. But don't worry, Ma, I'll be crossing my fingers—not my chest.)

Ed Traubner's father, Alexander—of Hungarian descent— had three sons and a daughter, and, as I said, was in the business of making white duck uniforms—for nurses, doctors, sailors, and the like.

The day I called Ed to get the Pals of Harmony band uniforms "for *gor*"—wholesale, from the Yiddish *far gornisht*, or
"for nothing"—he was terribly distraught and close to tears. It
seemed that a few weeks back his dad and younger brother
were going to the various hospitals to make their collections;
their car was sideswiped by a truck and Mr. Traubner was
dead on arrival at a hospital they were not visiting for that
purpose. His very vital and successful business was up for
grabs, and for a while the family, meeting in council, thought
of selling out. Ed said: "Let me try to run it; we can always
sell." They agreed, and for a month or so Ed had almost been
chained to the workbench of the factory. He had brought
about a miracle. Not only didn't the business suffer; he was
actually doing better than his own father.

Ed at first brush is not the most delicate of men. He is very
short and squat and totally unable to express directly the
warmth and sensitivity that make him the dearest and sweet-
est person imaginable—if you take the trouble to look. We
have been together for almost fifty years, and for all those
years I get notes from him signed: "Sincerely yours." I do to
this day.

To save the family business Ed suppressed his warm un-
derside and trampled over everybody, including his mother
and older brother. When he heard my voice on the phone he
said: "It's a miracle, Sammy. I was just standing here at the
cutting board, making patterns; I've been sleeping or standing
at this table for the last four weeks; I haven't smiled once, and
I was just thinking about the fun times."

"I'll be right there," I said, and I dropped everything and
rushed to his plant. He threw his arms around me and hugged
me, and we went out to a Chinese dinner—two thirty-five-cent
specials—the kind of special time that makes sure a friendship
never ends. Ed has had four marriages. I'm in my second; but
he and I have never been separated.

The first time I ever saw Ed it was at a resort called Saltz's in

Mount Freedom, New Jersey. I was barely sixteen; he was about seventeen. After we'd finished playing that night a bunch of us got in a car to ride over to Allentown, Pennsylvania, a famous red-light district, and Eddie—a paying guest at the hotel, one of the rich kids—went along for the action. After all, it only cost $2—unless I could get six of us for $10, which was mainly why I was taken along.

A not-so-funny thing happened on the way to that establishment. The car was crowded, there were a lot of horny bums in that band, not to mention Eddie, maybe the horniest of all, and I was hanging on the runningboard and, with all the laughing and hooting and hollering, I slipped off. After I stopped rolling they took me to a local druggist, who patched up what seemed like my whole body. On to the house. To this day I'll never forget that charming girl in that $2 crib mistaking my reluctance to disrobe for shyness. She said: "Don't you want to undress?" I said: "I'm exposing all that's necessary." She: "I think you'll be more comfortable if you undress." I: "You'll be sorry." And when I undressed and was standing there like an ad from Johnson & Johnson she agreed I could have left my clothes on.

Anyway, Ed made the uniforms wholesale, and he used to visit the band on its dates, while all this time I kept working at the United Dressed Beef Corporation, hating it. It was while we were driving back to the city from the Catskills one weekend that I said to Ed, "How I hate going back to that Beef Corporation." Ed said, "So why are you going back?" "My mother would kill me if I quit now"—because after candle boy came salesman, and as a salesman you had your own car and made $300 a week. Ed said: "How long will it take to become what you want, a hit songwriter?" That kind of naïve question deserves a naïve answer, so I naïvely said: "Oh, a couple of months." Ed said: "Okay, you're not going back to the meat plant; you're not going home; you're coming to live with me in the Bronx and try it." His family was away. He had the run of the house, and I went there with him. Ed was a marvelous friend. Every morning Ed gave me a couple of dollars to get through the day, and he never doubted or questioned—not then, not in the forty years since.

Eddie soon came to a total parting of the ways with his family. There was another council of war, and Ed was out. By this time I had started to make it, and Lou Levy and Saul Kaplan (Chaplin) and I had our pad on the corner of 57th and Sixth, and one day Eddie arrived to say that he had been thrown out of the business he had saved. Figures! I told him how happy I was that I had been given the opportunity to repay a friendship so swiftly; that now he could move in with us and he would find a few dollars every morning for his own. Eddie, being the type he is, said he didn't want any money; all he wanted was a place to sleep, the couch or the floor, and that would be repayment enough. So he moved in, and it was the floor because Lou Levy was on the couch.

One day Ed came to me and asked who took care of the business, the books, the taxes. Books? What books? What business? What taxes? I said we took our money, Saul and I, and divided it.

Well, Ed immediately took over the books. Today he is one of the most successful business managers in Hollywood; he handles people like Warren Beatty and Paul Newman—plus me. He insists I made it all possible for him. But it's the other way around. Ed Traubner took me out of the iceboxes.

Came the High Holidays. What does a Jewish boy who's running away from home do? He goes home, and, like the fella says, home is where you go, when you have no other place, and they gotta take you in. My mother was sitting there, in tears. She started to call me a bum or something and seemed about to hit me. I lifted my hand to protect myself. My father thought I was going to hit *her* and he came at me with the broom handle—only the second time he ever beat me. And, as I said, he was such a bad beater.

CHAPTER 2

"Rhythm Is Our Business"

Rhythm is our business,
Rhythm is what we sell.
Rhythm is our business,
Business sure is swell . . .

LONG-SHOT LOUIE LEVY, the vegetable man's kid from around the corner, existed by dancing at Roseland. Every Saturday night in the early thirties he'd win a silver cup and give it right back and they'd hand him something like $7. Or he would put on blackface and, along with a girl named Mary, also in blackface, dance with the Jimmy Lunceford band at the Apollo Theatre on 125th Street.

On the day I was selling my first song—"Shake Your Head From Side to Side," based on a shimmy headshake dance of the time. My father came with me to the music company of Judd and Brown, fly-by-night publishers in the Roseland Building, a haven for fly-by-night publishers. I was still a minor, so my father had to come along to sign the contract. We were standing there by an open door when Lou Levy came gallivanting down the hall. I gave a doubletake, he gave a doubletake. "Sammy! What are you doing here?" "Well, I have this song." "*You* write songs?" And that was the start of the "famous" Leeds Music Publishing Company, proprietors Sammy Cahn and Lou Levy, which Long-Shot Lou would someday sell for three million dollars to MCA—mainly because a lot of the long-shots didn't happen.

My mother, who had already despaired my making DLD (doctor-lawyer-dentist), was really upset by my association with Lou Levy, the dancing no-goodnik. And so one night she ordered him out of our home, and I said: "If he goes, I go." We both went. We'd sleep wherever we could, often on the couches or floors of offices. It was only after a long while that we finally took a single room together in the Elysée Apartments, Eighth Avenue and 57th Street. The Elysée Apartments had once been a fashionable New York townhouse, and the different floors had been cut up into rooms, so that whoever had a bedroom had a bedroom and whoever had a living room had a living room—with a sliding door connecting to the next tenant, so all these rooms ran together. The elevator was the classic original elevator which ran by pulling the cord, and, although there was no elevator operator, what they really needed was a priest or someone with rosary beads to bless each trip, which could very well be the last. Going up to the apartment in this "meet your Maker" contraption, Lou Levy would call off the various floors much as the operators do in department stores. Lou would yell out: "First floor— pimps, hookers, and dope peddlers. Second floor—just pimps. Fourth floor—just whores. Fifth floor, the lowest of them all—musicians and songwriters."

I have vivid memories of our apartment—make that "room" —those were the days. . . . Everybody came up to our room, and we wrote material for everyone you could imagine— mainly what's called "special material," more patter than melody—and all the while I was trying desperately to get through to music publishers and finding it extremely difficult.

"Shake Your Head From Side to Side" was the first and last song for which I wrote words *and* music. Lou Levy had encouraged me to the point where I started writing ten songs a day with a friend named Saul Kaplan. Every day we'd take one of these songs to the Brill Building and show it to Arthur

Piantadosi, a famous music publisher. Every day he'd turn the song down. After eight months of this Kaplan, who is brighter than I am, asked: "Why do we go back there?" I said: "Because he lets us in."

One day Lou came and said, "Jimmy Lunceford needs a special band number," and out of that came "Rhythm Is Our Business," which led to our first phone call from a legitimate music publisher. What a thrill, what a kick, what happiness! Mr. Georgie Joy of the Santly-Joy Music Company wanted to meet us. More important, he wanted to publish "Rhythm Is Our Business." He knew Lunceford had already recorded the song. We were later to learn that this very nice man was actually taking advantage of us, because what we didn't know was that Mr. Joy knew Lunceford had already recorded "Rhythm Is Our Business" for the Decca label and it was the flip side of "Stardust." Which meant an automatic sale of our song, which it did achieve, and by naïvely signing with Santly and Joy we were giving up half our royalties. On top of this, the authorship was divided between Sammy Kahn, as I then was, Saul Kaplan, and our first "cut-in," Jimmy Lunceford. A cut-in, in those days, was anyone who could get your song recorded, published, or played, which meant his name appeared on the song, and the big scam around the music business was and is that the greatest of all cut-ins was Mr. Al Jolson, who has his name on practically every hit he ever sang (or perhaps he'd never have sung). The second greatest must be Mr. Irving Mills, the famed music publisher, whose name appears up alongside Duke Ellington's on many of Ellington's songs. Another prominent cut-in was supposed to Mr. Billy Rose. I am not sure if Billy Rose really deserved that rumor, but I *do* know that Mr. Rose once, when hiring me to do one of his Aquacade shows, told me: "I can't wait to hear what we're going to write."

I don't have to tell you who Jimmy Lunceford was—just

about the single greatest leader of a black band that ever was, and I have seen and heard them all—but maybe I'd better tell you about Saul Kaplan when we first met, before he became Saul Chaplin. Of course, I was Samuel Cohen, but then I changed it to Kahn so as not to get mistaken for Sammy Cohen, a famous MGM comic of my youth, and finally to Cahn so as to avoid confusion with the even greater Gus Kahn—not only great but a *lyricist* yet.

It was while I was still with that Dixieland band, the Pals of Harmony, that Saul Kaplan came into my life. We needed a piano player for one of those little affairs at the Educational Alliance, down on the Lower East Side. It was a cold, wintry day, heavy with snow. I was outside looking for this piano player I'd never met, and here he came down the block, Saul Kaplan, from Brooklyn. I can see him yet. Skinny, 6'1", with a shock of wavy blond hair like King Gustav of Sweden, in a raccoon coat and, get ready—are you set?—plus a derby hat. He turned out to be and still is one of the great accompanist-pianists who ever lived, and what do you think he was doing? He was going to NYU to be an accountant. An accountant! This marvelous fellow who wore glasses behind which were eyes that rotated would never be an accountant if I had anything to do with it. I was around sixteen or seventeen years old and he was eighteen or nineteen, and I decided that he belonged to me. From then on he played with the Pals of Harmony and became the first wonderful collaborator I had—the guy who writes the music—in a line that included Jule Styne, Nicholas Brodszky, Axel Stordahl, Paul Weston, Vernon Duke, Sammy Fain, Gene De Paul, Jimmy Van Heusen. In my business these names speak for themselves. But when I saw the names on that first copy of "Rhythm Is Our Business"—Kahn, Kaplan—I said to him: "You're going to have to change your name." He bristled and said, "Why? It looks good." I said, "It doesn't look good at all. Kahn and

Kaplan, that's a dress firm." He said, "Why don't you change *your* name?" I: "That's fair. From now I'll be Cahn with a C." He: "Okay, I'll be Caplan with a C." I said: "Cahn and Caplan, that's *still* a dress firm. From now on it's Cahn and Chaplin."

The Pals of Harmony, now retitled Cahn and Chaplin, signed to play for the summer season at the Hotel Evans at Loch Sheldrake in the Catskills. It was there that we first met Phil Silvers—another of my best and longest friends—whom I'd seen at the vaudeville theaters as the little boy in the Morris and Campbell act.

The Morris and Campbell act was glorious: The enunciator identifies Joe Morris as the curtain goes up to establish a kitchen in a modest home. On the floor playing with a train is Phil Silvers, a little boy (fast outgrowing a little boy's suit). A harridan of a wife is screaming at a defeated Joe Morris, the husband. The gist of the wife's dialogue is: "And stay away from that theater. I know she's in town and you're dying to see her. When you go shopping, I warn you—don't go near the theater!" She gives him the shopping bag. He's about to leave when she decides he needs supervision and says, "Sonny, go with your father!" Abjectedly he says to Sonny, "Come on, Leech!" Enunciator changes to Flo Campbell, and out she comes. (I must say now that all comics in those days in vaudeville had this remarkable talent for finding the most incredibly beautiful women.) Bert Gordon, the "Mad Russian," had a girl that made me groan she was so beautiful, and here was Flo Campbell in the same mold. She sang two of the most popular songs and, at the end, into the theater box walked Joe Morris and Sonny (Phil) screaming, "Mama said you were not to come here." "Here's a quarter and shut up." This exchange of money to keep Sonny quiet led to a funny piece of business, when Joe ran out of quarters, Phil opened his jacket, revealing a motorman's changemaker, from which he extracted the quarter change. Joe Morris was one of the

Chaplin and I packing the Buick for our first trip to Hollywood! (Here is where Saul really looks like King Gustav of Sweden.)

The trusty Buick made it to Chicago (witness the Chicago Theater and the attractions there!) This is where we encountered Ted Lewis at the Chez Paree!

This is the after-effect of the Crash. I was too stupid to get hurt. The wounded are Lou Levy, Saul Chaplin and "Ukie" Sherin. (Yes! He played the ukelele and told the most awful jokes.)

There was a Hotel Evans in Loch Sheldrake, and musicians were allowed to act like guests.

Not to let anyone know we had a crash, we purchased another Buick (identical with the first) and continued to the land of the Oranges! Above: proof that we made it!

End of journey to Hollywood! Schwab's Drugstore!

(Photo: Stan Krell)

With Louis Armstrong and Saul Chaplin writing "Shoeshine Boy" for the Cotton Club Show.

Kenny Bowers, Jane Withers and me, when I went on stage to play the lead in "Glad to See Ya!" in Philadelphia.

(Photo: Bruno of Hollywood)

The original Chaplin, Levy and Cahn.

most incurable gamblers that ever played a vaudeville stage. I am sure that Phil comes by his talent for gambling from having studied with the champ of them all. Many years later when vaudeville had passed, Phil gone on to burlesque, and Joe come on hard times, Joe was selling socks. He once visited Goodman Ace, the writer, and tried to sell him some socks. Goodman appropriately said to him, "Still working out of a box!"

It was also at the Hotel Evans that Saul became attracted to a girl named Ethel Schwartz, who worked in the office there. On our return to the city we hired Ethel as our secretary in order to keep Saul around the office. Hiring Ethel was a rather extravagant plan because we were barely earning eating money. Not only did Saul hang around the office, he married Ethel, and they had a daughter named Judy. Judy is today Mrs. Harold Prince, wife of the Broadway producer-director. (Sammy Cahn–marriage broker without portfolio.) However, Ethel and I never really hit it off; that office romance would blossom into love for them and dislike for me. It taught me a lesson: You can't beat the pillow conference.

It was also in the Catskills that I met Axel Stordahl, at the Loch Sheldrake Hotel and Roadhouse Restaurant. He was a Norwegian, the most beautiful man in the world, and so Nordic that seeing him in the Catskills was much like meeting, shall we say, H. Rap Brown at George Wallace's house. Axel was a trumpet player then.

That Decca record of "Rhythm Is Our Business" in 1934 had brought Saul and me to the attention of Seger Ellis of Rockwell-O'Keefe Agency, and it also soon brought us to the attention of Mr. Jack Kapp, head of Decca Records.

I must pause here to tell you about Seger Ellis, out of Houston, Texas, a piano player and singer who was so handsome that people would stop on the street to look at him. He had that swarthy kind of look, with black hair that hung in ringlets, like a Greek god—or a Ramon Novarro, a Rudolph Valentino. He was so handsome that, legend has it, his was the first face ever printed on a phonograph record. It was the same Seger Ellis who discovered the incredibly successful Mills Brothers. It was he who brought them to Rockwell-O'Keefe —and Tom Rockwell rewarded him by taking away the Mills Brothers *and* his wife.

Ellis spotted some talent in me. In fact, he was the fella who paid the $25 a week which paid the rent on that little room in the Elysée Apartments. He took us to see Mr. Kapp, who soon became my guide and mentor. Kapp was a large man with a very open face, glasses, and a lovely manner, almost Talmudic; he used to love to philosophize to me. One thing he always sought to avoid was stirring up envy—even well-meaning envy. When Kapp moved the Decca offices from the old Brunswick studios at 799 Seventh Avenue to 50 West 57th Street, we both walked over there. It was a kind of loft. He showed me the corner where his office would be and another corner where his vice-president, Milton Rackmil, would be.

I said: "Jack, this doesn't seem suitable for the president of Decca Records. Your office and Milton's are alike."

His answer? That he didn't want anyone walking in and saying: "Jack, you're really doing sensational. Boy, am I happy for you." He didn't want happy envy or sincere envy or envy in any form.

I was also impressed when, in 1932, he told me he foresaw the period when Victrola records would be home entertainment. I'm talking about the time of the 78's. He suggested we should devote our writing to specific Decca artists. We wrote for Andy Kirk, Jimmy Lunceford, and Ella Fitzgerald. One song for Ella Fitzgerald was called "If You Ever Should Leave." I'll never forget how excited Jack Kapp was when he phoned me to say that Ella's record was well on the way to selling 40,000 copies. I never think of that triumph without remembering the day Ella recorded it. It was kind of a heartbreak ballad with lyrics like: "If you ever should leave, why would I want to live,/Darling, won't you believe, won't you try to forgive . . . ?" There she stood at the microphone in this dreary recording studio, singing as only Ella can, with a large hot dog with all the trimmings in one hand and a bottle of Coke in the other.

Because we were successful writing for all the Decca artists, Jack Kapp introduced Saul and me to Herman Starr, head of the Music Publishers' Holding Corporation (MPHC), a subsidiary of Warner Brothers. Herman Starr was supposedly the man the Warner brothers sent to the banks when the banks were going to take away the movie company, and he came back not only with the company saved, but with a loan. When the brothers asked him what he wanted as a reward, this very unmusical and un-show-business young man asked to be head of MPHC. His astuteness as a businessman soon proved itself. To this day MPHC has been the most profitable of all Warner Brothers assets, year in, year out. Anyway, Starr now also introduced us to Mr. Sam Sax, head of another Warner Brothers subsidary, the Vitaphone Studios on Avenue "M" in Brooklyn. And so we went to work for Vitaphone.

Vitaphone made short subjects, one-reelers, two-reelers, and if you wanted to run a Warner Brothers moie in your theater you had to take two or three of these. It was never a question of them having to be good, only of having to be *made.* Over and over they used to say to me: "We don't want 'em good, we want 'em by Tuesday." Our schooling in this "We want 'em by Tuesday" world was invaluable. We wrote for almost every entertainer known or unknown, because they all came through the doors of Vitaphone Studios. It was mainly my years of writing special material for the Vitaphone short subjects that prepared me for any eventuality.

One day a mailboy came in and said: "Mr. Cahn, my name

is Ralph Young and I'm a singer." I said: "Put down the mail
and sing, and I'll tell you if you're a singer." I picked up the
phone and asked for Mack Goldman of Harms, one of the
MPHC companies, a man renowned for his primness, one of
the most fastidious and impeccable who ever lived. "Anyone
need a singer?" I asked him. "Yes, Charlie Spivak needs a
singer." So Ralph Young put down the mail and started to
sing with the Charlie Spivak band. I waited thirty years for
Ralph Young to fulfill his promise of talent that day, and he
finally has; Ralph is half the team of Sandler and Young—you
know, the act where one sings French, the other sings American.

Which comes first, words or music? The phone call comes
first, always the phone call.

One day the phone rings and it's Roy Mack, a director of
these short subjects and brother of Austin Mack, who played
for Joe E. Lewis. He wants a love song for one of the shorts.
After a while I say to Saul: "How do you like this for an idea?"
'This is my first affair . . . so please be kind . . . Handle my
heart with care . . . oh please be kind.' "

The song is finished, it gains popularity, and we are called
to the offices of Mack Goldman. Singing to Mack Goldman
was no easy task, but I am no mean singer of my songs. I love
to demonstrate, to sell, my songs. Again, if I didn't get to
demonstrate my songs I would go into another business. I
must tell you that I consider myself the most expensive singer
in the world. I walk into the room without an orchestra,
make-up, or lights. Just me, a little guy with eyeglasses and a
mustache, to sing a song you've never heard, and if you like
what I sing you owe me. I really prepare for the moment of
truth. I wear a sincere outfit, a very plain tie. If I'm wearing a
ring, I take the ring off, if a flashy wristwatch, I take the watch
off. I don't want that fellow to think: "Where'd he get that

ring?" That can cost me. It's like a toreador in the bullring—
with a lot of show and terror, and hopefully enough style and
content to win the day.

So now, with Mack Goldman, I take my stance, as I always
do. I lower my head, one arm goes back, the other comes up,
so does my head, and I *lean in,* and I sing:

> *This is my first affair, so please be kind.*
> *Handle my heart with care, oh please be kind.*
> *This is all so grand, my dreams are on parade.*
> *If you'll just understand they'll never never fade.*
> *Tell me your love's sincere, oh please be kind.*
> *Tell me I needn't fear, oh please be kind.*
> *'Cause if you leave me, dear, I know*
> *My heart will lose its mind . . .*

And through those thin lips Mr. Goldman interrupted:
"What do you mean, your heart'll lose its mind?" I try to
explain the heart might be an entity all to itself. Goldman's
lips got even thinner, and he said: "You going to walk around
with the copies explaining it?" That taught me a lesson: Never
have a line you have to explain. Write a new song.

I was once doing a picture for Debbie Reynolds, *Say One for
Me.* So I'm singing one of the songs to Debbie Reynolds, and
it's a very odd song. It was written for a scene between Debbie
and Robert Wagner. He has just taken her home and tried to
make a pass. She rejects him and closes the door on him. She
now leans against the door, and we see that she is having
second thoughts. He also is leaning on his side of the door.
She sings reflectively:

> Verse *(almost recitative):*
> *I can see him right outside, grinning like a Cheshire*
> *Feeling he's applied, just the right amount of pressure.*

Chorus:
He's got a way of smiling when he talks
That shows self-satisfaction
He's got a nervous jiggle when he walks
That's not his main attraction
I'm well aware he doesn't care and he will drive
* me to distraction*
And yet, and yet, he's starting to get to me!

and suddenly Debbie is standing up and singing along with
me. Do you know the chutzpah that is? You do a thing like
that in B-pictures, right? The thrush joining in on the first
playing of a song!

Then Debbie got singing ahead of me. I stopped. When she
stopped I said: "When you joined me and sang along with me,
that wasn't too bad. But when you ran ahead of me . . ."

Another time she said: "Spare me your Jewish phrasing." I
wonder if she ever said that to Eddie Fisher or Harry Karl.

We wrote songs, songs of every type. Songs for bands,
songs for acrobats, songs for ice skaters—including one of the
worst *ever* written, "I'm a Musical Magical Man"—used in a
short that featured dancing trumpets. We wrote it for Georgie
Price, that little guy, a Jolson imitator—weren't they all in
those days?—who later became a stockbroker. Roy Mack, one
of the short-subject director–producers—and even more famous for being the brother of Austin Mack—would take us to
the warehouse and show us some costumes. Then he'd say:
"Write a song for that costume."

So by the late thirties we were working for Herman Starr
and for Vitaphone short subjects at the same time, and one
day, sensing that we had run the string out and could very
well be fired, I attacked Herman Starr and said: "If you don't
send us to the Coast, we're quitting."

Actually, some genius had already said: "If those two fellows can write hits for shorts, what might they be able to do for features?"—after all, "Please Be Kind" was the first song in the history of Vitaphone that made the Hit Parade. So Herman Starr sent us off with a letter to Leo Forbstein at Warner's in Hollywood, a letter which said: "This will introduce you to Sammy Cahn and Saul Chaplin. Please use them—they're gratis!" Once we got there Leo Forbstein would read that letter, say "Thank you," and we'd never get on the lot again. Two "gratis" kids from New York—who needed them?

But of course at the time we couldn't know that, so now Lou and Saul and I are taking our first trip to the West Coast, by car. Our first stop is Chicago, and there we go to the Chez Paree, where Ted Lewis is working with an act called the Radio Aces. We'd written for the Radio Aces. Now, as we're watching the act, one of the Aces signals me to come backstage after the show. When I do, there's Milton Pickman, a young New York lawyer. He says, "Sammy, I'm glad you came back. Ted Lewis wants to meet you," and takes me in to meet this amazing character, Mr. Ted Lewis.

Ted Lewis had a dresser, a black man with red hair. The dresser is saying, "Mr. Lewis, I think you should change your clothes," and Lewis is saying, "I don't think I'll change my clothes." "Mr. Lewis, your wife told me to *tell* you to change your clothes." Lewis, wistfully: "All right, I'll do it." "Mr. Lewis, I think you should take your pills." "I don't think I'll take my pills." "Mr. Lewis, your wife told me to *tell* you to take your pills." "All right, I'll do it."

Well, finally Lewis turns to me and says: "What are you doing here?" I say: "They told me you wanted to see me." "Did you write a song for me?" "No." "So what are you doing here?" "They told me you wanted to see me." Lewis: "Didn't you write 'Shoe Shine Boy'?" Me: "Yes." Lewis: "Well, I want another 'Shoe Shine Boy.'" Me: "So do I." He couldn't understand that I didn't have a song, but being the kind of guy I am and knowing the kind of guy I was dealing with, I suddenly remembered, and don't ask me why, the one song I was sure he would adore. It is, as I said before, the single worst song ever written: You guessed it: "I'm a Musical Magical Man." He asked me to demonstrate it, which is my *real* talent, and I do, making the necessary changes to make it suit him as I go along, which is one of my knacks. Where Georgie Price sang: "I can make you think you're hearing trumpets/Here's the proof I can . . ."—with a wave of the hand, to trumpets on the screen—I change it on the spur of the moment to "I can make you think that you're in Chi-na/Here's the proof I can . . ." and I put my finger in my cheek and my wave of the hand told the band to make the sound of a cacophonous Chinese orchestra.

Lewis says: "That's sensational! That's me!" I say: "Fine. Now who do I talk money to?" When I say the word "money" it's like I've taken the shaft from Ahab's whale and stuck it through the throat of Mr. Ted Lewis. "Money?" "Yeah," I say, "the stuff they pay you with, you know." Milton Pickman, hustling me out of the room, says: "Sam, this man is in third-degree shock. What do we do now? He's never paid for a number." I say: "I don't give a damn if he goes into fourth-, fifth-, or sixth-degree shock. If he wants 'Musical Magical Man' it'll cost him. I want $2500." Well, I finally got $1500—a lot of money in those days. But wait. While Pickman is making out the paper of transfer, Lewis insists he wants the movie rights.

Now the old "pushcart" comes out in me. I start to laugh. Picture rights? When would Ted Lewis be in pictures? Not ever. So, chuckling, I give away the rights to a song owned by Warner Brothers and blithely proceed on my way to Hollywood, California, where we couldn't get on the Warner lot and so returned, Saul and Lou and I, to New York.

Five months later the phone rings and its's Victor Blau, in charge of copyrights for Vitaphone and an old buddy. He says: "Hey, Sammy. Did you sell 'Musical Magical Man'?" I say: "Why?" "It's just been set into an MGM picture." "*That* song is in an MGM musical?" "Sam, the clearance just came through, it's in an MGM picture performed by Ted Lewis."

Now the fact is that I am a rascal though I hope never to hurt anybody, never to be mean just to be mean. But when I'm cornered, at least I know when to laugh. I tell Victor Blau the story I'm telling here and *he* starts to laugh.

It seems that MGM was making a war picture in which they needed a troupe of entertainers and an orchestra, and they went to see Ted Lewis doing his act, and the one thing in his act they liked is, you guessed it, "Musical Magical Man."

Victor Blau says, "Sam, don't do anything. Let me think of something." You know what he thought of? He told MGM that, unless they gave Vitaphone $5000, he'd have to hold up the picture. Since MGM never wants a picture held up, they gave him the $5000, which meant Saul and I got $2500 extra out of that (no thanks to my business acumen but to the high cost of holding up a movie production. MGM would rather pay than fight—which in dollars could mean a loss—since they'd lose costly production even if they won a lawsuit against Lewis and Vitaphone and me). Ted Lewis used that song for years and years, and Milton Pickman later sent me a clipping from the *New Orleans Times-Picayune*, a review of the Ted Lewis act, printed on the editorial page. "Last night I caught the Ted Lewis show. I recommend it to everyone because it contains one of the single greatest numbers ever seen." The editor so enjoyed that song from a short subject that he wanted everybody to go see it. Like they say, there's no accounting for taste. . . .

Saul and I made it back to Hollywood eventually, but never—no surprise—to the Warner lot; after all, I gave away their property and lived to profit from it. Our buddy Phil Silvers, who was then entrenched at MGM, got assigned with the Orsattis, number one agents because of their strength with Louis B. Mayer. They assured us we were "in." Not only weren't we "in," we were out. "Out" in Hollywood is no fun, so in desperation we went to an agent named Al Kingston and asked him to get us an audition with every studio—only when every studio had turned us down would we go back to New York. The first studio he took us to was Republic Pictures, to audition for Albert J. Cohen. For this Albert J. Cohen we eventually wrote the story, screenplay, and score for that gem, *Rookies on Parade* starring Bob Crosby and his orchestra.

Saul and I stopped working together around 1941, 1942. What happened is we used to write kind of easy together. I'd have an idea, he'd make a minor change in the melody, and we'd have a song. Then . . . I guess his wife thought he should be more assertive. One day when I ran in to sing a song he said: "Don't sing me the song, just tell me." And that was like the beginning of the end of a team. I was never going to walk out on him, but on another day he said he was unhappy and I said: "That makes two of us." So I called Morris Stoloff of Columbia and told him Saul and I had agreed to part, and I was out of work. A very low period of my life.

Saul and I remained buddies through the years, and not so long ago he—the fella in the raccoon coat and the derby hat—hired me to write the title song of *Star!* When the studio asked me to do it I said, "I'd like to do it with Saul. Ask Saul if he'll do it with me." Saul told them: "No, let Sammy do it with Jimmy Van Heusen." The guy I hired in the snow—forty years later he hired me.

Saul is divorced now from Ethel Schwartz, who married

some actor whose name escapes me, and Saul married a girl named Betty. You'll see Saul Chaplin's name on any number of motion pictures—*Singing in the Rain, The Sound of Music, West Side Story, Seven Brides for Seven Brothers,* I couldn't count them all—as musical coordinator. The night I won the Academy Award for "Three Coins in the Fountain" he walked on stage right ahead of me and got it for *Seven Brides.* I liked that twist of fate very much.

CHAPTER 3

"The Things We Did Last Summer"

The boat rides we would take,
The moonlight on the lake,
The way we danced and hummed our fa-vorite song,
The things we did last summer
I'll re-member all winter long . . .

PHIL SILVERS AND I go back more summers than we both care to remember. I've told you about watching him in his early vaudeville days, but I first came to know him well when Saul Chaplin and I were still together at the Hotel Evans on Loch Sheldrake. I was in the pit one night and Phil stepped out on stage. I was immediately taken with his apparently enormous ease of manner. He was and is for me one of the total stage creatures, and from that day to this he has given me more enjoyment than any man I've known in or out of show business.

Phil soon finished with his summer sabbatical—all burlesque comedians spent their summers working the Catskills before returning in the fall to burlesque, which profited from the months they spent honing and enlarging their skills—and was back on the vaudeville boards. At this time Saul Chaplin and I had our "office" on the premises of Al Beckman and

Johnny Pransky, who were to the Catskill Mountains circuit what MCA, William Morris, and all the rest combined are to all other aspects of show business. There are a few million Beckman and Pransky stories, but here is one of my favorites, set in World War II when it was very difficult to get cars for transportation up to the Catskills or to anywhere else. One day a performer with a new act comes to the Beckman and Pransky office for an interview.

Performer: "I have one of the most sensational acts in the world."

Beckman: "Do you have a car?"

Performer: "Yes, I have a car. . . . I come out with two girls balanced on each shoulder."

Pranksy: "How many people does the car hold?"

Performer: "Seven . . . I do a tap dance carrying these four girls on my shoulders and—"

Beckman: "Any spare tires?"

Performer: "Two . . . Then I change the shoulders and go into rope skipping—"

Beckman and Pransky, as one: "Be here tomorrow—*with pictures of the car.*"

Every comic and singer from Red Buttons to Henny Youngman to Danny Kaye to Jerry Lewis to Bob Alda to Jan Murray to Gene Baylos came through the doors of Beckman and Pransky; and Saul and I, being on the premises, had the good fortune to write for them all.

Down the street from Beckman and Pransky was the Gaiety Burlesque, at 46th and Broadway, where Phil Silvers was one of the top bananas, along with the legendary Rags Ragland. Every Monday there was a new show, and Harold Minsky, the entrepreneur, would pace in front of the theater while I asked him: "How's it look?"

He'd say: "By Friday we'll tighten it up and have a

smash."—and by Monday, every Monday, they'd have a new show.

For me to watch Phil Silvers on Monday start with an old, old almost cliché-ridden sketch called "Montpelier, the Lover"—well, it was art without the capital "A."

The set consisted of a cot—didn't they all?—and a door and a hat tree. The only accommodation Phil would make to the conventions of burlesque was to take a plain fedora hat and roll it à la Jimmy Walker and put it on his head, take a plain straight tie and make it into a bowtie, and carry a cane.

The sketch always started with a husband telling his wife that he'd just been called out of town on business: "Darling, I know how much you'll miss me." Wife: "I'll miss you *desperately.*" Hugs, kisses, exit husband. Door opens. Enter Montpelier, the Lover, played by Phil Silvers, who coming through the door says: "I thought he'd never go." He wildly embraces the errant wife and starts pounding the cot with his cane as he shouts: "Shall we?" Another wild embrace, out of which the girl, in disgust, announces to the world in general: "I cannot work with this ham." Phil, clutching his throat as though mortally wounded, rejoins: "Ham? Did you say *ham*? Why, I was playing at the Palace before you stripped your first bra." Now the "director" walks down the aisle, trying to placate his two "stars." But the girl speaks again: "I cannot work with this—this oaf." Phil, grasping his chest: "*Oaf!*" Whereupon, shattered, he lets her have it, followed by a solid *ta-ra-ra* from the band.

I think the best of Phil's bits were ad-libbed. For example, one evening during his co-star's ham–oaf business he abruptly went to the phone and asked to be connected with the theater where the long-running play *Tobacco Road* was booked. When the phone "answered," he asked for that play's mangy lead character, Jeeter Lester (James Barton), studying his co-star all the while with infinite contempt. Finally, after a long pause, the depraved old daddy of *Tobacco Road* "answered" the phone, into which Phil exclaimed, "Jeeter, I just want you to know I'm starring down the street opposite your mother."

For denouement Phil takes a sandwich wrapped in cellophane out of his pocket. It's white bread. "Lunch?" he says, offering it to the girl. "Are you mad?" she says. They then tumble onto the bed, and when their love bout ends he reaches for the sandwich—which now is toast—to the tune once again of a great big broad burlesque *ta-ra-ra* from the band.

Phil—like most comedians—never let unreasonable compassion muck up a chance for a boffo, as was painfully discovered by a young comedian whom Rags Ragland tried to help. Rags started to give the large parts in all Ragland's own sketches. Phil noticed one day that the young guy was trying to steal scenes. Rags soon observed that what Phil had said was true. When he did, he picked up this helpless third banana and said, "If you blink an eyelash the next time I'm speaking, I'll nail you to the stage."

This third banana wore shoes that were really boots strapped to his legs, with wide soles so he could sway comically and unnaturally in every direction. The next show, he promptly forgot—or chose to forget—what Rags had told him and began mugging through Rag's bits. Rags stopped the show and shouted: "Bring me a hammer and nails." They did, and he nailed this kid's boots to the floor. The way he was strapped in, the kid couldn't get out of his boots. The show proceeded all around him—dancers, strippers, singers. At one point Phil walked on and said, "What an interesting hat rack!" When the live show ended and the old fight movies went on, the third banana just stood there, nailed to the stage, until the theater closed that night. Mean, well, yes. But also deserved.

Remember, the theater—and burlesque *was* theater—had its
etiquette too. Wise guys proceeded at their peril.

There was once a stripper named Georgia Southern. When
"Rhythm Is Our Business" came out, lyrics by Sammy Cahn,
Phil with great joy ran to her with the orchestration. With her
kind of act, the architecture rocked, strong men cried. And
she considered music as necessary to her act as fuel to a 747.
She happily took the orchestration Phil gave her and went out
and demolished the theater, which she would have done if
they'd been playing "Ave Maria." She came off, knocked on
the door of Phil's dressing room as she was passing by, and
said, "Phil, that number went great for me. Thanks a million. . ."

Later, Phil and I shared a double room in the Piccadilly
Hotel on West 45th Street. I can't tell you by dimensions how
small this set-up was, but any Henny Youngman one-liner
will do—"You had to step outside to change your mind". . . "A
two-cent stamp fits the rug"—"It was tiny—but then again, we
only paid $15 a week *between* us."

One of my most vivid memories of the "spaciousness" of
that Piccadilly Hotel room was the morning I went into the
bathroom. I was leaning over the sink washing my face, when
I felt someone brush by me. It could only be Phil. Suddenly I
felt my left leg getting wet and warm. Still trying to wash the
sleep out of my head, I thought maybe it was water from the
sink splashing on my leg. Then, sleepy as I was, I realized the
water on my leg was warmer than the water that I was washing
with.

I straightened up, turned and faced Phil, who was at the
toilet, facing me—that, incredibly, was the layout. "Howahya?
You know how nearsighted I am." We laughed like hell,
because what else could you do?

Phil eventually made it to Hollywood. I eventually made it
to Hollywood. And there we met up with Garson Kanin in his

old RKO days. The most pleasurable year of my life was spent in the company of Garson Kanin and Phil Silvers, when we were all young together.

Garson had just left Broadway, where under the tutelage of the likes of George Abbott he had proved his ability, and now was the *Wunderkind* writer–director of the RKO lot. His first film, *The Great Man Votes*, with John Barrymore, attracted immediate attention.

Phil took me to Garson's home, where Garson lived with his mother. I walked over to the piano and found it badly out of tune. I went quietly to the phone and called a piano tuner, who came over to the house—nobody even questions a piano tuner—tuned the piano, was quietly paid by me, and left. That night Saul Chaplin remarked to Garson how wonderfully the piano was tuned. Garson said: "It's amazing, that piano tuner. I thought my mother sent for him. She thought I'd sent for him." This, forgive the indulgence, is to tell Garson, Saul, and Phil that I sent for that piano tuner. Yes, and *I* paid him. . . .

I had not yet started to make good in Hollywood, and Phil had come on lean times right after being presented at a newcomers' dinner in the MGM commissary—a dinner where neophytes like Tony Martin, Cyd Charisse, Kathryn Grayson, Virginia O'Brien, and Phil Silvers were presented to the brass.

Phil, accompanied by Saul Chaplin, had done his now classic "Old Man River" take-off and literally stopped the show, causing Louis B. Mayer in all his majesty to stand up and say: "I'm glad you did what you did, Mr. Silvers. Ladies and gentlemen, I brought this man to MGM because of his talent. He's been here two years, and nobody has used him. You should all be ashamed."

Phil came back in tears of delight to tell me about it. Next day he was let out of MGM. (Hooray for Hollywood. . .)

Garson Kanin, who was making his first major picture, the exquisite *Tom, Dick, and Harry*, with Ginger Rogers, Burgess

Meredith, George Murphy, and Alan Marshall, came to Phil and said, "Phil, I've got a part in the picture you could do—a small part not worthy of your talent, the part of a Good Humor man." Phil leaped in the region of Garson's throat and said, "I'll take any part," "I'll even walk in with a telegram."

While the picture was being edited, Phil pestered Garson day and night to "Please let me see my sequence, please, please!" Garson does not like to let his actors see the "rushes," or the work in progress, but finally, in a weak moment, he screened the picture for Phil at the RKO lot. During and after the Good Humor sequence there was what seemed to Phil a deadly hush. He got up and, as Phil will, went into his Hamlet bit: "Sorry, Garson, you shouldn't have risked it with me, I'll go back to New York. Sorry. Sorry." Garson blew up. "You sick clown! This is one of the funniest scenes ever made. *We've* seen it a hundred times, which is why *we* didn't laugh."

From that small magical bit part in *Tom, Dick, and Harry,* Phil Silvers got an RKO contract and was on his luminous way. And—I don't know exactly how to say this—but that year, with the booze and the broads and the fun, well, it was magical and one-time-only for Phil and Garson and me. We did it all—it won't come round again. Magic never does.

Phil is, or was, a compulsive gambler. Once he sent me a wire from Philadelphia saying he was off gambling for life, but would I send him $200? I called Ed Traubner and told him to wire Phil that Sammy wanted to send $200 but Sammy didn't have it and it would break Sammy's heart if he couldn't send it, so Phil should please thank Sammy and make believe that he got it. Wouldn't do to hurt Sammy's feelings . . . . Then I went down to Philadelphia and I found that Phil's theater is the original OTB—bookies in the wings, in the flies, in the orchestra pit. Phil *painfully* thanked me for the $200—always a trouper. Some time later Phil and Ed Traubner

and I were together and I asked Phil, "How about that $200?"
He rolled his eyes at Ed, as if to say: "Tell him, *please* tell him."
I damn near collected on that debt he never owed.

To me Phil Silvers is the complete funny man in the true
and deep sense. I never dreamed the day would come when
this man could also play a real-life combination Hamlet and
Lear—and yet he has, to the dismay of all who adore him.

He made one of the few apparently absolutely right moves
in his life when he married a Revlon beauty after a previous
marriage to a Miss America. He and his Revlon wife had five
daughters in four years. One afternoon he came home to find
his luggage in the driveway. Good-bye, Baggie Pants; enter
Hamlet's despair and our lament for a great comedic talent—laugh clown, laugh? That's what they say, especially the
ones who haven't been there.

The last time I saw him he came to my house with a
cane—not a burlesque prop—and a falter. Wherever Phil is
right this minute, I wish him smiles, I wish him applause, I
wish him loud and lasting yocks, because he certainly sup-
plied them to me. And, Phil, I'll say it one more time: I've been
there too, get rid of the cane, get rid of the falter, get rid of the
miseries. It won't do. You play a lousy old man.

CHAPTER 4

"Bei Mir Bist Du Schön"

> Bei mir bist du schön,
> Please let me explain,
> Bei mir bist du schön
> Means that you're grand.

IN THE OLD DAYS Saul Kaplan-Chaplin, Lou Levy, and I would periodically saunter up to the Apollo Theatre in Harlem. On the stage one night are two black guys. "Johnny and George," I believe, was the name of the act. They sing a song called "Bei Mir Bist Du Schön," in the original Yiddish. Don't ask me how or why they're doing this, but there they are. The song went something like this:

> Bei mir bist du schön,
> Bei mir host du chein . . .
> [To me you are grand
> To me you are charming . . .]
> Bei mir bist du einer auf der velt.
> [To me you are the first in the world.]
> Bei mir bist du git . . .
> [To me you are good . . .]
> Bei mir host du "It" . . .

(The last line shows a curious way the Yiddish lyric writers

worked: They would rhyme any kind of word. Here they put
in an English—or, at any rate, American—word, "It," referring
to Clara Bow, the "It" girl of the middle and late 1920s.)

> *Bei mir bist du teierer fin gelt.*
> [To me you are dearer than money.]
> *Fiel sheine meidlach hoben shoin gevolt nemen mir . . .*
> [Lots of pretty girls have wanted me . . .]
> *Un fin sei alle oisgekleiben hob ich nor dir.*
> [From them all I've picked out you.]
> *Bei mir bist du schön,*
> *Bei mir host du chein,*
> *Bei mir bist du einer auf der velt.*

That's the song, and these guys are standing there doing
this Yiddish song in front of this almost 99 percent black
audience. And about the theater—

I don't know if you've ever been up to the Apollo, but I can
promise you that, when the beat gets going there, it's the same
as in a cartoon. The building expands and contracts. I can't
explain it, but it's a frightening thing. The whole theater
literally starts to undulate, and you feel that this place is going
to cave in—it can't handle the excitement. I turned to Lou and
Saul and I said: "Can you imagine what this song would do to
an audience that understood the words?" We laughed at each
other.

Two or three days later I ran into Tommy Dorsey and he
said: "I'm going to open at the Paramount. Do you have any
ideas for a number I could do there?"

"I'm glad you asked," I said. "I heard a number up in
Harlem called 'Bei Mir Bist Du Schön'—"

"Oh, get outta here."

"Tommy, it's a Yiddish number—"

"Whaddaya mean, it's a Yiddish number?"

I tried to sing it to him.

"*Bei mir bist du schön, bei mir host du*—"

"Are you crazy?"

"Tommy, I'm *telling* you," I said. "It's a sensation. I don't know if you know it or not, but there are very few Jews up in Harlem"—this was before Sammy Davis—"and that audience went out of their heads! You do this song at the Paramount Theatre, where you get an occasional Jew, you'll kill 'em."

He stared at me and he kept saying: "You're out of your Goddamn mind."

I couldn't convince him.

On Second Avenue there used to be a little music store, the kind where you saw dozens of instruments hanging in the window. It was called S. Blank, Shimele Blank. This man came from a whole family of musicians. As a matter of fact, his claim to fame was that his nephew was the trombonist who used to make the trombone laugh. When Ted Lewis would ask "Is everybody happy?" Shimele Blank's nephew's trombone would go "Wah-wah-wah!"

So I walked into this music store and I asked: "Do you have a copy of a song called '*Bei Mir Bist Du Schön*'?"

He said "Sure," and I bought a copy for 35 cents.

Now I take this copy and I go back to Dorsey. You know me—relentless. He throws me and the copy out. He couldn't comprehend why I would want him to do this Jewish song.

So I put this copy on the piano in the office–apartment I shared with Lou Levy, and as far as I'm concerned that's the end of it.

Meanwhile, Lou Levy had been hanging around Jack Kapp of Decca Records and his brother Dave Kapp, and one day Lou brought the Andrews Sisters, Patty, Maxene, and La Verne up to our apartment. On the piano was this copy of a song in Yiddish. Patty, she was the talker, said: "What is this, a Greek song?" Because they were Greek.

"No," I said, "though it might as well be."

"How does it go?"

I played it for them, and they started to sing right along and to rock with it. "Gee," said Patty, "can we have it?"

I said, "Be my guest," and they took the song away.

Next thing I know they are in a recording studio at Decca Records, recording *"Bei Mir Bist Du Schön"* in the original Yiddish. Mr. Jack Kapp is sitting in his office, and he has a monitor. He presses a button and hears this group singing in Yiddish. He presses another button and says: "Hold it! Hold it! What're you doing, making a race record?" (Any song in a foreign language was considered a race record in those days.) "If you want to do that song, get an English lyric."

So Lou Levy asked me—then pleaded with me—to do an English lyric. I rebelled. I said: "Come on, I can't. What're you talking about—write an English lyric for this?" And I refused. I wouldn't do it. He kept after me, leaving notes in my shorts, in my shirts, in my jackets, on the roll of toilet tissue, saying: "Please, Sam, please!"

One night I happened to find myself trapped all alone in the apartment. There in front of me on the desk was a red-penciled "Please!" and the Yiddish song sheet. I took up the red pencil, I didn't even sit down, and I started to write:

> *Bei mir bist du schön,*
> Please let me explain,
> *Bei mir bist du schön*
> Means that you're grand.

That's the crux of that song. The thing about my work is that if I jump on a toboggan, who's taking the ride, the toboggan or me? I don't control what happens; I'm just on the slide, and I'm going to end up at the bottom, hopefully in one piece.

Bei mir bist du schön,
Again I'll explain,
It means you're the fairest in the land.

All right, I've rhymed "grand" and "land." In those days
there was a song called "Umbrella Man":

Tutta bella bella, tutta bella bella,
Umbrella man!

So the words "bella bella" were currently in the air. There
was also a song out called "Voonderbar." So I wrote:

I would say "Bella, Bella,"
Even say "Voonderbar."
Each language only helps me tell you
How grand you are.

I repeated:

I've tried to explain
Bei mir bist du schön,
So kiss me and say you understand.

Fifteen minutes later: "grand, land, understand"—genius! The
next day Lou Levy says, "Sensational, sensational!" I would
have settled for "great."

"But Dave Kapp asks would you please make the verse
twice as long."

The verse is the preface of a song, what comes before the
chorus, and all verses, if you really think about it, merely add
up to " . . . and *that's* why I say . . ." Try it with any song. For
instance, "Stardust." " . . . and *that's* why I say: 'Sometimes I
wonder why I spend the lonely night . . .' " Or, if you prefer,

"Swanee." " . . . and *that's* why I say: 'Swanee, how I miss you, how I miss you . . .' " Or any song.

Nowadays they don't use verses, but in those days they were important—and here was Dave Kapp wanting it twice as long. So what I did was double the verse. And the Andrews Sisters recorded the song.

But a curious thing happened. We wrote and recorded an English version of the song without anybody's permission. You just can't do that without permission of the copyright owners. Someone says: "You guys will have to get permission."

But I vacillate. You see, I'm still totally disenchanted with this whole idea. Nevertheless one day I picked up the music and I studied the name of the publishers: "J. and J. Kammen, 305 Roebling Street, Brooklyn."

Roebling Street, Brooklyn? I didn't go to Brooklyn when I was poor.

But one night someone said: "Why don't we go to Peter Luger's steak house over in Brooklyn, under the Williamsburg Bridge?"

Great idea. On the way we'll stop off at the J. & J. Kammen Company, right?

And this is what we did. We got in the car and went over the Williamsburg Bridge, turned under the bridge, found Roebling Street, and I walked into this storefront, "J. and J. Kammen Music Company."

J. and J. Kammen turned out to be Joseph and Jacob Kammen, small-statured identical twins. I called them the Jewish Tweedledum and Tweedledee. Both wore little black derbies and the typical serge suit of a certain light-blue color that people wore for about a hundred years. I can see them right now, standing there. They even alternated words as they spoke.

"What—" "Can—" "We—" "Do—" "For—" "You?"

So I asked while my friends were double-parked outside: "I would like to know how do I get in touch with Sholem Secunda." Secunda was the writer of the music.

"What—" "Do—" "You—" "Want—" "With—" "Him?"

"I heard a song that he wrote, and I think I can write an English lyric to it."

The song had already been recorded, mind you, and I was telling these fellows I *thought* I could write a lyric.

They said: "The song doesn't belong to him any more."

It seems that immediately after Sholem Secunda and his lyricist, Jacob Jacobs, finished writing the songs for a Yiddish musical the Kammens would print them. While the musical was playing, Secunda and Jacobs would stand in the lobby and sell the songs and they would get 100 percent of what they made. So let's say they sold the songs in the theater for four, five, six months or whatever was the run of the musical. When the show closed, they couldn't very well sell their own music in the lobby of another show, so they'd go back to the publisher with whatever copies of sheet music they had left and they would say: "We have five songs. What do you want to give us for them?"

"Well, I'll give you $150 for the whole thing," might be the reply.

So I said to the Kammens: "If you give me authorization I think I can write a lyric [which I'd already written] and maybe get a record [which we already had]."

They wrote out a little letter that said: "You are hereby authorized to write an English lyric of 'Bei Mir Bist Du Schön.'"

I left, went to Luger's, and enjoyed a wonderful steak. I waited three days. I called the Kammens.

"Hey! I think I got a great lyric!"

"That's marvelous."

I waited another three days.

"Hey! I think Decca Records is going to make a record!"

I wait another day.

"Hey, they've made the record!"

I wait another day.

"Hey, the record's coming out!"

As soon as the record did come out it was a smash hit—an international smash hit. Warner Brothers Music Company, for whom Saul and I had been supplying material, said: "How do we get to publish the English-version sheet music? Anybody know where Roebling Street is?" Boy, did I know where Roebling Street was! I volunteered to go back and see Tweedledum and Tweedledee.

So I went to the Kammens and told them Warner Brothers Music Company would give them five cents a copy if they gave Warner Brothers permission to publish the music. "Fine," they said.

What writers usually got for a song in those days was three cents a copy, but, because we were only doing a translation, Saul and I only got half of that. We had to split a cent and a half, and J. and J. Kammen were getting five cents.

There was something about this song, the contagion of this song—that was its own special magic. Once I stood in the Gaiety Music Shop on Broadway between 45th and 46th streets, where Benny Katz was the owner and a buddy of mine—he's still my buddy—and when people walked in the clerk didn't even ask them what they wanted; he just handed them the rolled-up copies, right and left. That's how big a hit it was, the number one song in the world for 1938.

Except now starts the big trouble.

Sholem Secunda and Jacob Jacobs are hollering murder, and there are big headlines in the papers: MILLION-DOLLAR SONG SOLD FOR THIRTY PIECES OF SILVER.

Warner Brothers is a big company and doesn't like all this publicity, so Warner Brothers calls in Secunda and Jacobs and gives them two cents a copy. Then Secunda and Jacobs turn around and go to J. and J. Kammen, screaming: "You did this to us!" And the Kammens also give them two cents.

That's four cents for Secunda and Jacobs, three cents for the Kammen brothers. God knows how much for the Warner Brothers—and a big three-quarters of a cent and the label "Thief!" for the fellow who picked up a red pencil one night and tried to explain *"Bei Mir Bist Du Schön."*

Some deal for such a smart rascal . . .

The first thing I did when *"Bei Mir"* broke so big was to find out the name of the first boat leaving for anywhere; I am a creature of wanderlust. It turned out to be a boat that made a Caribbean cruise, and I booked passage on it.

Our first stop was Havana. I didn't sleep all the night before we arrived there. I was the first one up in the morning. I was the first one off the boat. And the first words I heard when I set foot on foreign soil were: *"Lantsman, kenst mir helfen?"* This is Yiddish for, "Countryman, can you help me?" and it was spoken by a refugee waiting out his chance to get into the United States while peddling shoelaces, chewing gum, and other penny items for his survival. I beamed. I figured he recognized the famous lyricist who wrote the famous hit song, *"Bei Mir Bist Du Schön."* He recognized me, all right—he recognized at once that I was not a Cuban. Call me, at that point anyway, humble Sam . . .

CHAPTER 5

"I've Heard That Song Before"

It seems to me I've heard that song before,
It's from an old familiar score,
I know it well, that melody . . .

I WAS WITH a rascal named Harry Cohn, head of Columbia Pictures, for several years. Actually, I had a good deal of fun during those years, and, as most people will tell you, having fun with Harry Cohn was something very few people could honestly claim.

Al Kingston, a hot agent who had previously sold me to Republic, sold me to Cohn by saying: "I got this three-headed genius, Sammy Cahn: original story, screenplay, score." All you had to do was tell Harry he was getting three for the price of one and it was pretty much an automatic sale. So, with Saul Chaplin, I started working at Columbia Pictures around 1940.

At first there was no way I could get to meet headman Cohn. Every stratagem failed; but I did make friends with a very talented man, Morris Stoloff, head of the music department. I tried through Morris and his marvelous wife Elsa to meet Cohn, but no amount of "leaning in" brought me even close. I never saw Harry Cohn in all the time Saul Chaplin and I hung around just doing whatever B-film needed words (mine) and music (Saul's), although once I did bump into Cohn in the hall and he kindly said, "Get the hell out of my way."

There came the day, as I've mentioned, when the well ran dry and Saul and I parted. Then began one of the low points in my life, but luckily Morris and Elsa Stoloff had become like my West Coast parents. One night at dinner, just before the usual gin game, I explained my unhappiness to them—how I was out of work and would walk the streets of Hollywood and cry, literally. The frustration of being accepted by peers, such as Johnny Burke and Jimmy Van Heusen and Harry Warren Johnny Mercer, and watching them shine in the spotlight . . . well, it was a frustration I still remember. What made it even tougher was how nice they were to me.

When it seemed I'd hit bottom, the phone rang. It was Cy Feuer of Republic Pictures, now the Cy Feuer, who with his partner Ernie Martin, was responsible for all those major Broadway musicals. Cy was calling to ask if I would do a picture with Jule Styne—that is, write the picture's songs with him. Would I do a picture with Jule Styne? The way I felt right then, I would do a picture with Hitler, I told Cy. As a result I went out to Republic Pictures and met Jule Styne officially.

For the record, Jule Styne is one of the single most talented musicians I have ever worked with. I believe that songwriting ought to be a joyful endeavor, and with him it has been even more.

From the beginning it was fun. He went to the piano and played a complete melody. I listened and said: "Would you play it again, just a bit slower?" He played and I listened. I said again: "One more time, just a little bit slower." I then said, "I've heard that song before"—to which he said, bristling, "What the hell are you, a tune detective?" No, I said, that wasn't a criticism, it was a title: "I've Heard That Song Before." "Oh," he oh'd, and I continued with: "It seems to me I've heard that song before,/It's from an old familiar score, /I know it well, that melody . . ."

Now let me try to explain what my lyric writing is about.

First, I am not sure what brings about an instant title when I hear a melody, but it seldom if ever fails me—a title flashes into my head. It sounds strange and maybe even phony to people when I insist that I don't write a song as much as the song writes me. What I do is sort of trigger it with the title and then follow wherever it leads. I ask you to believe that when I began with the lyrics just quoted I didn't at all know that it would lead me to: "(BOOM-BOOM) Please have them play it again,/(BOOM-BOOM) And I'll remember just when . . . I've heard that lovely song before."

In any case, we had our first collaborative effort. I was hired to work three weeks for $1000—$333 a week—and after the songs were done Mr. Styne was done—with me. He dropped me, bang, like that. Jule went on to do another score—he was hot, having just written "I Don't Want To Walk Without You, Baby," one of the great "Baby" songs, with Frank Loesser. He also went on to do a score with Kim Gannon; then he left Gannon and went on to Harold Adamson and one other lyricist. Shortly thereafter I met Kim, and, like two jilted lovers, we commiserated with one another. "How did you like working with Jule Styne?" he asked. I said I liked it fine and I thought we'd had some fun. "Did you write a song about a song with him?" Kim asked. "Yes, I wrote a song about a song, and, you know, Kim, I think it happens to be one of the best lyrics I've ever written, if you consider the tune came first." Kim said: "Maybe you think it's the best lyric you've ever written; Styne thinks it's the wor-r-rst lyric he ever heard." Just what I needed.

So there I was, dragging my tail again down the Hollywood streets, until saved by a real giant of a music man, Big Sam Weiss, known to all as Rachmones Punim or "Pity Face"—the name given to him by Bing Crosby—Sam took "Heard That Song Before" to Harry James, who recorded it as the very last song before the great musicians' strike against the recording companies in the forties. The singer was Helen Forrest. It was released as the "B" side to a Burke-Van Heusen tune, and I thought grimly how lucky I was. Well, the "B" side turned out to be the "A" side, and life started to turn brighter because the phone rang and it was Jule Styne to say, "Hey, Sammy, I think we ought to write some songs." And some songs we wrote—a series of hits that were pure delight to work on.

They also brought us to the attention of the MCA agency, whose man, Harry Friedman, brought us at last to the attention of Columbia's Harry Cohn. The first time I met Harry Cohn I told him: "Mr. Cohn, let's you and I get one thing straight. You're not giving me ulcers. I've already *got* them." He looked at me for a long time. Then he said: "Don't worry, *you*, I'll give *something*."

So I was back at Columbia Pictures, this time with Jule Styne. A five-picture deal was negotiated by Harry Friedman of MCA for $10,000 a picture, $5000 a film for each of us! Life was good. Elsa and Morris, proud of my success with Styne, now began to ease me in with the "in" people; and slowly but ever so slowly I began to come to the attention of Harry Cohn.

I was alone in my apartment at the Sunset Towers when once again the phone rang. It was Harry Cohn. He said: "What're you doing?" and I smartly said: "Nothing," and he said: "Want to come over to the house?" and I said: "I'd love it." I lay back on the bed, grinning at the ceiling. That's at least one difference between Harry Cohn and me. I'm at least a smiling rascal. He was a serious rascal. And people get hurt by serious rascals.

One night at a dinner party over at Harry's there was this mutual friend of Cohn's and mine, Eddie Buzzell, a musical-comedy star turned director. Eddie leaned to me and said: "This man"—Harry Cohn—"is crazy about you. So play the game." I looked across the room at Harry Cohn. He'd just pulled out a cigarette. I raced across the room, pushing people aside, and lit his cigarette. Then I struck a pose, yelled back to Eddie Buzzell: "This what you mean?"—after all, a man needs his self-respect. I don't think I've ever lost it, even with Cohn.

After that I was like a son to Harry Cohn. He must have been ten or fifteen years my senior in real life. I was with him constantly, seven days a week, day and night. The day's routine would go something like this: The phone would ring and the studio would alert me that the Man was getting ready to leave his home on Crescent Drive, across the street from the Beverly Hills hotel; and that meant I was to be ready and waiting in front of the Sunset Towers, a legendary apart- ment–hotel up the street from the Players' Restaurant, which was owned by the great director Preston Sturges and was a hangout for me and all my chums: Phil Silvers, who was riding high at MGM and/or 20th Century-Fox and/or Co- lumbia, always as Blinky, the bespectacled friend of the hero; Frank Sinatra, already on the way to being a superstar—and stud—he is to this day; Frank's arranger, Axel Stordahl; Peter Lawford; Rags Ragland; and Gene Kelly.

Cohn would come tearing down Sunset Boulevard, and it always seemed that he didn't actually stop for me but that I had to get into the car while it was still in motion. Beside him was his famous briefcase—famous for the way it bulged. There are many stories, I'm sure mostly apocryphal, of Harry's near illiteracy. There was the one about the time he called in a story editor and wanted a certain writer fired. The writer was working on a movie about Richard the Lion- Hearted, and Cohn wanted him fired because, Harry said, "This son-of-a-bitch can't even spell a simple word like 'Sir.' " The writer had, of course, spelled it "Sire."

I never knew if Harry ever really read a script out of the bulging briefcase that never left his side. I only knew that I usually left him at two or three in the morning, and he usually picked me up at about eight or nine, so he was either a fast reader or a fast sleeper. . . .

But there we were, every morning—Harry, the bulging bag, and me, racing down Sunset to Gower and the remarkable Columbia studios, eventually called Gower Gulch because of all the Westerns made there.

Why do I say remarkable? Because by actual square feet Columbia was the smallest of all the studios in Hollywood: a tiny studio one block square, as compared to MGM, *miles* square, or Warner Brothers, *miles* square, or 20th-Fox, *miles* square. But from this tiny place came so many of the great motion pictures of all time. Harry had the instinct and the feel of a gambler, and when he rolled for a big one he could come up with Capra classics like *It Happened One Night, Mr. Deeds Goes to Town* or *Lost Horizon,* or others like *The Jolson Story* or *From Here To Eternity*—the film which would bring Sinatra back, not for altruistic reasons on Harry's part but because Harry "beat Sinatra's salary."

From this tiny studio, with its Columbia emblem of a very lovely girl holding a up a gleaming torch, came pictures that won Academy Award after Academy Award. I would guess that, with the exception of Disney, no one has ever won as many as Harry Cohn. The first time I ever entered his office I couldn't see him for a moment because of all the Oscars blazing on the desk behind his desk. To this day I have the feeling he had them spotlighted. The irony is that he fought the Motion Picture Academy tooth and claw, as was his nature, and he never was at peace with them, even when he took their Oscars year after year; he was decades ahead of George C. Scott, but maybe smarter; he fought the Academy but never refused the Oscars!

Be that as it may, from as far back as I can remember—even as a boy of ten who went to the Windsor Theatre on Grand

Street near Clinton, on the Lower East Side, when the manager would let two kids in for a nickel, saying "Who's got two?"—meaning pennies—or "Who's got three?"—even way back then I felt that when I saw the Lady With the Gleaming Torch I would see a really good movie.

And here I was, some eighteen years later, practically the son of the head of that studio!

We would arrive at the lot and I would go to offices on Beachwood Street in a little apartment house across from the studio proper—Columbia was already starting to burst out of its seams—and there I would start the day with Jule Styne. Jule and I would go through the ritual of discussing all the inside dope on Hollywood. Styne was a master at this. We would discuss anything and anyone and it would take us to lunch, which usually meant that we would go up to the private dining room to eat with the Man. For most of the people "condemned" to eat there, this was sheer hell; but for me it was great fun. I could have fun with Harry! I could disagree with him, and did, to the consternation of not only the condemned ones but the maître d' and staff, who might chuckle and enjoy but would also pay a price for any tiny infraction of Harry's rigid rules of cuisine, which, when reduced to the basic, meant lots of sour cream and rye bread with plenty of seeds.

After lunch, which was especially great because it was gratis, Jule and I would wander back to our office and the place would start to fill with all the chums, headed by Phil Silvers and his brother Harry.

I must tell you about Harry Silvers. He was like a mother hen to all of us, especially to Phil. He was our doctor, our lawyer, our jack-of-all-trades. It was Harry who would take the Coca-Cola empties back to the store to pick up twenty cents while Phil was at the track losing a thousand dollars. If any of us had a slight fever it was a sin not to call Harry, who

had a friend who had a pharmacy where Harry got his medical
education. Harry Silvers is gone from the scene, and this is to
tell him I love him.

So the little office would ring with laughter until it was time
for me to go back to Cohn's office to watch the dailies—the
special screening toward the close of every day of'all the
prints from all the films being shot on the lot. Harry would sit
there—always with one of his "assistants" or one of his writer
and/or director friends—and it was through the commentary
of these people that the fearsome Harry Cohn judgments were
made. And very smart judgments they often were. It always
amazed me, the power of a headman. He could walk into a
room—at the studio or at home—lift his hand, and the magic
would start. By which I mean a motion picture would go on. I
think that since the advent of television every man is now his
own Cohn or Zanuck. On the bus you hear two plumbers
going to work: "How'd you like the opening of the Carol
Burnett show?" "I think it could have been faster."

After the dailies we would usually go to Harry's marvel of a
house on Crescent Drive. His wife, Joan Perry Cohn, was an
immaculate hostess, but Harry was certainly not an immaculate host. I have seen him at the dinner table—a table set in
perfect taste with four beautiful candlesticks—I have seen
Harry with a single belch blow out two or three of those
candles. I always hoped to be present when he hit a home run
and got all four of them. It never happened.

Jule Styne and I had signed at Columbia to do five pictures—my words, his music, or his music and my words,
because there always has to be a note under every word—at, as
I say, $10,000 for each picture. Today I get around $15,000 to
do a *song*. Jule and I had started getting lucky with "I've Heard
That Song Before" back at Republic. Now we were writing for

Ann Miller, Penny Singleton, Kay Kyser, Janet Blair, Sid Caesar, Alfred Drake, Rita Hayworth. We had finished four pictures on the deal, with a fifth to come up, but Harry didn't seem to have an assignment for us. One day I was at his house, playing gin rummy, which was his complete avocation and my boredom—and playing for small stakes.

Harry broke off the game and said: "You'll have to forgive me. There are lawyers coming. I have to set up a trust fund for my two boys." I said, "Harry, if you really want to set up a trust fund there's a music company for sale, Crawford Music. It earns $30,000 a year from ASCAP and they want to sell it for $300,000"—a normal procedure, since any ASCAP firm usually sold for ten times its annual earnings. "Since you fancy yourself an old song plugger," I continued, because that's how he'd begun, behind the sheet-music counters at Woolworth's and Kresge's, singing the songs, and he loved being called that—"in ten years you'll have your money back and millions more, because of all the Columbia Pictures songs you'll be putting into the Crawford Music Company." Which brings us to Jonie Taps. Many people have wondered how a man named Jonie Taps got to Columbia Pictures—mostly the people at Columbia Pictures. When I started this book he was still there, as head of the music department. He lasted through I don't know how many regimes. And I used to think if the atom bomb ever hit Hollywood and the dust cleared, there'd be only two people left: Jonie Taps at Columbia and Lionel Newman in the same capacity at 20th Century-Fox. But at this writing Jonie Taps has at long last departed Columbia.

Jonie Taps is best described as a very short squattish man who has a laugh as loud and explosive as it is unexpected. A squat Babe Ruth. Fastidious dresser in the true music-man sense: white-on-white Cye shirt, Mele handmade shoes, Sulka tie, monograms, custom-made suits—all standard for the top man in the music business down to the errand boy. Jonie Taps was in charge of song plugging for Shapiro, Bernstein Company, one of the giant firms.

"Look," I said to Harry, "you wouldn't buy a plane without buying a pilot. Therefore you shouldn't buy a music company without the man to run it, and right now the number one music man in New York is Jonie Taps." So Harry said, "I'd like to meet him."

I called Jonie Taps in New York, and he said, "Well, I'll meet the man, but frankly I don't think this makes any sense. Why should I work on a music fund to make his kids rich?" But he came out to the Coast and met Harry Cohn—and from that moment on it seemed to me that they both tended to behave as though I was the enemy. They'd either whisper or walk away when I appeared on the scene. When Jonie Taps left for New York I asked him, "What about the deal? What about the music company?" He answered with whatever the 1940s equivalent was of "no way." As it turned out, though, it seems there must have been a way.

In the interim, one night at the Cohns' house after dinner Joan Cohn took me aside and whispered, "Harry's birthday is coming up. I have an idea for a party. It's a come-as-you-were-as-a-child." When she told me that real *goyishe* idea—maybe from where she came from it would be sort of cute, but where I came from it had been and still was torn knickers, wrinkled stockings, worn-out sneakers. I immediately said, in self-defense, "Joan, if you will allow me, Jule and I will put on a show for your party, a play called *A Day (And Night) in the Life of Harry Cohn*. Jule and I will write songs and parodies and sketches. I promise you it will be a sensation." For years I'd been doing such "evenings," and I still do, telling the story of someone's life in songs and parody. At the time Jule and I had been doing it for New Year's Eve parties at the Sinatras', so I felt pretty sure we could pull it off. We wrote a score of approximately sixteen songs, some originals but mostly parodies based on existing songs.

It began with Phil Silvers playing Harry Cohn—and if they'd given Emmys or Tonys or Oscars for such a performance, Phil would have taken them all. He was brilliant—he was at the top of his form—and, although I have seen him as Bilko, as the top banana, as everything, I don't think he's ever equaled that night. The rest of the cast was the kind you dream about. Frank Sinatra played Frank Sinatra. Peter Lawford played Peter Lawford. Gene Kelly played Gene Kelly. Judy Garland played Janet Blair, who was suing Harry Cohn at the time and was therefore *persona non grata;* Rags Ragland played Rags Ragland; Jule Styne played both Jule Styne and Hollywood columnist Sidney Skolsky—great casting size-wise. I played myself—no guts. And the guest stars were . . . Al Jolson and José Iturbi as themselves.

I had the unenviable task of telling Jolson we were putting on this "impromptu show," as I put it. Now Mr. Jolson was really not the nicest man in the world, though unquestionably a great entertainer. When singing "This Is My Lucky Day," no man sounded so lucky. Or singing of heartbreak, so heartbreaking. But *apart* from that and in real life . . . And here I had to tell him, unquestionably one of the world's greatest entertainers, that his part in the undertaking would be one word, the word being "Mammy," and just one chorus of the song of the same.

On the night of the party and show at Harry's house Jolson was in his standard white turtleneck sweater and white suit. He came up to me and said: "This Sinatra—is he a friend of yours?" I said yes. Jolson said: "He'll never have anything like this." And he whipped out five pages of yellow legal paper with his stock holdings listed on them. The first item was 10,000 shares of AT&T, in case of a rainy day. I don't know where Mr. Jolson is as I sit here remembering that moment—though I *do* know where he is, because I pass his elaborate gravesite with its splashing waters over a long series of steps every time I go to or from Los Angeles International Airport, and whenever I do I wonder if Jolson knows that Frank Sinatra now also has five sheets of yellow legal paper. If so, I'll bet he'd start swimming upstream.

Anyway, I told Jolson his one word and one song, and ran away.

Well, Harry Cohn was a captive audience at his own party, which made him quite a hero that night. He took it rather graciously. I think, if he'd known in advance what we were going to do, he wouldn't have been so happy or so gracious. But Harry laughed hilariously through the whole thing. Everybody started thinking: maybe we had him wrong.

The show began with Harry Cohn, played by Phil Silvers, in his office. Phil had this riding crop with which he'd beat the furniture and/or the people in the office. He was hard at work casting *The Jolson Story,* which Harry Cohn was then actually getting ready to make.

Phil went around the room yelling for Miss Missick, Harry Cohn's secretary—her real name, by the way, and a lovely girl, by the way. "Miss Missick! Send in Sidney Skolsky!" And in comes Jule Styne reading the *Hollywood Citizen News,* Skolsky's paper. Phil snapped at him: "Skolsky! Have you found a guy yet to play Jolson?" And Jule said: "I got this fella outside," and Phil: "Well, bring him in." Jule went to the door, snapped his fingers, said: "Boy! Boy!"—and in came the real Al Jolson. "Are you kidding?" says Phil, grabbing Jule by the lapels. "This guy couldn't play Jolson's *father.*" Jule looked at Phil and said: "But he sounds like Jolson. Please, let him just say one word." And then Jolson said: "Mammy." Phil said to Jule: "I'll kill you for this," and Jule said: "Please, please, just listen to him sing." Phil said: "Okay, but I'm warning you." Jolson took his stance. And then—

I've seen Al Jolson at the Winter Garden, I've seen him many, many places; but there was never ever any performance of "Mammy" as there was that night. Never. Standing backstage, all those talented people were awestruck.

Because what Jolson was doing was *auditioning*. He didn't want Larry Parks to get the role in the picture. *He* wanted to get it.

So he ended the song to a standing ovation, and Phil Silvers said: "Thanks a lot. Don't call us, we'll call you." And the minute Jolson walked off Phil shouted: "Miss Missick, get me 20th Century-Fox!" Then, on the phone: "Twentieth? Let me speak to Georgie Jessel. Hello, Jessel? You've got to dub this picture."

And now I come in, as me, and he started talking to me about another Columbia movie called *A Song to Remember*, starring Cornel Wilde as Frederic Chopin. I might add that to this day one of my favorite memories is looking at the bulletin board in the office of Morris Stoloff and seeing a notice that read: "Cornel Wilde is to be at the studio to learn *The Polonaise* from 2 to 3, the *Étude* from 3 to 4, the *Concerto* from 4 to 5." Which is remarkable, considering that Cornel Wilde wouldn't know what part of the piano to play if you sat him on the bench. What he was doing was learning to mimic the piano playing to be done by a great artist named Iturbi.

But Phil Silvers–Harry Cohn was asking me if anybody has been found to play the piano for "that Choppin picture."

I said: "It's Chopin, sir," and he said: "What's *your* name?" and I told him, and he said, "Keep talkin', kid," which became a running gag through the rest of the show. I said, "I think there's a fellow outside who plays the piano pretty well." "Have him come in." And, again, a snap of the fingers and "Boy! Boy!"—and in comes Iturbi. Who plays as memorable a *Firebird* as I've ever heard, followed by an ovation, followed by a "Don't call us, we'll call you." Exit Iturbi. "Miss Missick,"

Phil shouts, "Get me Harry Akst!" (Akst played for Jolson all those years and later for Eddie Fisher . . . I'd heard that one of Harry Akst's chores for Fisher was to hide under the TV camera during a TV show and point out the pauses in the music so Fisher wouldn't lose time. One day, on a TV show conducted by my buddy Axel Stordahl, Fisher lost his place —he had lost Akst. Axel took the orchestra out, Ken Lane the pianist helped Fisher find himself—and in the background one trumpet player, horn at the ready, turned to another trumpet player, also at the ready, and said, "I'm leaving here at 6:15 no matter *where* that so-and-so is!")

Anyway, Harry Akst came in and played "Kitten on the Keys" and Phil said, "Now *that's* a piano player." Finally the buzzer buzzed, Phil–Harry lifted it and said, or rather snarled, after a moment: "Janet Blair wants to to see *me*?"—and enter Judy Garland as the forbidden Janet Blair, who curls her lip at Cohn and, to the tune of the obvious hit:

JUDY: *I'll be suing you,*
    In all the old familiar places,
    True you gave my teeth these braces,
    But we're through.

PHIL: *(leaping from behind desk, and* à la Nelson Eddy):
    I took this unknown blister,
    Made her Eileen's sister,
    All of this I did,
    And never once at-tacked the kid.

JUDY: *I'll be suing you*
    Whenever skies are dull and gray,
    Whenever there is rent to pay,
    I'll always think of you that way.

PHIL: *(outraged):*
    You've ru-ined my en-tire morning
    With your Com-m-m-m-munist-ic view . . .

Judy says: "If that's the way you feel about it. This for you"—snap of fingers—"and that for you"—snap of fingers —"and *this*"—turns and lifts her skirt above her bottom—"for you!" Phil, after a smoldering look at her bottom, contemptuously:

> *I am gazing at your moon*
> *But I keep seeing . . . you!*

The people were rolling on the floor, and at this point we cleared the set, which now again became his home, and at the end of the day the great man relaxes by playing gin rummy with Sammy Cahn, as I told you.

I say there never was a gin game like the one I now played with Phil Silvers as Harry Cohn. We took Harry Cohn apart. Phil was sitting there at the table with a deck of cards and a platter of candy. I rushed in: "What's the crisis? I'm hungry." All he said: "Deal!" And he offered me the candy and then pulled it back, saying: "Candy is bad for you if you're hungry." Let me tell you about Harry Cohn, the real Harry Cohn in a real gin rummy game. If you shuffled he'd give you his pushcart snatcher's look and then reshuffle the cards longer than you had. So in the play I shuffled them *brrrp*, like that, and said, "No sense both of us shuffling." And this went on for half an hour, *brrrp*, me shuffling and he reshuffling. Then he played—and played—and played—and he ended up losing $11.60. On the back of the score sheet he wrote: "Miss Missick, give Sammy Cahn a chit for $11.60." I say: "Just once, I want to see something green, all you keep giving me are these papers. I'm winning what—paper?" Right then he said: "You know something? I think you'd make a hell of a movie producer," and he told me what a great idea he had for a picture for me to make about a returning World War II hero. He kept pulling back the markers, the score sheets, and I kept reaching for them, and this went on until at last he said: "You think *Lindbergh* had a welcome? When this guy comes home they'll give him such a ticker-tape parade—there'll be ticker, there'll be tape—such a welcome"—and he ripped up all my markers into confetti, and threw it all out the window, so to speak.

I jumped up and said: "Mr. Cohn, you are a *son-of-a-bitch*—but *since* it's your birthday"—and we all broke out into "Happy Birthday."

Immediately thereafter Cohn called our agent—Harry Friedman of MCA had taken us over from Al Kingston—and started to rehearse Friedman on how to give us the finger, Jule and me. What he had in mind was to sign us for five more pictures, but not for us to know it. Therefore the finger rehearsal. "Tell the guys there's an outside chance of five pictures at $75,000 for the batch"—a fifty percent increase. Harry Friedman, to his credit, came and told us what Harry Cohn was trying to do. I loved it. Harry Cohn, the pushcart snatcher. I said to Friedman: "Why don't you go back and tell him we'll do the first two pictures for $15,000 each, that's $30,000; and the next two for $20,000 each, that's $40,000; and the final picture—and who knows when? or if? for $25,000. It adds up to the same thing, especially if the fifth picture is never made."

Harry Friedman took the suggested counter-deal back to Harry Cohn. What do you think was the answer from this man I'd been with day and night for four years, in happy times for me and I think for him? *"Get those bastards off the lot."* This edict was delayed because we'd just finished a picture for Kay Kyser, and Harry knew if we were off the lot we couldn't finish the final recordings. So we kept coming to the studio. Harry Cohn's office was right over the main gate, and, though I didn't know it, he was up there, watching—and waiting.

On the last day, Jule and I went over to the Bank of America, kitty-corner from the Columbia lot, and one of us said why not go back and say good-bye to the cast and the other said, "Good idea." We walked back up to the front gate, and the cop there says, "You can't come in." It is impossible to explain what a shock this was—like being barred from your own living room. I said to the policeman, "You're kidding," and he in genuine embarrassment, said, "No, Sammy, it's the boss's orders, you can't come in here."

Three or four days later I heard from Morris and Elsa Stoloff. Harry had obviously again been playing pushcart snatcher. He had told Elsa Stoloff to talk to me, set me up.

"Sammy," she told me, "Harry feels badly." I said: *"He* feels badly? I've lost a studio." She: "Why don't you go see him?" "Go see him? I can't get on the lot." "Why don't you go to his home?"

Okay. So on a Sunday Jule Styne and I drive out to Harry's house. There he is, at the pool, pacing up and down like Napoleon on Elba. I didn't know whether we should stay on our side of the pool, or wait for him to walk across the water. After a while we joined him, and Jule Styne—blessed are the peacemakers—said: "Gee, Harry, it seems to me that, if you and Sammy had just put down the cards and talked for a moment, you could have come to some agreement." Harry said: "Do you mean if I'd left the agent out of it you'd have made the deal?" It was Harry Cohn's obsession that agents were put into the world to louse up everything. Jule got flustered and answered: "Yes," at which Harry kind of smiled. I kind of smiled also and said: "Now what are you going to do for a lyric writer?" Cohn became livid. "Get out of my house!" He kept pointing *out* until I thought he was on the verge of a stroke. I said, "Harry, I'm not a religious man, but it's a sin to throw a friend out of your house. I don't have to work for you. Why can't we just be friends?" The more quiet I got, the more enraged he got, and he kept pointing for us to leave. "Leave! Leave!" So Jule and I walked off, and then Jule Styne turned back to Harry, with what I think was the perfect exit line: "Gee, and we had such a great idea for your next birthday."

You know what makes it a poignant story? At Harry's next birthday they *read* the script of the year before.

A coda to my Harry Cohn story: Our next job was a picture for a gentleman named Samuel Goldwyn: *The Kid from Brooklyn*, with Danny Kaye and Virginia Mayo. Harry Friedman took us to see Mr. Goldwyn. It was Mrs. Frances Goldwyn who said, "How do you do?" I took my stance—as you know, the strange croaky voice that first demonstrates a Sammy Cahn song to a producer or anyone else is always Sammy Cahn's and it starts with the ritual described—left hand goes out, head goes down, right hand goes up, head comes up, I let go.

As I sang the first note of "It Seems to Me I've Heard That Song Before," Mr. Goldwyn slid off the chair and under his desk, hysterical with laughter. Mrs. Goldwyn, very embarrassed, said: "Sam, Sam, get up." He got up, Jule Styne gave me another arpeggio, and I started again. Out went the hand, down went the head . . . the first note—and again Mr. Goldwyn slid under the desk, hysterical. We tried a third time: same thing. So I turned to Mrs. Goldwyn, who I think is the real Sam Goldwyn, and sang the song to her. Result: we went to work for Goldwyn—our first job away from Harry Cohn—at $25,000 a picture.

I eventually made it back to that fabulous house of Harry Cohn's on Crescent Drive at the invitation of Mr. and Mrs. Laurence Harvey. Harry had died, and Joan Cohn had married Laurence Harvey. (Blame it on a compulsive songwriter's antic reverie, but I've more than once sort of wistfully thought that, if Joan had married Franchot Tone, why then her name would have been Joan Cohn Tone . . . A song. . . ? Sorry, Joan.)

I believe the key word to all my experience is paradox. Show me anything that can't happen and it will happen. Anything's strength is its weakness, and anything's weakness is its strength.

Paradox: Where once sat rough, tough, basic Harry Cohn, who could belch shamelessly at a formal dinner—to see, at his place, at his table, the elegance of a Larry Harvey . . .

Actually, I loved Harry. I think I understood what he was about. It was sadness to me that he apparently didn't know what I was about. After all, once upon a time I also snatched from pushcarts.

Harry Cohn. He was a real pistol.

The Swooners Softball Team. (We played the NBC staff, the CBS staff, the Les Brown Orchestra, etc.) The back row shows Tony Quinn, Barry Sullivan and Frank Sinatra. The front row from left to right shows Stanley Styne, Sammy Cahn, Jule Styne, and—an unusual pair—Hank Sanicola, Sinatra's manager, and Ed Traubner, my manager. We used the Beverly High Field on Saturdays and Sundays.

A much younger Jule Styne with a much younger Sammy Cahn. Barely concealing our joy after having won the Academy Award for "Three Coins in the Fountain!"

Early Cahn and Styne.   (Photo: Alexander Bender, New Yo

CHAPTER 6

"It's Magic"

You sigh, the song begins,
You speak and I hear violins,
It's magic.
The stars desert the skies
And rush to nestle in your eyes,
It's magic . . .

In 1942, when Jule Styne and I first were brought together, I was what I believe is called a wild swinging bachelor, living at the Sunset Towers with Axel Stordahl and beginning to come into some dough. Frank Sinatra lived a couple of stories above us; he had a terrace because he was a star. We'd yell back and forth to one another, and guess who was living down below? If you looked down from Frank's terrace you'd see, across the street, a series of little houses, one of them owned by Tom Kelly, a noted interior decorator; the occupant of that house was Ava Gardner. Just for mischief, Frank and I would stick our heads out the window and yell her name. She couldn't know, of course, that one of the voices yelling her name would someday make international headlines with her.

Jule Styne was born Julius Stein in London, England, on December 31, 1905—he thinks all New Year's Eve parties are his birthday parties—but he grew up in Chicago in the same area with another Julius Stein. Because they were both occupied with music in the Chicago area their mail started to get mixed up, so Julius Stein No. 2 asked Julius Stein No. 1 to change his name, which Jule did. And the difference today between Styne and Stein is, among other things, about $100 million, because Julius Stein is the president of the giant agency MCA, Music Corporation of America.

By the time Jule Styne was eight he was already a child prodigy, playing the piano with the Chicago Symphony, and soon thereafter in small jazz groups along with his brother Maurey, saxophonist *extraordinaire.* These groups included the likes of Benny Goodman and Glenn Miller, to mention but two. Jule went on from the small bands to the big bands and finally to just about running the Phil Spitalny All Girl orchestra at the then posh Edgewater Beach Hotel. It was in those days he wrote his first standard, "Sunday," as good a Chicago-type tune as there's ever been.

Jule married a marvelous gal named Ethel and migrated to New York, where he worked as a vocal coach. When 20th Century-Fox turned to making musicals they sent for Jule to be their vocal coach; from there he went to work as a composer for Republic Pictures, and his association first with Frank Loesser and then with me. By that time Jule and Ethel were the proud parents of sons Stanley and Norton—so Styne was the Married Man and I was the Swinger. What James Van Heusen was for the Methodists, I tried to be for the Jews.

One day the studio wasn't available for us to work in, so Jule suggested we work at his home. The maid opened the door, Ethel came to greet us—seems all my collaborators were married to Ethels—and immediately I was taken with her warmth, her *Gemütlichkeit.* You knew where you stood with this Ethel.

We couldn't work in my place because of the games and the broads and the wet towels, so we continued to work at his place. It was at 611 North Elm Drive in Beverly Hills, not an expensive home, and with the architecture typical of early Beverly Hills. I call it Moroccan—like the original fort in *Beau Geste*. I always approached it from tree to tree, afraid of getting picked off by an Arab. As I stood in front of his home, I realized that I was a fool the way I was living—this man had it made.

Jule and I were on the upward curve. We wrote rocking-chair songs, which means the kind of hits where the publishers sat and rocked while the songs did all the work for themselves. My old buddy Ed Traubner was now on the Coast. Then, as now, he was my manager, and he made our first deal with the Edwin H. "Buddy" Morris Music Company, perhaps one of the most unusual deals in the history of songwriting. In those days sheet music was the important sale, and, as I've said, the writers got three cents for each copy sold. Ed Traubner suggested, "Why not make it a sliding scale?" and further suggested three cents for the first 100,000 sales, four cents for the second 100,000, five cents for the third 100,000, and so on. It seemed a reasonable proposal from the publisher's viewpoint, because *"Bei Mir Bist Du Schön,"* one of the biggest smashes in history, had only sold 135,000 copies.

The war broke out and the first song Jule and I wrote, "Five Minutes More," went to 600,000 copies. "I'll Walk Alone" went over a million, and *Time* magazine did a piece on us in which they generously said: "Styne and Cahn are, next to Rodgers and Hammerstein, perhaps the most successful songwriting team."

One day I said to Jule: "It seems to me this war may end soon. I have it on the highest authority—Walter Winchell. We should have a song ready to welcome the boys back."

My idea was: "Kiss me once and kiss me twice, and kiss me once again./It's been a long, long time." Most songs have thirty-two bars; that one has only sixteen. I didn't realize that when I gave Styne the title I was giving him *half* the song. A reporter once asked me what my most profitable song was, and I told him it was "It's Been a Long, Long Time" at $75,000. He went home and counted the words—about seventy-five—then put it in his article that Sammy Cahn earned $1000 a word!

About this time Henry Spitzer, the professional manager at the Buddy Morris Company, asked us to come over to see him. We thought he was so happy with our success that maybe he wanted to give us a car. What he wanted was to renegotiate the contract. The irony is that the only reason we'd gone to Morris in the first place was to be with Big Sam Weiss, the man who had taken "I've Heard That Song Before" to Harry James—Big Sam, if not for whom I'd probably not be sitting here writing this book or you reading it.

A couple of years later Jule and I were signed by Michael Curtiz, the Hungarian-in-residence at Warner Brothers, to do a picture called *Romance on the High Seas*, with a screenplay by the very talented Brothers Epstein, Philip G. and Julius J. I want to tell you a little story about Michael Curtiz, pronounced Cur-teez. Jack Warner had gone to Europe and said to him: "If you will come to America and work for me, I will give you a welcome you will not believe." It so happened that the boat bearing Mr. Curtiz arrived in New York on a July 4. He saw the fireworks, the fireboats, water shooting up—all for him! He started to cry. Michael Curtiz is an emotional man.

At the time Jule and I were signed for a picture by Mr. Alex Gottlieb, who shortly thereafter married Polly Rose, sister of Billy Rose. A short squat man, Alex Gottlieb, hair slicked back over his head, wore metal glasses and had a habit of trying to see how many wrinkles he could get between his collar and his chin. One time I said to him: "I've got a great idea for a movie. Let's you and me write it." And we wrote it—*Two Tickets to Broadway*, one of the few screenplays I ever wrote. Mr. Gottlieb took it to RKO and sold it to Howard Hughes, and then he hired Jule Styne and Leo Robin to do the score. Nice fella.

But, prior to all this, Jule and I were to do *Romance on the High Seas*, for Michael Curtiz, and we were told to write the score for Judy Garland, the number one musical-comedy star in Hollywood—then, I guess, or since. But it turned out Curtiz couldn't get Judy Garland for the picture, so he told us: "Write for Betty Hutton." So we are writing now for Betty Hutton. So one day Curtiz comes to us and says: "Now we can't get Betty Hutton, but I have a genius idea. You'll write for her sister Marion"—who was then singing with the Glenn Miller band.

I said to Curtiz: "You know, Mike, when you talk about Judy Garland you're talking about a big star. When you talk about Betty Hutton you're still talking about a movie star. When you talk about Marion Hutton you're talking about a fine *band* singer. But if you want a band singer I'll get you the best." He said okay, and I rush to the phone and called a fellow named Alfred Levy.

Alfred Levy was a very personable fellow who had left the clothing business in the Midwest and come to Hollywood to make his fortune, working in the office of agent Jimmy Saphier. A group of us had a little round table at the Brown Derby, and it was there I met Alfred Levy. Not much later I told Frank Sinatra he needed someone around him like Al who would advise him and not exploit him, because Al was a *rich* boy. So Al Levy became Frank Sinatra's manager; eventually he left Frank to open his own talent agency, at which time I said to Al: "If I were going to open a talent agency, the first girl I'd sign would be Doris Day."

Doris Day was singing with Les Brown. She had had a hit record, "Sentimental Journey." (To this day I cannot understand why Doris Day cannot sing in front of people—she won't make personals—because that's what she did, perform as a vocalist with a band.) In those days we had a baseball

team called the Swooners, the "we" consisting of Frank Sin-
atra, Jule Styne, Sammy Cahn, Ed Traubner, Hank Sanicola,
Tony Quinn, Barry Sullivan, Stanley Styne (son of Jule), and
Harry Crane, a top television comedy writer, and Don
McGuire. We used to play on Sundays on the ballfield of
Beverly Hills High School, against teams of NBC or CBS pages
and orchestras like Les Brown's. One Sunday morning the
Swooners were playing at Beverly Hills High and Al Levy
came running across the field, yelling to me:

"I've just signed Doris Day!"

"Doris Day? That's great, just great!"

So, when I called Al Levy for Michael Curtiz's singer, it was
Doris Day I had in mind. I said to Al on the phone: "I'm here
with Michael Curtiz and he's talking about Judy Garland and
Betty Hutton. There's no way for Doris to get the picture, but
if you bring her around I'm sure we can get a technicolor
screen test out of this, and at least she'll meet Mr. Curtiz." I
hung up and told Curtiz about my idea, and an audition was
set for 1 P.M. in his office.

Doris showed up just as she was: no special hairdo, no
pretty dress. I said, "Okay, let's rehearse. Let's do the first two
choruses of 'Embraceable You.' " She did two bars and then
threw herself, crying, onto the couch. I turned to Al and said:
"Do you want to explain that?" Well, it seemed she'd just left
her husband, who was George Weidler, the brother of Virginia Weidler, the marvelous brat you may remember in the
movie of Philip Barry's The Philadelphia Story. And this was
their song!

I said: "Hey, Al, spare me all this. Get her on her feet, will
you?" Which he did, and after a bit I told her: "Mr. Curtiz is
expecting a Betty Hutton sort of a singer, kind of bouncy."
Doris, to her credit, said, "I don't bounce around. I just sing."
So I tried to think of a bouncy song to give her, and finally
settled on "What Do We Do on a Rainy Night in Rio?"—a
Latin song by Leo Robin and Arthur Schwartz that might

make her move a little bit. She sang it, but just standing there, with perhaps a little finger snap. I said: "Look, you've got to move at least a little." She said: "Betty Hutton moves because she doesn't sing."

At that point we had to go in to see Curtiz, who looked at her and says: "You sing, dolling." She did "Embraceable You." Michael Curtiz looked at me as if to say, "This is very very good," but to her he said, "You move a little, dolling." She did "What Do We Do on a Rainy Night in Rio?" and you could detect a tiny sway. At that—I swear to you—this eminent Hungarian got up from behind his desk and walked over and put his hands on her hips and moved her as she sang again. And then he finally said the fateful words: "We make screen test."

I knew I'd at least done my part.

One day they screened the tests of the three girls. First came Marion Hutton; she was not earthshaking. Then came Janis Paige—by comparison, excellent. Then came Doris Day —and the projection room, when they ran the film, exploded.

Jule and I started going through the script of *Romance on the High Seas*, and as I was reading he was fooling around at the piano with this waltz and then this tango he always warmed up with. We needed a song for a scene in which Jack Carson is to take Doris Day to a nightclub in Cuba. Suddenly I began to listen to the tango and I said: "What's that?" and Jule said: "Just something I've been playing for two years," and I said: "Play it again, *slowly*." And he did. "Once more, *slower*." He did, and we wrote "It's Magic."

Three years later Doris Day was queen of the Warners lot, and a dozen years later Jule and I had changed positions: I was married, with two children, and Jule was divorced. This divorce also broke us up at the time. Jule wanted to go to Broadway. I said: "I can't go to Broadway, I got a wife and two kids." He said: "I *had* a wife and two kids." And he left. Love and marriage . . .

CHAPTER 7

"Guess I'll Hang My Tears Out to Dry"

When I want rain, I get sunny weather,
I'm just as blue as the sky.
Since love is gone, can't pull myself together.
Guess I'll hang my tears out to dry!

In 1943 Jule Styne and I were approached by a man named David Wolper—not the David Wolper who produces documentaries but his uncle, who used to be in the café business—to do a Broadway show. It was a terrible book and we declined the proposition. But Wolper did the show. It was called *Follow the Girls*; it had Jackie Gleason, Tom Patricola, Buster West, Gertrude Niessen, and it was quite a hit. But this was during the war, and *Follow the Girls* was a brassy, hokey musical, which took a low-level approach toward the war effort—in fact, it was all pretty low class. Jule Styne said to me, "Huh! We sure blew that one." I said, "No, we didn't. We don't want that kind of hit."

And again David Wolper came to ask us to do a show. He gave us a book titled *Glad to See Ya!* because that was Phil Silvers' catch-phrase and it was hoped he would play the lead. It was, I thought, absolutely the worst book I'd ever read. Then he handed us a second book, by the respected Guy Bolton, who would subsequently write *Anastasia*. I liked Bolton's book, but it was the other one that everyone wanted us to do. So they said: "You like the Guy Bolton? Come up to MCA and tell both stories."

So I did. And I also did one of my pushcart shticks—disastrously. I got up before seven or eight people in the room, and, instead of telling the Bolton story first, I started with *Glad to See Ya!* I told it fast, to get it out of the way—snap, snap, snap! Then I said: "Now I'd like to tell you the story that I like." I launched into Guy Bolton's book, a little slower and little more studied, with more care. Only toward the end did I realize my error. By comparison the Bolton book seemed dreary, dull, stilted. I suddenly thought to myself: "Why am I involved in this idiocy, trying to sell this audience?" By the time I finished they were ready to leap at me. And before you knew it Jule and I are involved in doing a score to a book called *Glad to See Ya!*

Phil Silvers was going to play the lead. Lupe Velez, the Mexican actress around whom the *Spitfire* series of motion pictures was made, was going to be one of the stars (this is during her Gary Cooper period). Busby Berkeley was going to be the director.

We went to New York to write the show.

Subsequently Phil Silvers was not allowed to do the show because they needed him for a picture at 20th Century-Fox. Lupe Velez was found dead—by suicide. And there we were with Busby Berkeley.

The new selection for the leading man was Eddie Davis, who was one of the supreme performers at a night club called Leon and Eddie's on 52nd Street. People used to come from all over the world to go to Leon and Eddie's and see this man on the stage, Eddie Davis, one of the great song men. Everyone thought that it was a great victory for us to get him. Also we wound up with Jane Withers—once a child star who became the lady plumber in TV commercials—and an actress named June Knight.

Now, we had an Eddie Davis who was the star and we had a second Eddie Davis who was the co-author of this script—a cab driver. Eddie Davis the cab driver had a good sense of humor, but he was almost totally illiterate. He used to haunt the big hotels where the stars would stay, and when he'd get a guy like Eddie Cantor in his cab he'd say: "Mr. Cantor, my name is Eddie Davis; I got some great jokes." And he'd give them jokes. From that he progressed to being a comedy writer, and then he wrote this show.

He wrote the show with a man called Bill Thompson. Thompson was an Englishman who had written many shows in England, and he was a good musical playwright, something that Eddie Davis needed. But temperamentally they were completely opposite men.

That was the cast of characters.

This was the first Broadway show for the team of Styne and Cahn. It was 1943, and I remember vividly that, at a meeting early in the proceedings, Jule said: "You know, I don't know how to time a book, but I've put a stopwatch to the songs we've written, and we have an hour and a half of music. That's too much. So I think we should cut now."

Busby Berkeley replied with the first of what were to be his many remarkable statements: "If it's good it can run until two in the morning." And, instead of someone saying right away, "you're fired!" they left everything in.

We opened in Philadelphia.

Before we left New York a Broadway actor sat us down and gave us a lecture on how to conduct ourselves. I wish I had taped that talk and saved it, because what he said should have been published and kept for every performer who's going out of town. One of his sagest bits of advice was: "Stay away from the showgirls, the tall girls, stay away from the stars. Find yourself a nice little chorus girl. They don't yell, they don't tell, and they're grateful." I listened very carefully to everything he said.

We got out of town and immediately Jule Styne showed up with one of the tallest showgirls I'd ever seen, just like he hadn't heard a word that had been said to him. The first night in Philadelphia he walked in and said, "A terrible thing happened!"

"What happened?"

"My girl, they stole her coat. I had to buy her a coat."

That's how he opened, right? He had to buy someone a new coat.

I, on the other hand, picked out a lovely small chorus girl and was very happy.

By this time, however, Mr. Busby Berkeley was having hard times with the show, and all the performers in the show, who couldn't follow his direction were looking past him at me. He started to sense that they were doing this, so he barred me from the theater.

I was relieved. One good reason for my relief was that I had found him one day in the pit with a viewfinder of the kind that a photographer uses for framing his shots. He's doing a Broadway show, what's he doing with a film framer? So I said to myself, "We're in a lot of trouble," and was happy, indeed, to be barred.

We opened in Philadelphia. The show ran until 12:15 in the morning—three and a half hours, when it should have been no more than two and a half.

This was on a Monday. In that Wednesday's *Variety* three musicals on the road were reviewed. One was *Glad to See Ya!*, opening at the Shubert Theatre in Philadelphia. The second was *On the Town*, in Boston, with music by Leonard Bernstein, lyrics by Betty Comden and Adolph Green, dances by Jerome Robbins. And the third, also in Boston, was *Carousel* by Rodgers and Hammerstein. According to *Variety* the latter two shows were in trouble, but all our show needed was some pruning. Some pruning!

The producer decreed, "We've got to bring it down to a respectable running time. Rip an hour out of it." Which is what they did—literally ripped an hour out of it. They never were able to put it together again.

I now risk telling the plot of this beauty:

A comedian goes to the USO to try to get a job entertaining. He's so bad that he can't get a regular job, so he figures maybe the man at the USO will let him entertain the troops. He is rejected. At the same time a young couple, a song and dance team, also tries to get a job there; they also are rejected. The comedian and the young couple are sitting in the waiting room consoling one another when in walks the great—I forget his name, I'm glad to say—the great . . . Zoroni, an Italian fellow who has two young people as his assistants. He's going to go out on the USO tour because he's one of the greatest magicians in the world.

As he's about to pick up his papers and passports, two guys come in and tell him, "If you show up in any of these places, people will be waiting for you because you're wanted in each of these countries for the terrible things you've done in the past."

He runs away and leaves behind all his papers and other materials, and the incompetent comedian and the other two young people pick them up and go in the place of the magician and his assistants. Wherever the comedian goes he has to evade people who try to kill him, mistaking him for the other. . . .

That's the plot, I swear. Some *pruning?*

The show played its first week. Sunday morning I was snuggled up nice and warm and comfortable with this lovely small girl and life was good, just like that actor fellow told me.

The phone rang. It was the theater calling me. I had to get down there right away.

I said, "Hey, you got it all wrong. Remember me? I'm barred from the theater."

"You don't understand. You've got to get here right away. Immediately—there's been a terrible accident."

I put on my clothes and I ran over to the theater, where everybody was standing around.

Eddie Davis the star had been hurt in an automobile crash the night before while going home from the theater.

Usually you have an understudy, but not the first week. And, even if you have an understudy, how are you going to make the show work without the star?

They asked: "Can you do it?"

I said: "What do you mean? You've got it all wrong. It's not, *can* you do it? It's, *will* you do it? And the answer is no."

"*You've* got it all wrong. Because if you can do it you will do it because you must do it."

"Look, nothing in the world will make me walk out on that stage."

"Answer one question: Can you do it?"

"I can do it. But nothing will make me walk out on that stage."

The conductor of the show was a man called Max Meth, a very famous conductor of musicals. Max and I had become friendly. Max said, "Can I see you alone, Sam?"

"Sure."

He got me in a room and said, "Sammy, can you do this thing?"

"Sure, I can do it."

"Then why won't you do it?"

"Max, look at me. I'm a little Jewish boy from the Lower East Side in New York. I'm not a leading man. If I walk out on that stage and someone says something—like, 'What's that Jew doing up there?'—I will die. I will literally die."

"Are you insane? You must be crazy. No one talks that way

in the Broadway theater. What do you think you're in, burlesque? This is the Broadway theater. Is *that* your concern?"

"That's my concern."

"If that's what your concern is, I promise you, I give you my word of honor on everything I hold sacred in the world, you can dismiss that from your mind. If *that's* what your concern is—I don't know how to guarantee it but I promise it. Sammy, if you can do it you must do it, or this show closes this week."

Of course I realized he was referring not only to the hopes of dozens of people but also to the investment. In those days such a show cost around $200,000.

"—Please, Sammy."

"Okay."

I walked out on the stage for a run-through of my songs. Jule Styne got in the pit and gave me the introduction. On my first number I lifted my finger and opened my mouth to sing out . . . and I froze.

I'm hung up on the first word—I'm blank!

And I heard this voice behind me. It belonged to Jule's big showgirl that I didn't like. "Oh, this is great!" she said. "This bum wrote the lyrics and he doesn't even know them."

But I was still just hung up there, couldn't move. I was looking at Jule Styne, and finally he said: " 'The'!"

I burst out with: "The fact is that we got to do a—" And I zoomed through all the songs.

Now we were going to do the scenes. Busby Berkeley didn't like me from before. Now he hated me because *he* wanted the part, which I didn't know at the time.

As I put my foot on the stage for the first entrance Busby Berkeley said, "Just a moment."

I said, "Buzz, please, Buzz, if you think you're directing me, I ask you, please, not to. I think I can do this whole thing if you'll let me. I may not go to the exact spot in some instances;

I may not say the exact word in some instances; but if you let me I think I can do it. But if you start directing me, I don't know."

So he sat down and I went through the scenes.

This was Sunday in the Shubert Theatre in Philadelphia, December 1944.

The leading lady was June Knight, one of the most beautiful women in the world. She was in pictures at Paramount, and she was the girl who introduced "It Was Just One of Those Things" in the Cole Porter show *Jubilee!*

I think I wanted to sleep with June Knight more than I ever wanted to sleep with a woman. She was everything in the world that a little boy from the Lower East Side could ever aspire to. But there we were. You want a better dream than this? I'm the leading man in a show with June Knight! (I never made a pass at her, though. I felt, down in my gut, that during our affair, if we had one, at the very height of it she'd stop and say: "I could use another half-chorus.")

I remained faithful to my small chorus girl.

It got to be Monday, and I was in the dressing room of Eddie Davis, the star. He was a man of six feet one, easy. I am five seven and a half—eight, if I stand tall, though even five seven's taller than Jule Styne. They hadn't got any wardrobe for me. I had to wear Eddie Davis's wardrobe—they were even putting extra stocks inside his shoes to make them stay on my feet.

Eddie Davis had a black dresser who had a profound contempt for me. He was a giant of a man, and he kept shaking his head and pouting his lips and blowing air past them, "Phuh! Phuh!" I could read it in his face: "You're the lowest, you're the lowest!" He wouldn't help me with anything. He just gave orders. He'd say: "Stand up." I'd stand up. He'd say: "Put your pants on." I'd put my pants on. I was now acting like a robot. I think the enormity of what I was about to do was beginning to sink in. He'd say: "Turn around." I'd turn around. He'd walk away, as if to say: "Look at what I'm stuck with."

There was also a man named John McCauley in the show. He played all the would-be assassins in each of the countries visited by the comedian and his friends, which meant that he handled something like eight parts. McCauley was a master of make-up, so they sent him in to make me up. Now you know what kind of shock and terror I was in, and as he proceeded to apply my make-up he also began to hum something and then said, "You know, I sing too." In the middle of my special agony this actor is trying to get a song! Showbiz. . . ?

Meanwhile, they had sent out calls to California. They wanted to get Jack Oakie or Eddie Foy, Jr., for the replacement. One of my best friends is David Shelly, stepson of the late Buddy De Sylva, lyricist and composer. Dave had heard that Eddie Davis was in an accident and he called up and said, "By the way, who's going to do the part in the mean time?"

They said, "Sammy."

He dropped the phone, and he and everybody left for Philadelphia. At the same time Billy Rose's *Seven Lively Arts* was playing in Philadelphia, and most predicted it would be one of the season's big hits. Every big star, Bert Lahr, Milton Berle, more stars than I can remember, were in it.

Finally I was dressed and the dresser directed: "All right, stand up." He looked at me, again blew some air, "Phuh! Phuh!" and said, "Walk." I walked. He said: "Turn left." I turned left. He led me to the stage. I was the mechanical man—a comic sketch in myself.

Then I stood in the wings waiting to go on. I looked across the stage and in the other entrance I saw all these big stars— Bert Lahr, Milton Berle, all watching. By this time I wasn't scared. I was wetting myself.

When the overture finished, the clockwork in me started up again, just enough so that I was about to step on stage—when somebody grabbed my shoulder. At first, I didn't know why. Then a fellow walked out on the stage and said, "Ladies and gentlemen, if you've read the paper I'm sure you're aware that the star of this show, Mr. Eddie Davis, was in a terrible automobile accident and cannot possibly continue in the role. But we think you're going to watch some history made here tonight. We have a young man who, if you've read your playbill, you'll know has written the lyrics for this show. He's never appeared on a stage before, and he's now going to play the lead."

The ham in Sam liked that. The adrenalin started to flow again. I felt good—after all, he hadn't told them that Gene Kelly wasn't going to dance out there and not to look for Cary Grant. He'd told them an amateur was going to walk out there. I took heart.

Now the show started and I walked out.

I think I made one error.

I had a very simple way of playing this part. I figured that if someone spoke to me I would answer in the context of the play, which I had read numerous times. I hadn't memorized the lines but I had written the songs, I knew what the plot was about, and if someone spoke to me I would answer the best I could and in context.

So there was one scene where two people were, as usual, chasing the comic who was taking the place of the magician, and as they were rousting me about one of them whispered to me, "You're doing great! You're doing great!"

And I stopped and said loudly: "What?"

When I did that I also threw him, so that he muffed his next line. I could see him wondering: "Why is this idiot asking me 'What?' "

Finally I pulled myself together and went on with the play.

After the curtain came down there was a cheer from the cast

and they carried me around. Jule Styne was strutting about saying, "Well, if I don't get my way around here I'm gonna pull my star outta the show."

I'd always respected performers I could hear clearly. I didn't know what they did to project, but I said to myself: "I will have to project. If the audience doesn't laugh at anything I say, at least it won't be because they didn't hear me." I was really belting the lines out.

Meanwhile, they had hired Eddie Foy, Jr., to come and play the part. This was Monday and he was going to arrive about Wednesday, and it was their hope that he would go into the part at the Saturday matinee.

All through that week I kept trying to find ways to improve my performance, but because I had set my level of projection so high I was practically shrieking out my lines. And with each performance my voice deteriorated a little more.

Then it was Saturday. They said to me, "No, you'll have to play it again today. Eddie Foy, Jr.,'s not ready. He'll go in on Monday."

That night my parents came to see me. (Incidentally, the deal was that the producers wouldn't pay me anything for this stint. I just wanted them to buy my mother a fur coat.) My parents were going to be sitting in one of the front rows. By then my voice was pretty far gone and they had doctors looking down my throat, but as far as I was concerned everything was fine. I was going to go out on the stage for my last time, in a Saturday-night performance in Philadelphia, in a big Broadway show.

The performance began. I was going:

"I'M FROM B 'POSTROPHE" . . . and I was screaming. In the pit was Max Meth, looking up at me with his hands pressed together, as though pleading "Please save your throat." I thought he was crazy. What the hell did I want to save my throat for? This was my moment. This was my last show and I was doing it for my parents. I didn't care if I never made a sound again.

Later it turned out that—as usual—Max knew better and that I would have to continue in the role until Wednesday; not until then was Eddie Foy, Jr., going on. I was just blowing my voice and everything.

After the performance I was sitting in my dressing room, really bushed, sitting there at least feeling like Lee J. Cobb after his performance of *Death of a Salesman*. My father came in and I panted, "Pop, what did you think?"

He looked at me with great love and said, "Son, you were better than Menasha Skulnick!"

Menasha Skulnick was one of the great Jewish comedians. My father had paid me the highest honor he could bestow.

While I was in the show it was being rewritten by a fellow named Cy Howard, who later would be famous for his *My Friend Irma*, the motion picture *Lovers and Other Strangers*, and the very funny Broadway comedy *Nobody Loves an Albatross*.

I have a simple rule. When you say such-and-such fellow is going to do such-and-such, I ask, "What are his qualifications? What has he done?" And on this occasion they said to me, "You remember Al Bloomingdale, the department-store magnate, who had a show called *Allah Be Praised*. When the show was in trouble they sent for Cy Howard and asked him, 'What do you think we ought to do?' and he said to Al Bloomingdale, 'Close the show and keep the store open nights.' "

Many people are reputed to have said that line—George Kaufman, Billy Wilder, some other brilliantly funny men— but I know that it was Cy Howard because George Kaufman told me that Howard said it. So now I replied, "That was a very, very funny line, but I'm not sure one line qualified you to doctor a play."

They said, "He's going to be great."

On Wednesday matinee the show, rewritten by Cy Howard, went into performance with Eddie Foy, Jr., in the lead. We were still in Philadelphia. I was out of the show and standing in the back of the theater.

Eddie Davis, the cab-driving playwright, had a terrifying asthma condition and with the show being in such trouble he had been hospitalized. But the doctor granted him permission to see this matinee.

The show had never been a beauty, but it had seemed to work. The review in *Variety* had said all we had to do was prune it and we had a chance. But when that hour was jerked out of it at such a late stage, it was like someone trying to alter a suit by pulling on it in only one direction. It just couldn't be done.

In the middle of the first act, when it was really sinking, Eddie Davis the playwright ran down the aisle of the Shubert Theatre yelling at the top of his lungs, "I didn't do this! I didn't do this!"

The show was booked to go to Boston.

When a show is ailing, really ailing, you find that there are not really very many nice people in the world. When you might have a hit they help you; when you're ailing they run away from you. We went to Boston and they booked us into the worst possible place, the Boston Opera House. It was huge, cavernous, and we were playing to empty houses.

Finally, it was obvious to everyone that the show was too far gone to be saved and that we were going to close on New Year's Eve in Boston. As good a time as any, I guess. That same Christmas week *On the Town* was opening in New York, and by December 29 its advance ticket sales would reach $250,000—$50,000 more than the cost of our production. Later, in April, *Carousel* would also open in New York, for the first of 899 performances.

A girlfriend of mine—a rather large girl—came to see the show, and I told her it was closing.

I was a single man, Jule Styne was a married man. I said, "Hey, Jule, what're you hanging around here for? You're a married man; you got two kids; it's Christmas. I can close this for us. Who needs you to close the show? Go home for Christmas with your family. If I had a family that's what I would do."

So it was decided that he was going home. He said to this girl I was with, "How do you like this? I'm going to be in a drawing room all by myself on the *Super Chief* all the way to California."

This tall blonde said, "Boy, what I'd give to be going back to the Coast on a train."

Jule said, "C'mon, go with me!"

And we all laughed at the thought of this big beautiful babe with little Jule Styne. She was about two feet taller. She's my girl, right? We're laughing. *I'm* laughing.

I said good-bye to Jule at the station, and as the train started pulling out he called, "By the way! I ran into George Abbott, and Abbott says to open with the closing!"

A week or so later I called the Coast, and Ed Traubner, my buddy, answered and he said, "Hey, Jule Styne came home. I picked him up in Pasadena from the train. You want to hear something funny? Your big blonde was on the train with him, and he didn't even know it!"

My girlfriend went to the Coast on the train with Jule.

But that's okay, that's part of what life's about. You just have to learn to laugh—or cry—in the right places.

Meanwhile I was thinking about those parting words: "George Abbott says to open with the closing!" George Abbott was at that time the number one theater man in the world. A top playwright and director. "George Abbott says to open with the closing!"

If a show is dying and it's going to close and someone says, "Why don't you do it sideways and run around the corner and stand on your head," what's the difference? A person would do it, right? So I ran back to the theater from the station and I said, "Hey! Jule Styne saw George Abbott. Abbott saw our show. He says we should open with the closing."

So, all right. All that means is that you do a flashback, the last scene first.

If you were to ask what were the two most horrible sights I ever saw, I'd have to say that the first was the *Normandie* after it capsized in the New York City harbor in 1942. I wanted to cry. Here was this huge, formerly alive, formerly beautiful 83,000-ton French liner, the first of the thousand-footers, that had caught fire while it was being converted to a troopship and had flopped over on its side where it lay sick and helpless.

The second most horrible sight was this show when we opened with the closing.

Glad to See Ya! closed in Boston on December 31, 1944, without making it into the New Year. Some pruning!

CHAPTER 8

"Love and Marriage"

Love and marriage,
Love and marriage,
Go together like a horse and carriage . . .

IN THE DAYS when Jule Styne was very much married, and I was a bachelor and beginning to contemplate the error of my ways, Frank and Nancy Sinatra bought a house at Toluca Lake. Near Lakeside—Gentile country-club territory. The Los Angeles Country Club, most prominent of all, doesn't exactly throw its arms around Jews, blacks, or actors—which could strike out, for example, Mr. Sammy Davis, Jr., on all three counts.

Sinatra and friends used to have sixteen-handed gin rummy games, eight to a side, with a captain for each side, usually Sammy Cahn and Jule Styne, and a guy to keep score, like at a bowling alley. We used to play far into the night and on into the morning.

One of the guests one night at the gin game at Sinatra's was Eileen Barton, whose father Ben Barton owned a little music company called Barton Music, with Sinatra and Sinatra's pal Hank Sanicola as partners. Eileen was a singer who had been a child star as "Jolly Gillette," the sponsor's daughter, on the Gillette radio show with Milton Berle. She had just outgrown being "Jolly Gillette," and, on this particular evening, she had brought along a girlfriend from her days at a Hollywood acting school for kids. The friend's name was Gloria Delson.

I had noticed that all the women you'd meet at Sinatra's home—except his wife Nancy—tended to be, how can I say, women accustomed to being attended to. Now I quickly noticed that this very young girl Gloria Delson was different. It is an evening I remember vividly: She so gracious and attentive, taking away ashtrays, asking, "Can I bring you a drink?" Old-fashioned things like that. It was the first inkling I had of how special this young girl was. And how beautiful. As I've already told you, my bed at Sunset Towers was seldom cold, I've known lots of females. Gloria was something else.

It was 1944. I was thirty-one going on thirty-two, Gloria was eighteen going on nineteen, and Nancy Sinatra became a matchmaker.

It's always been a lifestyle with me that, if anybody says "Anyone want to go anyplace?" I say "Sure" before they finish. So when Harry Meyerson of Victor Records was going up to San Francisco to record the San Francisco Symphony with Pierre Monteux and asked if I'd like to go along for the ride, I said "Sure." Harry Meyerson also, like Jule Styne at the time, had an enviable married life. I'll never forget, I was in the upper berth, he was in the lower (after all, he was paying). I leaned over and said: "I just made up my mind. I'm getting married."

"*What?*" said Harry Meyerson.

"I'm getting married."

"Anybody I know?"

"You might know her. Gloria Delson."

"Gloria *Delson?* Have you ever taken her out?"

"No."

Back in Los Angeles I called Gloria. I had never met her parents.

Gloria is the daughter of Sydelle and the late Abner Delson.

She had a sister named Audrey, around three years older. They were both lovely, but even Audrey knew that Gloria was the real beauty.

The Delsons were Jewish, originally from Chicago, in the knitting-mill business, and had come out to California to put their daughter Gloria in the movies. Mrs. Delson, who I guess saw in both girls her own chance for celebrity, decided that of the two Gloria was the most likely to satisfy her own ego. So it was perpetual schools for singing and dancing and whatever else was needed to achieve the goal—stardom for Gloria; and if Audrey had to go to the doctor and there was a casting call for Gloria, the car took Gloria to the studio for the casting call and Audrey either took the bus or walked to the doctor. Audrey, an angel, never complained. Not once did she ever show what would be a reasonable tinge of jealousy. She loved her sister. Ironically, I think Gloria might have traded places willingly with her older sister—Gloria never really showed the kind of drive and ego it usually takes to reach stardom. Come to think of it, of the three Delsons, mother and two daughters, the mother would probably have been the best prospect—which is a double irony, considering her motive in pushing Gloria in the first place. (Do you remember in Charlie Chaplin's *Modern Times* where Paulette Goddard steals a few bananas and gives them to two little girls? Well, Gloria is one of those little girls. And the other is Gloria de Haven—the two Glorias.)

It happened that Mr. and Mrs. Jule Styne were celebrating their twentieth wedding anniversary with a big party in the Coconut Grove of the Ambassador Hotel. During the party Nancy Sinatra passed me a note: "Dear Sammy, ask Gloria tonight. This is the time."

So I took Gloria out on the dance floor, and I said, "Don't get startled. I'm going to ask you something. If your answer is yes, just keep dancing. If your answer is no, just shake my hand and leave the dance floor. Will you marry me?" She just kept dancing, and I gave Nancy Sinatra a victory smile. The orchestra was playing "I Don't Know Why I Love You Like I Do." Shows you my luck. They weren't playing one of my tunes.

When we came back to the table the news was going down the line. Next thing I know, before you can say Cy Feuer, big-mouth Styne is at the microphone announcing "Sammy's engagement." It immediately broke in the newspapers, which offended her parents, because what kind of a man gives an engagement party without inviting the girl's parents? I tried to explain that it wasn't my party and we weren't engaged—that I was not quite that graceless—but I could not make them understand.

Finally, in anger, I called them and said: "I'm sick and tired of you people treating me like a Nazi or something." I also said, "I'm a very nice fella. All I want to do is marry your daughter and give her the best I can. I'm never going to see your daughter again, and if I do," I added—now in fury, "it'll be because *she* wants to see *me.*"

I wasn't as successful a songwriter then, and they didn't see how I could contribute to their dream for this girl. Abner Delson, as a matter of fact, turned out to be the most penurious person I ever met in my life. I don't like to say this—and the man is gone—but he never bought me a dinner in eighteen years, and he could never pull up to a gas station and say "Fill 'er up." The Jack Benny character is a total spendthrift by comparison. During the war Mr. Delson had three dress shops on Hollywood Boulevard, very lucrative, and, when rent controls went off at the end of the war and the landlord wanted an increase, Delson went out of business rather than give in to him. I think going out of business and having nothing to do probably shortened his life. . . .

One night I was at dinner with Doris Lilly in the Players Restaurant in Hollywood, the Doris Lilly of *How to Marry a Millionaire*. How she did her research running around with a penniless lyric writer I do not know. Anyway, who should come into the restaurant but Gloria Delson and Eileen Barton. Gloria cried . . . . so I walked over and sat down and we chatted. She said she didn't care what her parents' feelings were; she wanted to see me and she loved me. We decided to face her parents once and for all.

It wasn't an easy meeting, and the best I could get was an agreement on all sides that Gloria and I would wait a year. Jule Styne and I had been working hard preparing a Broadway musical which suddenly came into focus—*High Button Shoes*, to be produced by Monte Proser of the Copacabana and Joe Kipness of Seventh Avenue, and now they needed us in New York. What a chance for a honeymoon! Gloria had never been to New York, my town. I went to her parents and said: "Look, I'm not a young boy; I can't wait a year. Here's an opportunity . . ."

And Gloria and I got married—at the Ambassador Hotel, where I'd proposed—and went to New York on a honeymoon. Danny Thomas was the act at the Martinique on 57th Street, so we went to the Martinique. Sitting across the table were Martha Raye and Polly Adler, the famous madam. I'm on my honeymoon, you understand. Gloria asked, "Who's that?" and I said: "Martha Raye." Gloria said, "I know that's Martha Raye, silly, but who's that with her?" I said, "Her mother."

Gloria and I went back to Hollywood, where we lived in Sunset Towers, Axel Stordahl having considerately moved upstairs to let us have the apartment. And life was just beautiful, full and rich, the Sinatras and the Cahns and the Stynes together all the time. After two years my wife was pregnant. My son Steven was born in 1947. My daughter Laurie was born in 1949. And *High Button Shoes* became a hit and ran two years on Broadway at the Shubert. Oh, yes, life was beautiful. Except for what happened with Gloria's sister Audrey.

Audrey had married a fellow named Duke Marchiz, a soldier she'd met from New Orleans; a football hero out of Duke University and a handsome guy. Duke's father had an elegant men's custom-made clothing store in New Orleans. Duke wanted to stay in Hollywood and go into business with his father-in-law, Audrey and Gloria's father. No way. This man was so rigid. This man would spend hours cogitating on whether to buy or not to buy an apple. So Duke and Audrey went back to New Orleans.

More than anything in the world Audrey wanted to have a baby. She tried more than once, and more than once lost the infant in childbirth. It shattered me to learn that one of the stillborn infants was an almost perfectly shaped boy. They told her not to try again because it could mean her life, and finally she and Duke adopted a baby boy. Life for her seemed to be heaven.

By this time Gloria and I were married and we were beside ourselves with joy for Audrey. I'd been feeling some sense of guilt that the happiness Gloria and I shared couldn't rub off on Gloria and Duke. Maybe now it would all change. Letter after letter glowed with happiness: the baby was doing this, the baby was doing that, everything was so marvelous.

We kept after Audrey to please run away for the summer from the sweltering heat of New Orleans, and she finally consented and came to visit us, bringing Jeff, the little boy. How we looked forward to it! And how shocked we were when we discovered almost at once that Jeff was a spastic child. I will never forget the terror that gripped me. A tragedy such as I've never seen.

Audrey, never by look or voice, showed the slightest sign of anything being wrong. Jeff, her manner said, was every bit as

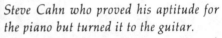

Steve Cahn who proved his aptitude for the piano but turned it to the guitar.

Laurie Cahn, who still loves wheels—she drives a school bus in the San Francisco area.

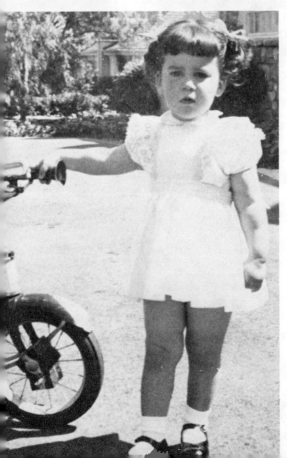

normal as our Steve and Laurie. It broke my heart to watch her with this little boy, and I went to bed many nights and cried and prayed for God to be kinder to Audrey, even if it meant He had to take a share of my own happiness. When Audrey left for home I took a long walk and just stared up at the sky and asked, Why? *Why?*

Well, all I can tell you is . . . Audrey went back to New Orleans and died. No, not a suicide. I think heartbreak.

Duke married another marvelous girl, and this girl took over the chore of taking care of Jeff. And then, my God, Duke died.

Audrey and Duke, I love you. I miss you.

With Laurie and Steve (1951).

My eternal loyalties to Frank Sinatra are based on "Anchors Aweigh." When the MGM powers wouldn't hire two unknowns to do the first multi-million dollar musical, Frank said, "If they are not there Monday, I won't be there Monday"! So there we were—Frank and Gene Kelly (back row), Jule Styne, Sammy, George Sidney, the director, and Axel Stordahl.

CHAPTER 9

"All The Way"

When somebody loves you,
It's no good unless he loves you
All the way . . .

Happy to be near you
When you need someone to cheer you
All the way . . .

I UNDERSTAND I'm considered to have "put more words into Frank Sinatra's mouth than any other man." My earliest recollections of Frank go back to the days when, having established myself somewhat as a writer of "special material," I was called to supply such for Tommy Dorsey. That reconnected me with Axel Stordahl, who was playing trumpet for Tommy, singing with Jo Stafford and the Pied Pipers, and doing fantastic arrangements that became the Dorsey trademark.

When people speak of the sudden emergence of Frank Sinatra it tickles me, because of the clear memory of what it was like then whenever the Dorsey band played at the Paramount.

They'd always open with the show-stopper "Marie"; then go on to trumpeter Ziggie Ellman, a show-stopper all by himself; on to singer Connie Haines, a little Southern girl who would do a solo and tie it up for a while; and next to Jo

Stafford and the Pied Pipers. If that wasn't enough there'd be drummer Buddy Rich to really break it up. If you thought nothing else could happen after that, you'd be right—except for this young, blade-thin, poised, and in-command young man named Frank Sinatra. In his early twenties, he'd step forward to do magic things with numbers like "South of the Border" and "I'll Never Smile Again."

I've been fairly close to many orchestra leaders—Jimmy Lunceford, Glen Gray, Jimmy Dorsey, Red Norvo, Andy Kirk and His Clouds of Joy—but I don't believe there was ever one with the consummate good taste of Tommy Dorsey. To watch him lead the rehearsal of a new arrangement was to see a display in which he drew out every lovely nuance of the music, so blended and yet personal that even the arrangers didn't recognize the arrangement.

As a trombonist Tommy Dorsey was one of the most total and special instrumentalists who ever lived. It came from his tremendous chest cavity and breath control. Dorsey could take a deep breath and play eighteen bars, two bars beyond the bridge or halfway through the chorus, whereas others could play at best only eight or ten bars before taking another breath. What this did was give his music a beautiful legato flow.

Sinatra has said he attributes his own fluidity and style—I speak of the early Sinatra—to his love of Heifetz. I've also heard he attributes some of it to Dorsey. Whatever Frank thinks, I like to think it all came from Dorsey. After all, Frank's instrument is a wind instrument—his voice—as opposed to a bowed instrument like a violin. I doubt even Heifetz could play half through a chorus with one bow—as a semi-violinist I'm maybe qualified to say that.

I also believe one of the hidden keys to Sinatra's phenomenal success is his breath control, learned from Dorsey. Frank can hold a tremendous phrase until it takes him into a sort of paroxysm—he gasps, his whole person seems to explode, to release itself (the same kind of thing used to happen when you watched Marilyn Monroe). Next time you see Frank, watch for this.

Tommy Dorsey, and I say this with great affection, was one of the truly notable swingers—cocksmen, to an older generation—but he always had the sense to know when he was going overboard, which was when he had to take a breath between the eighteen bars. Right then he would lay off his two favorite B's, booze and broads, and go back to tennis and physical training.

A lot of people think that when Sinatra came into his own he changed. Sinatra never changed. If Tommy Dorsey was late to a rehearsal Frank Sinatra acted as substitute orchestra leader. When Dorsey arrived, Sinatra would fix him with a glare of "Where the f--- you been?" Dorsey would apologize that he'd been tied up in this and that and Sinatra'd say something quaint like "bullshit." Dorsey was then around thirty-two, at least ten years older than Frank, who at this time was thinner than all the jokes, including the one about how he used to moonlight working in an olive factory filling the olives with pimento—from the inside! Yuck. The heavy character analysts say that if Sinatra had sung with Glenn Miller he'd have turned out a different character because Glenn Miller was something of a scoutmaster. I wonder. Matter of fact, I don't believe it. He'd have changed Miller.

By 1941, I had finally made it back to Hollywood and was in one of the low periods in my life. I was living with Axel Stordahl at the Castle Argyle, a transient apartment hotel on North Argyle Avenue behind the Hollywood Palladium, where the Dorsey band was playing. All the orchestras would stay at the Castle Argyle because it was so close to the Hollywood Palladium, where they were all booked.

One night I was sitting chewing it over with Frank during a

break. It must have been sometime in 1940. A lot of people thought he broke up with his wife Nancy because he became a big star, but he was a restless soul even then. He told me how unhappy he was being a married man. I gave him the George Raft syndrome. "George Raft has been married all his life. Put it this way—you're on the road all the time, you at least can go home to clean sheets." He kind of understood that. Still, he was so unhappy just sitting up there on the bandstand. "I've got to make my move," he said, "because I'm going to be the best singer in the world, the best singer that ever was." I said, "There's no question in my mind you can do that, there's no way they can stop you.". . . "Do you really mean that?" . . . I said I did.

Some time went by. Jule Styne and I had just written "I've Heard That Song Before," and things were looking up. One night the phone rang in our room at the Castle Argyle. It was Frank calling Axel to say that he was leaving Dorsey and that Axel should come and join Sinatra in New York. I said to Axel: "You've got to go." He did.

I came to New York too. Frank was holding forth at the Paramount while doubling into the Rio Bomba, where the Martinique would later be, on 57th Street between Fifth and Sixth avenues. He was a sensation, doing extra shows, and I went to the 2 : 30 A.M. show with a stop first in his dressing room. The moment he saw me he put his arms around me and said, "Did I tell ya? Did I *tell* ya?" I said, "Don't tell me anything, let me see."

I walked out and watched the show. Let me tell you. In that audience, at two-thirty in the morning, there weren't any teenagers or bobby-soxers and if there weren't any of *those*, just who was Frank Sinatra supposed to play to? In fact, it was one of the most cosmopolitan, varied audiences you can imagine—the kept girls, the rich, the famous, the infamous, sports figures, hoodlums . . . you name it, it was there.

I kept watching the bandstand. The lights dimmed, the timpani started to roll and a voice said: "The R-r-r-r-io Bomba pr-r-oudly pr-r-r-esents Frank Sinatra!" And now Frank, all ninety-wet pounds of him, instead of entering from behind the bandstand, as is customary, made his way by wending through the tables from the back of the room. He looked around and around, and, when he'd thoroughly sniffed them and they'd measured him, he proceeded to stare them down and went into his act.

I think I know a superb instrument when I hear one, and over the years Sinatra's voice has deepened from violin to viola to cello. This particular night, though, it was full pure Stradivarius, with a unique, beautiful fluidity. I remember an incident during one of the songs, "Old Black Magic," I believe. A giant gorilla of a man in the audience—he must have been six feet six and 250 pounds—gave a cough just as Frank came off one of those sustained breath-control passages. Sinatra almost imperceptibly looked at him and the guy—he could have picked up Sinatra and spun him into space—started to shrink and fell back into his seat. Sinatra may have scared him—I doubt it. What he did, more likely, was embarrass him into quiet so an artist could perform, and Sinatra has never been more artist than he was that night.

Of course, after that show we all hugged and laughed and shouted. For us it was proof that the "B" group now had an "A" singer, which was the wire I promptly sent to the other members of the "B" group back on the Coast. (The "A" group of that era was Bing Crosby & Co.)

I went back to Los Angeles, further spreading the good news, engineering an appearance of Frank before 18,000 people at Hollywood Bowl and a benefit at the Mocambo to bust him through to the industry. He was signed to do his first film, the score of which had already been written by Jimmy McHugh and Harold Adamson. It was to be the only movie in which Sinatra wouldn't have complete control over such personnel, which leads, I think, to the definitive Sinatra story—at least it is for me.

He was next signed to do *Anchors Aweigh* for MGM, the first multimillion-dollar musical—all of *two* million dollars!—co-starring with Gene Kelly and Kathryn Grayson. Joe Pasternak called in Frank and asked who he wanted to do the score—Kern, Gershwin, Rodgers and Hart . . .

Frank casually said, "Sammy Cahn." Silence. Then: "Sammy Cahn? We don't mind hiring him, but *who is he?*" Frank said, still very cool, "Since you aren't doing the singing and I am, let me be the judge of who writes the words I sing."

MGM wasn't quite ready for this, and the first of the many Sinatra Scenes unreeled. It came to such an impasse that Lew Wasserman, head of MCA, came to me to plead, "Unless Frank gives in, he'll lose the picture. Won't you talk with him?" I of course went to Frank and said, "Frank, you've already done enough for me. Why don't you pass on this one? There'll be others." He looked at me—and this is where it will always be between us—and said: "If you're not there Monday, I'm not there Monday."

I was there Monday. So was he.

I'm not sure many people know this, but Frank Sinatra never turned down a song of mine. I'll never forget when Jimmy Van Heusen and I wrote "All the Way" for the Joe E. Lewis film, *The Joker Is Wild*. Van Heusen and my agent Lillian Schary Small and I went up to Vegas to sing it for Sinatra. We were told he would hear it before breakfast, which meant four in the afternoon. Came 4 P.M., we were in the living room and he emerged from the bedroom looking like *all* of the Dorian Grays. He looked at me much as he'd looked at Dorsey so many years before, grimaced and said, "You before breakfast—yechh." I looked back. "Hey, from where I'm standing, I'm not sure who's being punished more."

The "theatre" is Sinatra's transformed living room in his and Nancy's Toluca Lake home. Each year we gave a New Year's Eve musical revue, with complete score and sketches. Among others on Frank's stage are Phil Silvers, Frank, the late Bill Goodwin, Pete Lawford, Harry Crane, Axel Stordahl and Paul Weston. This became the "in" event of Hollywood.

Rehearsal for the Sinatra-Presley TV Special from Miami, Florida. Left to right: Cahn, Joey Bishop, Nancy, Jr., Sammy Davis, Jr. and Nelson Riddle (naturally Sinatra isn't there!) (Photo: Bill Mark, New York)

Sammy, Frank and Sammy working on "Robin and the Seven Hoods."

Here I am with Frank during production (the only one I ever produced) of one of his ABC-TV specials—the one on which Eleanor Roosevelt appeared.

Dean Martin, Sammy Davis, Sammy Cahn, Frank Sinatra and Bob Hope at one of the countless Friars affairs.

Van Heusen gave me an intro and we went into "All the Way." When I'd sung the last immortal word and note, Frank turned and said, "Let's eat." We had a marvelous meal—lunch for us, breakfast for him—and left. Outside, Lillian Small had tears in her eyes. "How could he not like that song?" I said, "Oh, he loved it." "How do you know?" she said. "Because he loves them all." His reaction to all our Sinatra songs was the same—"Three Coins," "High Hopes," "All the Way," "Call Me Irresponsible," "Love and Marriage." All of those also won the Oscar.

One day during a very hot spell in Los Angeles the phone rang and it was Jule Styne to say, "Frank wants a Christmas song." Most Christmas songs, I should say, are written in the heat of June or at the latest July, in order to give the singer, publisher, the record company, the promotion people, and the weather a chance to get together.

"Jule, we're not going to write any Christmas song," I said. "After Irving Berlin's 'White Christmas'? The idea's just ridiculous."

Jule said: "Frank *wants* a Christmas song."

So we met in Jule's apartment. Jule, as I've mentioned, always used to warm up with a tango and a waltz, and as you know we'd already made "It's Magic!" by slowing down his tango. Now I decided to go for the waltz. "Hey, Jule, has there ever been a Christmas waltz?" He said no. I said, "Play that waltz of yours." He did so. "Again, Jule, just a little slower." He played slower. "Just a little slower please, Jule." He slowed it way down, and I started writing the song that begins:

> *Frosted window panes,*
> *Candles gleaming inside,*
> *Painted candy canes on the tree . . .*

and ends:

Merry Christmas, may your New Year dreams come true.
And this song of mine,
In three-quarter time,
Wishes you and yours the same thing too.

You'll notice there's an impure rhyme in that lyric, "mine" and "time." If I had written that song with James Van Heusen—purist, rigid, all Methodist—I wouldn't have gotten away with it. But since Jule Styne is neither rigid nor a total Methodist, you could get away with an impure rhyme. We did agonize over it, though. I tried:

And the sleigh bells chime
In three-quarter time . . .

And this little rhyme
in three-quarter . . .

And this song sublime
In three-quarter . . .

This song sublime? The hell with it. We decided to let "The Christmas Waltz" be only 99 and 44/100 percent pure.

I did have one great disappointment with Frank Sinatra in my life. In the film *Robin and the Seven Hoods* a song was needed for the scene in which Barbara Rush, ostensibly the daughter of an Al Capone who has been slain by a henchman, comes to Robin—or Frank—seeking revenge. She was to come at him the way Sinatra came at a broad, pouring liquor into him, looking at him very seriously. It was a song that had to be reprised four times as she goes in turn to Dean Martin, to Victor Buono, and so forth. I drove around for days searching for a clue to the song, and it was while I was driving, coming home to Holmby Hills from the doctor's, that I got the notion . . . "I like to lead when I dance . . . I like to steer the car whenever I drive . . ."

As soon as I reached home I typed out the lyrics and gave them to Van Heusen. He went to the piano, I heard a melody and thought it sensational. "Hey, what is that?" "It's a tune for that lyric you've written." It was a tune he had written the day before, and, remarkably, it fitted word for word. I've no idea if that ever happened before, but this time it happened. Magic, right? Special chemistry, alchemy—who knows, except I was sure it was *something* unique.

Some songs Sinatra liked better than others, but, as I've said, he had never not liked a song of mine. I knew he would love this one. I could taste it. It was definitely the single best Sinatra song I'd ever written . . . I usually don't go to the studio to hear a song put in, but *this* song I wanted to go for. I arrived at the studio on a Friday to hear him sing and shout. There was something a little funny in the air; they were a little uneasy. Were they going to do the song? Well, after lunch; Sinatra wasn't around. "What do you mean he's not around?" I went to Howard Koch, the film's producer, "I can't wait to hear—"

"That song is out," Koch said.

"What? If you're kidding, it's a bad joke. Frank cannot *not* do that song."

"Well, he won't do it."

I later found out that Frank was hungover or hadn't re-hearsed or whatever and felt he wasn't able to sync the song that day. Meanwhile, I went to him and asked, "If not on Friday, why not Monday?" The trouble is that in pictures you never have time and Sinatra never had patience. He wanted to do the picture and get it over with.

I then wrote him a note: "Please don't let this one get away. We're not up at bat that often and don't often get that big fat pitch. If you don't do the song we'll all be punished."

That was as much of a threat as you can threaten Sinatra with. Also, that Sunday his son was kidnapped—I thought they'd find that note and come after me.

In the finished movie the song was reprised three times—just the music. It was never sung first, which to me —naturally—is like making love first and kissing the lady afterward.

I have been in show business since I was ten years old, and I'm sixty years old at the present writing. I've seen them all, but I do not recall any performer since the beginning of show business, *any* performer, who so long and so constantly has held the public imagination.

At one time we had a real falling-out. Someone told Sinatra that at a dinner party at my house his name was, as I believe they say, taken in vain. He thought I should have slapped the offending person's face. Now, unless you're Sinatra you don't slap the guy or punch him in the mouth and throw him out of your house. Then, too, the whole thing wasn't that serious, and Frank should have known I was his friend, his real friend, no matter what.

We didn't speak for about a year. Shortly thereafter came the low point of his career. I was in Palm Springs one day and the phone rang. It was Frank calling me—Frank himself and not one of his boys. Usually when Frank called I would go to the phone expecting to speak to Hank Sanicola. (Hank Sanicola was a piano player and, to put it most accurately, a bull of a man. He and Frank were very close from the beginning: He used to rehearse Frank, teach him the songs—he was almost his alter ego. You remember that picture *Not As a Stranger*, in which Robert Mitchum gets to throw Sinatra up against a wall? In the theater when it was sneak-previewed somebody called out, "You wouldn't do that if Hank were here!")

I picked up the phone and Frank said, "Hi." "Hi, how're

you doing?" "Okay, I guess." "How're you feeling?" "Pretty good." "Pretty good? I'd been hoping you were great. I've been reading that you're going into the Copacabana."

Going into the Copa was a try at a comeback for him. And, like an old firehorse who hears the bell, I had started to think of the kind of numbers I would write for him if we were buddies.

Frank said, "That's what I'm calling you about. I need some songs."

I said I had three or four ideas; I'd write them and mail them to him. One of the numbers was a take-off on Frankie Laine, complete with whip and goose horn. I sent the material along, and as a rule that's all I needed to do for Sinatra. He was and is very perceptive about usable material, and I didn't think he needed me.

Again the phone rang. The stuff was marvelous and would I please come to New York. I said, "Frank, you don't need me, it's all there. Just do it." "Please, come to New York. Please . . ."

These were the days before planes. I took the *Twentieth Century Limited*, arriving at Grand Central at eight in the morning. Frank was at the Hampshire House. I rushed to the hotel at eight-thirty, only to be informed that Mr. Sinatra had left a note saying he was not to be disturbed until one o'clock.

I had four hours on my hands, so I bought a dress for my baby daughter and went over to Abercrombie & Fitch for the whip and the goose horn. I met Frank at the Copa at 2 P.M.—at one he was still in his bedroom, just awakened.

I felt I shared the success of Frank's opening at the Copa. The next day I was going back to California, but I had to see Frank before I left. I wanted to talk with him badly.

I went to the Hampshire House and he was in the bedroom, just awake.

I told him, "I want to talk to you. You and I haven't talked for over a year. Maybe we won't ever talk again, but you must hear what I have to say. For a year now I've agonized over your inactivity. You're not number one. . . ."

On the dressing table, I remember vividly, there was a picture of Franklin D. Roosevelt, a picture of Ava Gardner, a picture of his children.

"I've seen every second-rate singer pass you. If I called a music publisher and said, 'Do you have a number for Frank Sinatra?' they'd hang up on me. Frank, I'm doing very well —I'm making $100,000 a year—but I'll quit what I am doing and stay with you. And we both know I'm not being altruistic, because if you do what you're capable of I'll make twenty times that."

He kept saying, "I know, I know. . . ."

"You're like a horse with three jockeys. Please unload and head out again." End of speech. I left him and took the train back to California.

Later, when he was going into the Empire Room of the Waldorf for the first time, he called me again. He was then staying at the Gotham Hotel on the corner of Fifth Avenue and 55th Street. I went over there and we laid out his act, opening with "They've Got an Awful Lot of Coffee in Brazil." Opening night was an event. I had a table about two feet away from Frank, so that I could be his idiot card if necessary, throwing him a line should he forget. I whispered to him, "Hey, you know what's a cute idea? Come out with a cup of coffee for that first number." He just looked at me, said nothing.

The lights went out, the orchestra went into its vamp, and Frank came out singing about Brazil and sipping coffee from a cup. Wow! I was mouthing the lyrics, but when it came to "Embraceable You," I knew Frank knew the words and so I turned my head to relax my neck muscles. Frank kicked me in the ankle and said, "Pay attention.". . . Not so sweet, but nobody ever said Sinatra was all anything—including heart.

Which brings me to one of the many faces of Frank Sinatra . . .

He once said to a group of us, "Who do you think is going to walk into this room?" and he named a lady who will be one of the great luminaries of the screen as long as movies are shown. Also one of the great all-around bedmates, with particular skill in the specialty lately made public by the alleged Linda Lovelace—an amateur, it is said, compared with the lady he spoke of.

I was somewhat skeptical. "I'm not so sure the lady's going to walk in," I said, "but if she does and sees six or eight of us sitting around, she'll certainly leave." Sinatra said: "Screw her, let her leave."

I was wrong. The lady walked in, smiled demurely, allowed Sinatra to take her hand and lead her into the bedroom . . .

Frank Sinatra is convinced—I believe the evidence mostly supports him—that somebody is waiting for him in just about every men's room in the world. He'll be minding his own business and all of a sudden some character will materialize, asking for his autograph or offering uninvited comment. Frank will say something provocative, and usually the dialogue gives way to fists. . . .

Another occasion, at Ruby's Dunes in Palm Springs, Sinatra was at his special corner table with his back to the wall. In the corner diagonally opposite was a fellow at the bar who seemed intent on mesmerizing Sinatra. Sinatra, leaving off from his soup, was caught up by this.

Now ensued a kind of duel, eyes-to-eyes. "I wish that guy would stop staring at me," Sinatra muttered. I said, "Frank, that's paying your dues. Who do you *want* him to stare at, Sam the tailor?" Sinatra tried to get down a spoonful of soup, couldn't. "Forget it; relax," I said. He tried two more spoonfuls, no luck. He stood up. Sinatra is about to be Sinatra. He walked across the room. Friends ran over to stop him.

Sinatra grabbed the guy by his lapels. They were now eyeball-to-eyeball. *"What are you staring at?"* Sinatra demanded. "Hey, Frank, I love you, I love you," the guy said. "I'm your number one fan in the world, I love you . . ."

Sinatra set him down gently like cotton wool. "Give this guy anything he wants." Homage properly paid was properly, promptly rewarded.

What else could it be with Frank Sinatra?

Frank called a few years ago and said he'd been asked to attend a party in Spiro Agnew's hometown of Baltimore and would I write some parody lyrics for the occasion. He made it sound like a private party to honor a local boy who at the time seemed to have made good. I sat down and knocked off a parody to the tune of "The Lady Is a Tramp." This, in part, is what I had him sing to then Vice President Agnew—which reads in the perspective of hindsight like heavy satire rather than parody.

> *There's no one like him, but no one at all,*
> *I mean his power is like wall to wall.*
> *So he's erratic when he hits a ball,*
> *But still the gentlemen is a champ . . .*

Even then that little effort caused me a lot of flak when it turned out the party wasn't quite that private. Everyone seemed to know immediately I'd written it and the story broke in the news magazines and on TV.

One day not so long afterward, in the lobby of the Plaza Athénée in Paris, my new wife Tita and I met up with Pat Lawford and Mrs. Rose Kennedy. Pat, never one to mince words, waggled a finger in my face and said: "You wrote that for Agnew?" I swallowed hard and said, "I wrote what *for* Agnew? I didn't even know he sang." I hadn't written it for Agnew, I'd written it for Frank, with no apologies. I'll always write for Frank Sinatra whenever he asks me.

People ask me about Frank being a split personality, and, as you've seen, it does seem to be true to some extent. It goes, though, beyond my own experiences and those of some others I've related. When the late Bennett Cerf was alive and presiding over the affairs of Random House, Frank used to love to call him and be with him and his literary friends. He loved the ambience of being around a man like Cerf, whose professional career involved close contact with such great writing talents and personalities as Sinclair Lewis, William Faulkner, and John O'Hara. Frank genuinely, I think, likes a touch of class (you should forgive the borrowing from my own repertoire), except he pretty soon gets restless with all the heavy class and decides he'd rather be hanging out with the guys at Jilly's, a favorite saloon on Manhattan's Eighth Avenue, which preference tends to last about as long as it takes for him to remember the other life and wish he were there. Or somewhere . . .

He has hurt me more than once, Frank Sinatra. He was not at the bar mitzvah of my son. He was not at the dinner at the Hilton given for me by the Henry Street Settlement—he was not there, he was two blocks away. He didn't sing "Three Coins" the night it won the Academy Award, and he *was* there. Most all my friends from the Coast have gone from the plane to the Golden Theatre to see our show *Words and Music*. Frank, to my knowledge, has never showed (and I'm sure if he had, we'd have known it). Why? Maybe to test our friendship by straining it? . . . I don't really know. I do know, though, that in the way it counts the most for me, he is a relentlessly good friend.

I'm not a sycophant or masochist. I've never, ever "run" with Sinatra. I'm certainly not knocking the ones who have and do, but for me it's all a bit too much; it tends to take over too much of your life, too much of the phone ringing and a voice saying, "Now hear this, Frank wants . . ." We have a kind of unwritten rule between us—he doesn't expect me to be "around" (he doesn't *need* me around); I don't expect to be around. That way nobody gets confused or disappointed. At the same time, I am attracted to dynamic, talented people, and Frank Sinatra more than qualifies on both counts.

Especially, though, whenever Frank needs a lyric you can bet I'm there. I have been, ever since *Anchors Aweigh.* You can also bet that the day he asks somebody else to write his lyrics I'll know it's changed for us. Until then, we're tight in the way that I think we both feel counts the most—mutual respect for each other as professionals, and as men.

If I had to sum up Sinatra, I would say, his has been the ultimate dream, matter of fact, I'm not sure that one day Frank wouldn't like to open his eyes back in Hasbrouck Heights, N. J., and be able to say: "Well, wasn't *that* a dream . . ."

CHAPTER 10

"The Tender Trap"

You see a pair of laughing eyes
And suddenly you're sighing sighs
You're thinking nothing's wrong, you string along
Boy! then snap—
Those eyes, those sighs
They're part of the Tender Trap!

I'M NEVER "with song," like "with child," but in forty years it has never, ever deserted me.

If people don't ask, "Which comes first, the music or the words?" they ask, "Where do you get ideas for songs?"

The process is so elusive. There seem channels of disaster everywhere. A movie or show with a good script or "book" (story) helps, of course. The personality and role of the star, the need of the producer and the director, they all add in. Mostly, though, if a fella sits down at a piano and plays a pretty melody, sooner or later it comes for me.

James Van Heusen really knows how to lure a lyric out of these bones. He's patient and will play the melody in every form—light, heavy, quick, slow. After that we *know*—if it doesn't come, we close the piano and walk away.

In the case of "The Tender Trap," the title started it off and so the lyrics came before the music. It really started, though, as always, with the phone call: Frank Sinatra, we're told, is doing a film called *The Tender Trap*. Now when I heard the word "trap" I also heard the word "snap." Think about it— "trap" and "snap" and you're almost home. I went over to Van Heusen's and to the typewriter:

> *You see a pair of laughing eyes*
> *And suddenly you're sighing sighs,*
> *You're thinking nothing's wrong, you string along*
> *Boy! then snap—*

I was about to add:

> *You're in the Tender Trap!* ["*trap*" *and* "*snap*"]

but something compelled me to add (and don't ask me why):

> *Those eyes, those sighs*
> *They're part of the Tender Trap!*

I handed over the piece of paper to Van Heusen and he went to the piano. I should have mentioned here that Van Heusen and I complemented each other in more ways than as composer and lyricist. Pace is also involved, and whereas I tended to speed up Van Heusen, he in turn slowed me down some (he was accustomed to the painstaking lyrics of Johnny Burke, which came very slowly). At the time, though, we really weren't adjusted to the effect our styles had on each other; we were just feeling each other out on our first song. What happened was that he proceeded, under my pressure, to write what I thought was one of the worst melodies I'd ever heard. I was chagrined, but made no show of it. After all, as I said, it was our first collaborative effort. I decided to just ride with it and started to write the second section:

You're hand-in-hand beneath the trees
And soon there's music in the breeze
You're acting kind of smart, until your heart,
Just goes "Whap!"
Those trees, that breeze
They're part of the Tender Trap!

Just at this moment Johnny Burke came into the room, which broke the tension for me but was also an embarrassing moment. Here I was working with the man who had been inseparable from Burke for more than a decade. We made some small talk . . . (I wasn't overly fond of Burke, although I later came to feel some empathy for him, as did two other Van Heusen aficionados, Ada Kurtz and Jackie Gale, who in Johnny Burke's last years did all but save his life—unfortunately neither they nor anybody could manage that, which was a pity, because personal feelings aside, Johnny Burke was a real Irish poet, a real talent.) . . . After very little of the small talk with Burke, I left and promptly went home to agonize over the tune that Van Heusen had come up with. The next day when I returned to work on the song, Van Heusen—thank God—said, "That tune last night wasn't very good, was it." "Wasn't very good?" I said, "that was one of the lowest . . ." He then said, "Listen to the way it goes today," and he proceeded to play the present melody you may know for the song and which sounds as though it had always been there.

As I mentioned, Van Heusen tended to go slower than I did, and he really didn't especially like to be speeded up. Many times after I'd left a writing session with him, completely happy with what he'd done, he would privately rewrite. I must say—I'm *glad* to—that he was incredibly good when he was left to his own muse (as first so well-demonstrated to me in the instance of the melody for "The Tender Trap"). Thanks to

Charles (Chuck) Walters, "The Tender Trap" went into the film and proved out to be one of the all-time most successful main titles for a movie. Matter of fact, if you watch the Late Late Show of a night, you're likely to see a speck in the distance and hear the voice of Frank Sinatra singing:

> *And all at once it seems so nice*
> *The folks are throwing shoes and rice*
> *You hurry to a spot, that's just a dot,*
> *On the map—*
> *You wonder how it all came about,*
> *It's too late now, there's no getting out*
> *You fell in love and love, is the Tender Trap!*

Every time Jack Benny sees me at a party, before he even says hello, he will say, "How could *any*one [you probably can hear Benny's famous mock emphasis] write a song called 'The Tender Trap'?" And then he won't leave or let me alone until I play it, again and again.

I think the four songs by Jimmy and me for the televised *Our Town* (1955) are the best writing I've ever done. We began by rambling around the room, thinking and talking about Mr. Thornton Wilder's play. As you may know, the first act is called "The Daily Life," the second act, "Love and Marriage," so at some point I turned to Jimmy and said, "Since we're doing a musical, Mr. Van Heusen, would you *please. . .?*" Whereupon he went to the piano and started thumping out *oompah, oompah*—which led to "Oom-pah, oom-pah, Love and marriage,/Go together like a horse and carriage . . . Love and marriage, love and marriage,/It's an institute you can't disparage . . . Ask the local gentry,/And they will say it's element'ry . . ."

I don't think I've used the word "disparage" six times in my life. I *never* use the word "gentry." Even Van Heusen, who has a college education, didn't come up with words like these. Speaking of unlikely words born of the necessity of rhyme, we once also needed a rhyme for "lady." Well, there are very few rhymes for "lady." What are you going to use? "Shady"? "Brady"? I came up with, "Tipped his straw cady." Van Heusen said, "What? Cady? What the hell is that?" I said: "Look it up. It means 'tipped his straw *hat.*' " I'm still damned if I know where I ever got that from.

Songs can and do come out of the most inane lines. I'm sure Mr. Thornton Wilder could not have suspected a lyric in the words "love and marriage." (Maybe he still can't.)

It was in 1954 that Frank Sinatra suggested that Van Heusen and I do the score for *Our Town.* For years people had been saying that Sammy Cahn's meat-and-potatoes lyrics and Jimmy Van Heusen's polka-dot-and-moonbeams music made for a happy combination. It seemed a good marriage for the romantic yet down-to-earth story and mood of Wilder's *Our Town,* a play about a typical small New England American town—its people, their births, lives, deaths, and meaning in the scheme of things.

I was on the high seas, on the *S.S. Constitution* headed for New York, having promised the brothers Warner, who had reached me in Naples, that I would take the first boat out of Lisbon and the first plane back to the Coast to start immediately on the songs for the last or the first of Mario Lanza's comeback pictures, with music by Nicholas Brodzsky. (Why didn't I take a plane straight from Europe to Los Angeles? I'd flown in everything down to single-engine rubber-band jobs, until one day I got frightened. I was flying off from Los Angeles to Vegas; my wife was pregnant and I saw her waving good-bye. It occurred to me I might never see this woman again, or my unborn child. So I then and there made an arrangement with God never to fly again. And I didn't—until God, in the form of Jack Warner, required me to.)

When the *Constitution* docked, there was Mr. Van Heusen at the gangplank, and he promptly told me we were on our way to the offices of Fred Coe, producer of the NBC Producers' Showcase series. Van Heusen asked if I were familiar with *Our Town*, the Wilder play and subsequent movie. I told him I was as familiar with it as anyone could be who had not seen or read it in seventeen years. Oddly enough, though, Robert Griffith, the stage manager and assistant to director George Abbott on *High Button Shoes*, had often discussed with me the possibility of doing a musical *Our Town*. As we were riding in the cab, Van Heusen handed me the play and said, "You've got an hour to read it."

I started, and my first question was, "What does Sinatra play here, the stage manager [the narrator and central figure in the play] or the young boy?" I should have known it was the stage manager, because ever since I've known him Sinatra likes to stroll on and stroll off, just like that stage manager does throughout the play, telling the audience what's what.

It was to be an hour-and-a-half special done *live* (no tape or retakes). "This story should have no more than four songs of any size, and maybe three or four incidental songs," I said. With Jimmy in agreement we cabbed over to NBC and met Fred Coe and Delbert Mann, who was to direct.

As I've since discovered, if a notion is blessed by the gods of the muse, nothing seems to go wrong no matter how hard you try. I took the floor, told how the songs should be done, where they should go, who should sing them, and they said, "That's how we'll do it."

So Van Heusen and I wrote the songs.

I must say here and now to Thornton Wilder that in a sense his name, too, should have been on the songs, because he couldn't have been a more active collaborator if he'd been there. When you write lyrics to Broadway musicals with books by Broadway writers—well, that's one thing. When you confront the genius of a Thornton Wilder, you must react more deeply, and react we did. I believe it is our best writing.

The teleplay was by the talented David Shaw, brother of novelist Irwin Shaw. The producer was Henry Jaffee, a very knowledgeable man who produced the Dinah Shore shows. It was happy times. Would you believe the cast? Frank Sinatra as the "stage manager;" Eva Marie Saint played the girl. And old blue eyes—not Sinatra, Paul Newman—played the boy.

I'll never forget the way Paul Newman auditioned. He came to the studio, slouched down at the piano and sang, to his own accompaniment, one of the raunchiest smoker-room songs I'd ever heard. No man was ever able to make a room as blue with language as James Van Heusen. His talent for making a room blue with language was right up there, in its fashion, with his musical gifts, and when he heard young Newman's rendition he was suitably and profoundly appreciative. "That's the most be-f---ing-yewtiful thing I ever heard." No prude am I, as by now you've gathered, but I was appalled by this audition song of Newman's, though it was a clear winner with Van Heusen. Still, I'm pleased to say that in the actual show Paul Newman sang "The Impatient Years," one of my favorites —and bearing no resemblance to the X-rated ditty Paul used to win over my earthy collaborator.

The score was written in Hollywood Hills in Van Heusen's pad, once the home of Robert Stack's mother. It was set on the edge of a mountain, and it had four stories and the most amazing appliances, including elevators (unheard of in those times). Jimmy is a couch composer. Lying flat out with his arms in back and cradling his head, he'll listen to a lyric and say, "Yeah, yeah, it sounds all right," and then after about fifteen minutes he'll get up and go to the piano and start to noodle out the notes that fit.

The first time we sat down with Sinatra to play him the *Our Town* songs was in the home of his ex-wife Nancy, where he'd gone, Sinatra fashion, for a home-cooked meal. He kept following the songs intently—when Sinatra is in deep thought he has a habit of stroking his lower lip with the back of his thumb—and when we were finished he looked up and said, "Gee, it's good." For him, that's high praise.

Things rolled along like that right up to D-day, 6 P.M., in Burbank Studios. Standing in the control room, Delbert Mann raised his hand, pointed a finger, and confidently expected that for the next hour and thirty minutes a cast of thirty people, an orchestra of forty musicians led by the staunch Nelson Riddle, more stagehands than I can remember on a single show, lighting and sound technicians, grips, and all the other assorted wonderful people that go to make up a *live* television presentation would each do his or her job without falter or hesitation. I still remember thinking it insanity that Nelson Riddle and the orchestra were in a studio across the hall, with Nelson watching the TV monitor, checking the actors, and leading the orchestra, the music sent through speakers into the stage. The isolation of the orchestra was for balancing purposes, separating it from the voices.

Like I said, the project was blessed from the beginning, and it turned out Delbert Mann was more than justified in his great expectations. Remember, there'd been weeks of rehearsal for everyone but Sinatra, who typically—in real life as well as in his stage role—strolled in and strolled out. Well before the televising of the program the songs were already popular, thanks to Sinatra being Sinatra.

I'm not sure who saw or remembers this production of *Our Town*. In accordance with the wishes of Thornton Wilder, it was never shown again. For some mysterious—to me at least—reason he exercised his contractual right to make sure that every vestige of it disappear. I got the feeling he'd have wanted the video tape, if there'd been one, burned. Maybe we watched two different shows that evening—at least we watched one show through two very different sets of eyes. It's his creation, though, and he is more than entitled . . .

Immediately upon the conclusion of the show the phones started ringing. I'm proud to say that one call was from my old buddy Bobby Griffith—half of the Griffith and Prince team that produced *Pajama Game* and *West Side Story* (subsequently he was sadly taken from us by a heart attack). He and Hal Prince and George Abbott wanted to bring our *Our Town* show to Broadway, having had no hint of what Thornton Wilder's reaction would be—nor had those of us directly involved.

All I know is that I can't be too upset. After all, Thornton Wilder did help (though inadvertently) give birth to "Oom-pah, oom-pah, Love and Marriage . . ."—which is the only song that's ever won an Emmy Award. As far as I'm concerned, Mr. Wilder is someone no one can—you should forgive the language—disparage.

Songs are kind of delicate creatures. I usually can sense, for example, if somebody else's came easy or was trouble. In the case of *Pocketful of Miracles*, it came tough for Van Heusen and me. Frank Capra had called us in New York to say he'd just finished a picture called *Pocketful of Miracles* and now he needed a song for it. "Isn't this call a little late?" I said. "And in any case, can't we see the picture?" He said we could that night down at Loew's Sheridan (which as of this writing is a hole in the ground with a garden on it). I went to see the film out of courtesy to Mr. Capra, because I had no intention of writing a song entitled "Pocketful of Miracles." It happened that Jimmy Van Heusen and Johnny Burke had written a song entitled "Pocketful of Dreams."

(Professional songwriters are aware of the literature on words and music, or they should be. Although I respect and admire the Beatles, I would not, for example, sit down and write a song called "Yesterday." Jerome Kern wrote "Yester-day." I would also not, as Stephen Schwartz of *Godspell* did, entitle a song "Day by Day." Sammy Cahn, Axel Stordahl, and Paul Weston wrote "Day by Day." I'm sure Stephen Schwartz doesn't want to be paid for my work, and I don't want to be paid for his. When Van Heusen and I did *Robin and the Seven Hoods* we needed a Chicago song. We didn't write "Chicago, Chicago, dada-dada-da"; we wrote "My Kind of Town." The trouble is that you can't copyright a song title —something about not copyrighting the English language. It might help keep things a little straighter, though.)

Van Heusen and I saw the picture, the heroine of which was Apple Annie, and I then told Van Heusen we couldn't write a song for it. He said, "What do you mean?" and I told him what I meant—that he and Burke had already written "Pocketful of Dreams." Van Heusen rejoined, "If I wrote that song with Burke, I can also give you permission to write another with me."

That pretty much took care of my concern about *l'affaire* title, so we went to work—Van Heusen in his characteristic prone position. Finally we came up with a word that took the place of "dream"—"practicality," which sort of made sense because if you're not a practical person you tend to deal in dreams, etc. That was the key to the song. We used the word "apple" to take care of the Apple Annie in the picture—"The world's a bright and shiny apple that's mine, all mine."

We finished the song and Van Heusen said, "What do you think?" I said, "I think it stinks." If you don't like a Jimmy Van Heusen song it's vengeance unto the seventh son, but I stood by my pencils and said, "If I have to get up and sing it, I have to *like* it." The trouble was that each line began with an *umph*, which meant you'd need a choreographer to help the singer. Singers have enough trouble without having to count. Finally Jimmy said, "How about putting a word there? Instead of

'Umph, practicality, umph, doesn't int'rest me,' something like 'Real practicality sure doesn't int'rest me.' "

" '*Real* practicality'? '*Sure* doesn't int'rest me'?" It didn't send me. Then I had an idea. "Pee-racticality dee-uzn't int'rest me . . ."

Van Heusen said, "What's *that* mean?"

I said, "If two people ask what that means, I'll throw it out." No one did—not then or since.

Later my daughter, Laurie, said, "You blew it," and I think she was right. I should have followed through. The song goes:

> *Pee-racticality dee-uzn't int'rest me,*
>   *Love the life that I lead.*
> *I've got a pocketful of miracles,*
>   *And with a pocketful of miracles*
>   *One little miracle a day is all I need . . .*
> *Tee-roubles, more or less, bee-ahther me, I guess,*
>   *When the sun doesn't shine . . .*

It should have been:

> *Pee-racticality dee-uzn't int'rest me,*
>   Lee-uv *the life that I lead . . .*
>
> *Tee-roubles, more or less, bee-ahther me, I guess,*
>   Wee-en *the sun doesn't shine . . .*

The song was nominated for an Academy Award. It didn't win it, which is all right, but when the song comes up for renewal or copyright, twenty-eight years from 1961, I'm going to change it . . . for Laurie.

James Van Heusen was born Edward Chester Babcock—the name used by Bob Hope in all his *Road* pictures with Bing

Crosby and Dorothy Lamour—on January 6, 1913, five months and twelve days ahead of yours truly.

As a young man he was a radio announcer in Syracuse, New York, where they said, "We can't have an announcer named Edward Chester Babcock." He looked out the window and saw an ad for Van Heusen shirts.

Of German–English background, and, as I've said, a strict Methodist, he is nonetheless one of the true free souls of the world—in World War II he opted not for the entertainers' USO but for the heady and dangerous and freewheeling role of test pilot.

When I first met him he was rehearsal pianist for the Remick Music Company in the RKO Building, working under the legendary Mousie Warren, brother of the legendary Harry Warren. In addition to playing piano as prettilty as anyone *can* play piano, he was reputed to be an incredible swordsman with the ladies. He was, in fact, the leading whorehouse piano player for all the top madams, including Polly Adler (he was also one of the few people at her funeral).

He and his partner Johnny Burke tested their talents against one another as they wrote such songs as "Imagination" and "Oh, You Crazy Moon"—and then went off to Hollywood while I stayed back in the East. In Hollywood at the time Bing Crosby was the king, and Burke and Van Heusen soon became his crown prices. When I finally made it to Hollywood I was welcome in Burke's home, but I confess I felt uncomfortable there. Everyone tended to be "Meyer" in his jokes.

One of Burke's buddies was a Barney Dean, a cute bald little guy who was sort of court jester to Crosby and to Hope. He was also a comedy writer, but his main job was to keep everyone's spirits up. One day he was playing gin with one of the stars on the set. The director had come to a line in the script where someone was referred to as being "cool as a cucumber." The director hated the cliché and called for Bar-

Cahn and Van Heusen

Here on the Mike Douglas Show are Van Heusen (at the piano); me
holding forth as usual; and would you believe Mike Douglas, Ozzie,
Harriet Nelson and Totie Fields?

Robert Wagner, Cahn, Crosby, Van Heusen and Debbie Reynolds
working on "Say One for Me!"

Crosby, Bob Wagner and Cahn
—also "Say One for Me!"

(Photo: Al Morch)

Crosby, Van Heusen and Cahn.

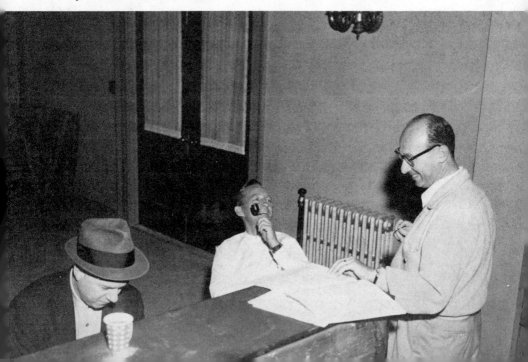

Cahn and Van Heusen composing the score for the musical version of "Our Town" starring Frank Sinatra—an NBC spectacular.

A dream realized—here I am doing a score for a "road" film for Crosby and Hope: "The Road to Hong Kong." Van Heusen had done all of them with Johnny Burke, and finally I got my chance.

Ed Sullivan honors Berlin (center).

Left to right—Harold Allen, Adolph Green, Betty Comdon, James Van Heusen, Jerry Herman, Ethel Merman, Irving Berlin, Ed Sullivan, Dorothy Fields, Stanley Adams (President of ASCAP), Burton Lane, Jule Styne, Sammy Cahn and Noble Sissle.

Sinatra singing special lyrics for Edward G. Robinson's birthday during the filming of "Hole in the Head."

My daughter Laurie and Van Heusen accepting the Oscar from Shirley Jones for "Call Me Irresponsible."

ney to come up with a socko word to complete the line, "this character is as cool as a" — dead silence while Barney Dean reflected earnestly and said happily, "How about cucumber?" Funny man . . . Barney, like Burke, also used to call everybody "Meyer." Somebody once said to me when I commented on this, "What do you mean? Some of his best friends are Jews." I said, "Some of his best friends also probably call *him* 'Meyer.' "

At the time Crosby was just getting over his alleged reputation as a drinker and was reputed to say, "When the sun goes down I run away from Van Heusen like the plague." Jimmy Van Heusen does like to drink booze, as well as write songs and spend money—he used to fold his money and stick it so loosely in a side pocket that when he reached for it, it tended to spill out—a really open guy, a free soul, like I said.

Van Heusen is a good drinker, charming even when drunk. I once asked him, "How come you never drink with Jackie Gleason?" He said, "Gleason? I can't drink with Gleason. I can't drink with anyone who gets sick at the table." (Subsequently Gleason, Van Heusen, and I did get together, in a show—not as drinkers—and were responsible, each in our fashion, for the Academy Award for "Call Me Irresponsible," about which more later.)

Van Heusen got married a couple of years ago—a shock to everyone. He married Bobbie Perlberg, widow of producer William Perlberg, and has since built himself a place in Yucca Valley, over the mountain from Palm Springs.

I said to him, "Well, you've finally done it. You've found a way to get rid of all your money."

By the way, he's also a monumental hypochondriac. He has absolutely memorized the *Merck Manual*, a compendium of all the recorded knowledge of medicine. If a doctor can't help you, go to James Van Heusen. He also has a preoccupation with surgery; he likes to be operated on. I'd be writing a song;

he'd say, "Excuse me a minute," and go to the icebox, take out a disposable syringe, drop his pants, and give himself a shot of Vitamin B-12.

Writing title songs is an ancient and honored business in Hollywood. I know I'm supposed to write "all" the title songs. I try to, but I don't. How can you write a title song for *Woman Disputed*? "Woman disputed, I love you"? *A Kiss Before Dying*? "Give me a little kiss before dying, will you, huh?"

One day the telephone rings again (thank God, I think—I never forgot the times when it didn't). It's Ross Hunter of Universal Pictures. He's calling to say he's doing a film called *Thoroughly Modern Millie* and needs a song. I say to Van Heusen, "He can't want a title song called 'Thoroughly Modern Millie'. Sing it? You can't even *say* it." When we get to the studio and walk into Mr. Ross Hunter's office he leaps from behind the desk and asks (demands), "Isn't that the catchiest title?" Trapped like rats . . .

Van Heusen and I go home and actually manage to write a song called "Thoroughly Modern Millie," but I got even because I used the title but once in the entire song. They also got even and turned it down. We went away to write another. Write a second? I never believed we could write a first.

I decided we shouldn't sweat it too much—after all, it was mission impossible—and so said to Van Heusen, "You know, I think what they want is a song that sounds like it's already been a hit. I mean, you've got to forget that you're James Van Heusen and we'll write an old-fashioned, really corny melody." Being the great composer he is, Van Heusen in utter disgust went to the piano and plucked out a ricky-tick old-fashioned tune. "You can't get cornier than *that* . . ."

I said to him, "Do you mind if I put some words to your 'Da-da-dadadle-da'?" "Be my guest," he said, and it became the song you know (I hope), with the title intentionally buried at the very end.

> *Everything today is thoroughly modern*
> *(Check your personality),*
> *Everything today makes yesterday slow*
> *(Better face reality),*
>
> *It's not insanity, says Vanity Fair,*
> *In fact it's stylish to raise your skirt and bob your hair.*
>
> *In a rumble seat the world is so cozy*
> *(If the boy is kissable),*
> *And that tango dance they wouldn't allow*
> *(Now is quite permissible).*
> *Goodbye, good goody girl, I'm changing, and how,*
> *So beat the drums, 'cause here comes*
> *Thoroughly Modern Millie* [note: first time title used] *now!*

Verse:
> *There are those, I suppose, think we're mad*
> *Heaven knows, the world has gone to wrack and to ruin*
> *What we thought was chic, unique and quite adorable*
> *They think is odd, and Sod-om and Gomorrable—but*
>> *the fact is . . .*

That song went on to win two gold records and, happily, to finance my second marriage.

Jimmy and I kind of separated for a while; in fact, we haven't written anything together for a couple of years. At the very beginning I said to him that we shouldn't get into the kind of relationship we couldn't dissolve easily; that when we were no longer producing songs that pleased the public we should shake hands and say, "Well, it was fun" and walk away friends. For years—many traumatic years—Jimmy Van Heusen and Johnny Burke stayed unprofitably together. I didn't want that to happen to us.

There was one problem when I was working with Van Heusen. He'd keep saying, "Where are you going with this song?" I'd say, "I don't know where I'm going." That wasn't the way he'd worked with Burke, and I think it was something he never was completely at ease with.

One of the most honorable men I've ever met was Glen Gray of "Glen Gray and the Casa Loma Orchestra." He was the head of that band, but he was not in a true sense a bandleader. Glen was a saxophonist who sat in the orchestra itself while a fella named Mel stood in front with a violin and conducted. The manager of the Paramount Theater, Robert Weitman, later variously head of MGM and Columbia Pictures, asked me if I could write a number for Glen Gray and the Casa Loma Orchestra to indicate subtly to the audience that Glen wasn't the guy conducting in front with the violin. Mike Neidorf of the Rockwell O'Keefe talent agency, who handled Glen, also liked the idea, and so, of course, did Glen. In fact it originally was his idea.

So I wrote a number which told the story of the Casa Loma Orchestra:

> *Once there was an "ork" organization*
> *That decided to become a musical corporation,*
> *And when it came time to vote*
> *All the trumpets hit a note . . .*

At which point the trumpet guys would stand up and Glen would stand up and the trumpets turned to him and played a riff.

And now if he'll leave his seat,
We'd like to have you meet
Mr. Glen Gray, president of the Casa Loma Orchestra.

There are all sorts of reasons for writing songs.

One of my strongest copyrights is "I Should Care," which is the title of this book and which was written in 1944 with Paul Weston and Axel Stordahl when the three of us were sharing an apartment. Paul Weston, *né* Paul Wettstein, is a non-Jew who changed his name because people thought him Jewish rather than the devout Catholic he is. He's now married, incidentally, to the marvelous Jo Stafford.

I came into the apartment one day to find Paul and Axel sitting at the table heaped high with their arrangements of "I've Heard That Song Before" for Tommy Dorsey. "There he is," they said. "Fifteen minutes for *him* to write it and hours for us to arrange it." Like most arrangers, they resented the drudgery of it. They'd ask me if I'd wanted a long or short introduction and I said, "Who cares?" You know what the introduction of "I've Heard That Song Before" is? One note: "*Duhh,* it seems to me I've heard that song before . . ."

So now I asked them, "Why don't you fellows write a song with me?" They played this melody of theirs, and the moment I heard the first three notes I also heard in my head, "I should care." When they'd finished I said, "What do you fellows call that?" They said (thank heaven) they didn't call it anything. It became "I Should Care."

Now if you say, or write, "I should care, I should go around weeping," you *must* by necessity say, "I should care, I should go without sleeping." Because can you say, "I should go around leaping"? You just open the door, it's just like walking into Shangri-La—opening the doors to heaven. Which in a way is what's been happening to me all my life.

"I Should Care" became a big hit, and it still is. And Paul and Axel come back to me like two kids who'd just found a pot of gold and want to try for a double. "Hey, Sammy, let's write another hit!" . . . "Okay, fellas, no sweat if you've got another hit melody." Whereupon they started to play this lovely melody. I listened and—sorry if it sounds made up but it's true—a title came into my mind. I said, "How do you like 'Day by Day' for a title?" They said not so bad and so I pushed on with . . .

> *Day by day, I'm falling more in love with you*
> *And day by day my love seems to grow,*
> *There isn't any end to my devotion*
> *It's deeper, dear, by far than any ocean*
> *I find that day by day, you're making*
>   *all my dreams come true*
> *So come what may I want you to know,*
> *I'm yours alone and I'm in love to stay*
> *As we go thru the years,*
> *Day by day . . .*

We had that song in less than an hour. Again, I never should allow anyone to watch me write; they wouldn't pay me. I have more fun than the boys who played in the band at my bar mitzvah. "Day by Day," by the way, has been a hit at least three times—first with Dorsey, next with Sinatra, and last time with the Lettermen.

CHAPTER 11

"Three Coins in the Fountain"

Three coins in the fountain,
Each one seeking happiness,
Thrown by three hopeful lovers . . .

IT WAS Frank Sinatra who, in 1954, brought Jule Styne and me back together again to work on a picture called *Pink Tights*, the first Cinemascope musical, for 20th Century-Fox. It was to star Frank and Marilyn Monroe, with direction by Henry Koster, dances by Robert Alton. When we were all set with the score, Marilyn Monroe took off to Japan with Joe DiMaggio. You can see how long ago I'm talking about.

So Jule and I were sitting around, on the beach, as it were, when one afternoon Sol Siegel walked in and asked could we write a song called "Three Coins in the Fountain." I told him we would write a song called "Eh!"—but what was the picture about? Could we see it?

Can't see it. No script. No book. Three girls go to Rome, throw coins in a fountain, hope to find love. Period. Sol Siegel departs. It was 2 P.M.

I went to the typewriter. I stared. After a moment I wrote:

Three coins in the fountain,
Each one seeking happiness,
Thrown by three hopeful lovers,
Which one will the fountain bless?

I gave the lyric to Styne. He stared at it. Finally, after twenty minutes, he produced a melody we agreed was the right sound for this kind of picture. Which meant Styne was three-fourths done with the song because the theme repeated three times. I'd said all I had to say with those lines I'd written. Jule asked me to mention Rome, so I added:

> Three hearts in the fountain,
> Each one longing for its home,
> There they lie in the fountain,
> Somewhere in the heart of Rome,

Now the song was really finished, but Styne pleaded for a bridge, the passage that links the themes that repeat. I stared some more. This was the hardest part. Finally I wrote:

> Which one will the fountain bless?
> Which one will the fountain bless?

Styne was incredulous. The same line twice? We argued. He went to the piano in frustration and pounded out some music that I hated. I said it stank. He said, "Of course it stinks. The same line twice?" Finally, he changed the tune to what most people are now familiar with.

We'd finished the song! Siegel walked in; he wanted to hear it. We asked for time to learn it. "Learn it? You wrote it." Well, after a little while we took a deep breath and sang it for the first time: "Make it mine! Make it mine! Make it mine!" He loved it and rushed us to play it for Zanuck. "Make it mine! Make it mine! Make it mine!"

Zanuck adored it. Would we make a demo (demonstration record)? I asked Sinatra to make the demo. He was in a good mood; he agreed. I asked Lionel Newman if there would be any musicians available the next day. "It just so happens," he said, "we'll have sixty musicians here for *The Captain from*

Castile." Could Lionel whip up an orchestration? He could and would.

Next day Sinatra learned the song. We walked over to the sound stage, I opened the door, and Sinatra viewed sixty men sitting there. Sinatra said something poetic like "What the f--- is this?" I less poetically said that they happened to be here, they happened to have an orchestration. He gave me the ray, the blue-eyed ray. I said that if he'd rather just do it with Styne at the piano, I'd have the orchestra take five. "Take five?" he said. "It'll take them an hour just to clear the hell out of here. Let's hear it." Sinatra recorded the song and it became the title theme and the number one song in the world in the number one picture—*and* it won the Academy Award.

An ironic epilogue: In all this excitement, in the twenty-four hours from 2 P.M. on one day to 2 P.M. the next, giant 20th Century-Fox forgot a small detail. *They forgot to make a deal for the song.* There's nothing on paper—no contract. Which meant that Jule Styne and Sammy Cahn owned the number one song in the number one picture in the world. Enter Sol C. Siegel, producer of *Pink Tights*, which, double irony, was never made.

"Fellas," says Sol in nice-guy conspiratorial, "we're in great trouble, we forgot to make a deal for the song and of course—"

"What that means is *you're* in great trouble," I said with open face and hands.

"You *can't* own the number one song in the number one picture in the world."

"We do," we both said.

Siegel pleaded with us to give the song back. We refused. He pleaded. Jule and I conferred. We gave him *half* the song back . . . So now, whenever you hear "Make it mine! Make it mine! Make it mine!" . . . *Half* of it is ours. And, believe me, that's not so bad.

Another irony, beginning with another phone call. It was

Ed Traubner, to ask if I would write a song with Gene de Paul, a composer who "needs cheering up." I said I might write a song with Gene that would depress him more than ever, but Ed insisted and so I invited Gene to the studio.

Bit by bit we worked out a song called "Teach Me Tonight." Since I was working for the studio, the studio had first refusal of the song. And they refused it first.

De Paul took the song to other studios, and at long last got Decca Records to record it with "some talented young girl." It sold three copies. He bought one and I bought one and she bought one.

Two years later I was sitting in Dean Martin's dressing room at Paramount when Alan Livingston of Capitol Records called to tell Dean he must make a cover record of a song that is breaking for a big hit. (A cover record is when a big record company discovers a hit made by a small record company and gets a big star to rush it out. In this way they can maybe steal it.)

I asked Dean what song they're discussing. "Teach Me Tonight."

"That's very funny," I said. He didn't understand. Actually, I wasn't at all sure it was *our* "Teach Me Tonight"—after all, you can't copyright a title. It didn't have to be ours. I asked Dean who recorded it; he didn't know.

I went to various record stores, no luck. Finally in desperation I called my buddy Willie B.—disc jockey William B. Williams. Did he know of a record called "Teach Me Tonight"? Yes, he'd been getting calls for it. Did he have a copy at hand? He did. Who had recorded it? The De Castro Sisters. Now, under the title in those pretty little parentheses, what does it say? "It says: 'Cahn–De Paul.'" I asked him to play it so I could hear it over the phone. He put it on.

Starting with the ABC of it,
Through the XYZ of it,
Solve the mystery of it,
Teach me tonight . . .

Gene de Paul would be undepressed for quite some time to come.

Doing a Broadway show is an entirely different proposition than writing a song for the movies as an individual artist. I've done two with Jule Styne (*High Button Shoes, Look to the Lilies*) and two with James Van Heusen (*Skyscraper, Walking Happy*). The biggest hit was *High Button Shoes*.

It goes something like this . . .

They hand us a script, *two* scripts, one for Jule, say, and one for me. He'll take his script home and I'll take my script home. That night I start reading, and everywhere that I see even the slightest chance for lyrics I will fold the page. Jule does the same, thinking, of course, of music.

Then when we get together, if there are many pages turned down—a musical script usually comes to 110 pages—we know we have a chance at musicalization. I've read many scripts where I've not turned down one page, and in such cases the question is, should we *tell* them?

Usually, though, we have the script dog-eared at thirty, forty, fifty places. We then try to space the songs, placing them where we actually want them and they seem to fit. It's not rigid; there's no absolute formula. If there were, everybody would be in show business. We do, however, generally speaking, try to space them about ten pages apart. The point, along with pacing, is to see that our contribution will not only enhance the plot on a particular page, but also be singable—and a good song on its own.

In Hollywood you don't go out of town to pre-test a show

on the road, where you can continue to fix it up. On Broadway, if you're with talented people, you proceed to rewrite. A Broadway musical—that's where you do tend to separate the men from the boys.

One devastating experience—which nearly separated some of us from our senses—was *Skyscraper*. It was in 1965, and starred Julie Harris, who had never been in a musical and was directed by Cy Feuer, produced by Feuer and Ernest H. Martin, with book by Peter Stone, and songs by Jimmy Van Heusen and myself.

We were trying it out at the Fisher Theatre in Detroit, and one night we went to the traditional hotel room and co-producer Ernie Martin, who is succinct, said: "We have no show." He also said the first thing we should do was get a new "book." Peter Stone, who had written the book, is really a considerable talent, as well as a good soldier—if I ever go into the trenches again I want to go with Peter. He locked himself into a room and wrote a different act every two days of the run.

At the end of three weeks we came to New York, where the consensus was: We have a first act.

Julie Harris, a great actress, is not a great singer. In fact she is not a singer, though at this time she was trying to prove otherwise. (Some say that Rex Harrison is also not a singer, but Rex Harrison is one of the greatest musical talents ever to walk on stage. He's a *talking* singer, which I guess is uniquely important for the musical stage; la-la-la-la-la doesn't count. You aren't interested in what a character has to sing if you're not interested in what he has to say.)

It was often my hope with *Skyscraper* that Julie Harris would not sing. Her feeling, of course, was, Why is this idiot telling me not to sing? The only reason I'm doing this show is to sing. Each time she sang, I couldn't help it—I left the theater. (Usually in the theater when the book [script] is playing the songmen leave the theater, and when the song takes over the book author leaves. Julie Harris reversed tradition.)

We'd arrived in New York with half a show, for which a benefit audience was going to pay $100 a seat. For the preview performance of the night before the opening, Van Heusen and I wrote a song called "Haute Couture." They put it in and it started to stop the show. Then the fellow singing it "went up"—forgot the lyrics. Cy Feuer literally became nauseated. The next day at seven o'clock we had a special rehearsal for this actor and the song. Again he "went up." Result: the song was not in the show on opening night, though we managed to put it in later.

The late Dorothy Kilgallen, in her piece in the late *Journal-American*, delivered the coup de grace: "I had my Thanksgiving turkey early."

Nevertheless, when I walked into Sardi's on opening night everybody stood up and applauded. Opening night on Broadway is the closest a man comes to understanding childbirth. Only he has labor pains twice: out of town and in town. The most painful thing in the world is to stand in the back of a theater and take your lumps. And I stood in the back of the theater that night with Cy Feuer and Ernie Martin, and we took it.

There's a song from *Skyscraper*, "Ev'rybody Has the Right to Be Wrong at Least Once," that explains more than a little what I'm all about, what I think life is at least partly about. It's not Spinoza, but it's not egg noodles either, and for me it signifies:

Everybody has the right to be wrong, at least once.
Everybody has the right to be dunce-like, once-like.

Not being too smart is no disgrace.
What sets you apart is smiling with egg on your face.

It's naïve to make believe that you're right;
    it's not bright
Only fools go walking on thin ice—twice!
You and life can skip the strife and you'll both get along.
All it takes is simply saying you're wrong when
    you're wrong!*

And everybody has the right to be,
It can be a sheer delight to be,
And I'd fight, fight for the right to be wrong
At least once.

---

* Every time I sing this song on the stage of the Golden Theatre, when I come to this line I have the strongest impulse to add: "Mr. Nixon, for Heaven's sake, please!"

CHAPTER 12

"Please Be Kind"

This is my first affair, so, please be kind.
Handle my heart with care, oh, please be kind.

FOR ALMOST TWELVE of the eighteen years of my marriage we had absolute Camelot. I existed solely for Gloria and our children Steve and Laurie. People would say to me, "What do you do for a living?" and I'd say, "I'm married." Yes, but what do you *do?*" "I'm *married."* I took my children to the movies, to the playground—and also took any other children who were around, which is how I won over most of the Wasps in the neighborhood.

I became known as the Pajama Man because every morning, no matter how exhausted, I'd take the kids to school in my pajamas. The birth of Steve really changed my whole lifestyle. I would wake at 5 A.M. to watch him sleeping and to be there when he opened his eyes. When Gloria became pregnant again I hoped it wouldn't be another boy, for fear of arousing jealousy in Steve, and my hope came true with the birth of Laurie.

We were married on September 5, 1945, and on the fifth of every month I gave my wife a present; I always carried with me a card listing her and the children's sizes—from shoes to hats to bras to slips and sweaters to rings to gloves to you-name-it. I would be meeting with the likes of Jack Warner or

Sam Goldwyn, but, when it came close to school letting-out time, I'd say I had to rush off to the dentist or whatever and take off instead for the school. (The *compleat* father, you say, cynically? Well, maybe so, but all I can say is I did it because I *wanted* to, not because I thought it was the thing to do. I *loved* doing it.)

Everything was going remarkably well. When we moved into 175 South Mapleton Drive I found that the man next door was A. P. Giannini of the Bank of America. Corny, I know, but I couldn't resist knocking on his door and saying, "I'm your new neighbor and I'd like to borrow a cup of money, please." The answer was: "You'll have to go to the bank. I never do business at home." I guess I had my nerve—but he said it with a straight face . . . To our right lived Art Linkletter. Across the street was Humphrey Bogart. A few doors from him were Sid Luft and Judy Garland—the Garland children in a sense were raised in my home. I waited almost fifteen years for Liza Minnelli to become the star she is today. By Vincente Minnelli out of Judy Garland . . . there was no way she would not be magnificent. (Speaking of Judy and the memories she invokes, eight years ago Jimmy Van Heusen and I were signed to do the songs of *Journey Back to Oz*, a full-length animated feature film, with Liza singing her mother's part, Ethel Merman the Wicked Witch of the West, Rise Stevens the Good-Witch, Danny Thomas the Tin Man, Mickey Rooney the Straw Man, Milton Berle the Cowardly Lion, and the voices of Herschel Bernardi, Paul Lynde, and the late Jack E. Leonard in supporting roles. I understand the picture—eight years in the can, meaning unreleased—is finally to be released, perhaps around the time this book is published.)

Bing Crosby also lived down the street, and I remember one Academy Award night when all of us were up for an Oscar—Humphrey, Judy, Bing, and myself. I was rooting for all of us and I had decided that if we all won I'd see to it that Mapleton Drive would be changed to Academy Drive. As it turned out, I was the only winner, but I did get a priceless bonus in the form of a wire from the other three: "Thanks for not letting the street down." Classy folks.

Life was fun. Life was exciting. In 1952, we purchased a home in Palm Springs, just like all the "in" people were doing. We had an apartment in New York too. I existed for my lady's happiness. And then one day the lady woke up disenchanted, and all the king's horses and all the king's men couldn't put it back together again. Camelot collapsed. And the lady couldn't quite say why.

It was the hardest shot of my life. I understand about Camelot. I understand life is imperfect—because it needs to be. To exist you have to swing somewhere between the highs and the lows. If you wake up everyday with the sun shining and the birds singing and everything right with the world —you've got to be dead or deluded. Still, I would have gone all the way to the wire with Gloria, but I wasn't prepared for this.

What was the problem, the real problem? I can only conjecture. When we were married Gloria was nineteen. (These days she's married to a tennis player twelve years her junior.) Maybe she felt she never had the fun she was entitled to. True, she had the house, the apartment, the servants, the kids, the successful husband in the Hollywood ambience . . . and maybe it was just too much of a much—and too soon. I'm not sure, I can't explain it to you, but I could have *written* the dialogue for us. "Sam, something's not going right." . . . "I know. Shall we try? Shall we try again? Just tell me what I can do. . . ."

No such words were spoken. Camelot was crumbling and I was fighting for my life. I would go away for months at a time to give her a chance to try to find herself. I sent *her* on trips. I redoubled all efforts to make her happy in the only ways I knew. No way. Slowly but slowly I came to the conclusion that I would have to leave.

I've opened each chapter of this book with a portion of one

of my songs—and indeed they do seem to frame in so many ways the content of my life. Any divorce is a heartbreak, but consider the case of the admitted sentimentalist who wrote, "Love and marriage, love and marriage, go together like a horse and carriage" . . . or, "Time after time, I tell myself that I'm so lucky to be loving you" . . . or, "When somebody loves you, it's no good unless she loves you all the way" . . .

When I could no longer take it I decided to go all the way—to New York. First the news had to be broken to the children. Steve is by nature shy and introspective while Laurie is outgoing and humorous; but when I tried—no doubt clumsily—to explain that just as they, brother and sister, sometimes had problems, now Mommy and Daddy had problems and Daddy was leaving for a while, Steve the moody one began cracking jokes and Laurie the comic began to cry.

I packed and took the "red eye" special flight at 11:30 P.M. to New York. On the plane was the late Marty Tananbaum, president of Yonkers Raceway, whose more interesting claim to fame was that as an orthodox Jew he'd married an Irish lass who now became known to the world as Kitty Kelly Tananbaum. He asked me what was taking me to New York and I told him about Gloria and myself. Marty, like most everyone, immediately refused to believe it. The happiest marriage in Hollywood . . . over? No way . . . I said, well, it was a trial separation, and now I'd have to look for a place to live while in New York. "What do you mean, look for a place?" said Marty. "You now live at my place, the Navarro, on Central Park South. I'm never there . . ." So I moved in and lived at the Navarro off and on for nearly a year. I'd returned to the scenes of my bachelorhood, but I wasn't the man I was, not nearly.

During all this my daughter was instrumental in maintaining my sanity. She kept in constant touch with me—came to visit me, spent her holidays with me. My son stayed with his mother, which I guess is par for these things. What also saved me was that I kept working all the time, *never* stopped working. And, at a certain point, I did what I always do, I called my buddy Ed Traubner. "I'm in trouble, Ed, I can't handle it. I'm fighting inside my body like a son-of-a-bitch." Ed sent me to a psychoanalyst in New York.

The analyst and I talked. I told him I was angry. "How angry?" he asked. "So angry I could bite the teeth out of my mouth." He said, "Did you ever hit this woman?" I said, "I've never hit anyone in my life. As a matter of fact I have a recurring dream in which I want to hit someone and I can't." The analyst said, "That's your problem." And then he said, "Lie down on the couch face down. I want you to do something for me. Please start hitting the couch." "Why?" "Because I'm asking you to." "It's silly." "Please hit the couch." Well, he was the doctor, so I starting hitting the couch—and I started crying. He asked me why I was crying, and I said, "Here I am, Sammy Cahn, age fifty, big success—and I'm hitting a couch." I was so ashamed, but I guess that particular little flow from the tear ducts was beneficial.

Work—blessed anodyne! Jimmy Van Heusen and I were asked to do a movie score together, and I went back to the Coast, where I moved into the Beverly Comstock, an apartment hotel about four minutes from the house on Mapleton Drive. It seems that somebody had also convinced my wife to try an analyst, and she was going to the reigning champ in Beverly Hills. Gloria and I were also trying to keep it cordial between us; one day she phoned to say her doctor wanted to see me—alone. You may know that scene.

I went, not feeling very comfortable, but actually when we began I found it wasn't so bad at all—until he told me that Gloria had a right, among other things, to hate her parents. As I've indicated earlier in this story, I had some pretty strong reservations myself about the Delsons, and I had increasingly come to suspect that one of Gloria's reasons for marrying me was to get away from her parents. Still, it seemed to be quite another thing to hate your parents so much that it took you

over, hurt you, and to make a big deal out of somebody—
forgive me, a husband—who thought that maybe this wasn't
the best way in the world to go about handling the problem.

The psychiatrist suggested that I wasn't the one to be
making these judgments, and I suppose he had a point. I'm
not exactly a graduate of Harvard Medical School and I admit
I never read much Freud. I have lived a lot of emotion, though,
including those early days on the Lower East Side, and I told
the doctor that I knew one thing for sure—nothing good ever
comes of hate, including and maybe especially hatred of your
parents. It might feel good for a while, like when your eye
itches like hell and you rub it and it feels so good that you rub
it some more—then you pay like hell for your momentary
indulgence with a sore and puffed and maybe infected eye for
days to come. I think it's that way with hate. I think it's an
enemy and you have to watch it doesn't take over. Like I've
also said earlier on in this book, I'm old-fashioned in some
ways, and I just don't go for this modish jazz about hate-
your-parents as the root of all evil. I fought with my mother,
but loved her. My father was a dear man; he couldn't even
apply a proper whack with his hand. Each day when he was
sick, one of my four sisters—all are married and all have
children—went to see him. I don't know if they loved every
minute of it, but I know damn well that they *felt* better for
doing what they did. That's what I was trying to tell Gloria
when we talked about her hatred of her parents, and that's
why I got sore at the psychiatrist when he told me I didn't have
a right . . . Maybe I was *all wrong*, but he wasn't *all right*. . . .

Still, I made other visits to him. On one such visit, when I
walked into his office, who should be sitting there but Gloria.
"Excuse me," I said, and started to leave, but he said no, there
was no mix-up and would I sit down, please? I did, and he said
to me, "Mr. Cahn, I want you to go home"—home to my wife,
that is.

Now I wanted to go home in the worst way in the world, but

not because *he* wanted it. I pointed my angry finger at him. "I don't want *you* to want me to go home, I want"—moving the finger from him to Gloria—"*her* to want me to come home." He smiled that smile that some analysts smile which seems to say "what fools you mortals be" and said aloud, "That's exactly what's wrong with you. Do you imagine I'd tell you I want you to go home if it wasn't what your wife wanted?"

I think he was dead wrong. It was up to her to tell me herself, and, if she couldn't or wouldn't, I should have marched out and gone back to the Beverly Comstock. But I did like *he* said and went home.

For a while we played at Camelot revisited, but instead of interludes for the joust Gloria took up tennis. Still, it was fun and life was good, we told ourselves, and the happiness of our friends over this apparent reconciliation also made it seem worthwhile. We started using Monte Vista again, our Palm Springs home, and worked at generating the excitement of our life before.

It was the time, also, of another Camelot in the making: the campaign that would lead to the election and inauguration of John F. Kennedy.

Frank Sinatra had gotten us together with the Kennedys, who asked did we have a song that could be a campaign theme. Did we have a song that could be a campaign theme? I said, "We sure have a title"—Van Heusen and I had just finished a song called "High Hopes." They loved the title, and Van Heusen and I went to work on a Kennedy version. We had trouble; the name Kennedy just wouldn't fit anywhere. We tried and probed but no dice. After some hours Van Heusen said, "All right, big mouth, how're you going to lick this one?" "What the hell, why don't we spell it?" I suggested. So where the original lyric said: "Just what makes that little ol' ant/Think he'll move that rubber tree plant/Anyone knows an ant/Can't move a rubber-tree plant,/But he's got *high* hopes," we now wrote, "K-E-double-N-E-D-Y,/Jack's the nation's favorite guy./Everyone wants to back/Jack,/Jack is on the right track/And he's got *high* hopes . . ." I looked at Van Heusen, spread my arms, and smiled my pushcart smile—not so inappropriate when you think of it; after all, old Joe Kennedy and I didn't exactly start out with silver spoons in our mouths.

So we were on the Kennedy team, and the song went on to be a big hit. The original, from the movie *Hole in the Head,* won an Oscar. Frank recorded the special campaign lyrics, and, before you knew it, it was President John F. Kennedy and we were assigned to write for the inaugural gala. Van Heusen and I really leaned in, gave our all for this one.

Around two o'clock the afternoon of Inauguration Day, the snow began to fall rather softly and quietly, almost stealthily, in Washington, and it continued to fall and fall and fall. We were all inside and had no awareness of the snow until around sevenish someone asked, "Have you seen what's happening out there? The snow's up to your ears." And it fell and it fell and it fell. All anyone could say was, "How do you explain it, all that snow?" I said, as I still say today when the occasion merits, "That's God reminding Frank Sinatra that he's still around." It's even my profound explanation for the Agnew downfall: God is again reminding Frank Sinatra.

After the gala all the performers were given a party in a private dining room. Frank asked would I please sit at his table because he wanted me to be with Ella Fitzgerald, who was always terribly nervous at such affairs. This meant my wife was seated apart from me at a table with the Milton Berles. As it turned out I was seated beside an empty chair, because Ella, out of nervousness or whatever, never showed up. Suddenly we heard the announcement: "Ladies and gentlemen, the President of the United States." We all stood and applauded and in he came, without Mrs. Kennedy. He came right to our table and sat down in Ella's chair.

There we sat, Sinatra and JFK and me. The President loved little cigars, which he smoked rather surreptitiously, and he was doing so now. Finally I said, "Mr. President, I feel a little uncomfortable sitting here." He smiled and asked me why I felt uncomfortable. "Well," I said, "I see three men here, and I think I could replace myself with something far more attractive and break the monotony of the seating." I stood up, walked across the room, and went to my wife, asking her to come with me. I led her over to the President and said, "Mr. President, my wife. You will agree it will dress the table a lot more attractively." I then left and took Gloria's former place with the Berles. A picture was taken of JFK, Frank Sinatra, and Gloria. And that was our brush with the larger Camelot.

I think the separation had been an even more crushing blow to my four sisters than me, so Gloria and I went on a second honeymoon to New York to show them the glorious flag of reconciliation. We all went to dine at La Fonda del Sol, and it was a determinedly fun, *hamish* evening, if that word fits with La Fonda del Sol. That night, back in the apartment, I said to Gloria, "I feel kind of funny, kind of stuffed." She said, "Perhaps you ate too much," and I said, or rather, said to myself—No, I think I feel some kind of tumor or something growing inside me. In a way we were both right. I'd taken in, held in too much. I was stuffed, all right, and something dangerous was growing inside me.

Our charade was over. The lady, as I say, was unable to tell me what I was doing wrong. In me, there was a change. I was able to speak out more, but it didn't help as things got progressively worse.

At one point I went to my friend Gene Wyman—I'm a very wealthy man in my friendships—and asked him please to get Gloria a lawyer because she was walking around seemingly incapable of doing anything for herself at the time. Afterward

Gene came to me and said, "Sammy, I don't think I'm violat-
ing the lawyer–client privilege in what I'm going to tell you
because Gloria's not my client, but I took her to this lawyer
and she insisted I stay. The lawyer began to ask questions . . .
'What kind of a husband is Mr. Cahn?' 'The finest husband in
the world.' 'That's hardly grounds for divorce. What kind of
father?' 'There couldn't be a better father.' "

I tell this not to demonstrate what a great husband and
father I was—I know I wasn't all perfect—but to suggest the
sort of thing that topped off my frustration about the whole
tragic business. I just couldn't get answers, except the kind
that said it shouldn't have happened.

The night it ended I'd just had an affair with a woman—my
wife—who lay passive. I felt as though I didn't exist. Maybe
for Gloria I no longer did, and this was her way of telling me in
the way I'd understand best. If that was her meaning, I got the
message. I lay there for a while in the darkness on my side of
the bed, and then I began to get the shakes. I got up, wrote a
note to Gloria—"I can't live like this"—and called Ed Traubner
at a hotel in La Jolla. It was 4 A.M. Ed said, "Just come up here
right away." I went up and stayed with him for three or four
days. Finally we went to a lawyer, who said to me, "Why did
you leave the house? It's your house. But obviously you can't
stay in the same room with your wife." So I moved back
home—in a manner of speaking. It was my house. My castle. I
saw every nail go into it. Now I was living in the guest house of
my own home.

After a while it got too rough for the children, too impossible all around, so I moved out for good. It was our last affair,
and "please be kind" would have been a nice line to accompany it. Except it was already very late for such sentiments. It
was time to get up and start living again.

But first I had to come very close to dying.

CHAPTER 13

"Until the Real Thing Comes Along"

I'd work for you, I'd slave for you,
I'd be a beggar or a knave for you,
If that isn't love, it will have to do
Until the real thing comes along . . .

It was a day in 1958 at the house on Mapleton Drive in Holmby Hills. The gardener and I waved at each other. He came up and said, "Mr. Cahn, I understand you know about ulcers. I have ulcers."

"Sit down and listen to me," I said, "and when you get up you'll be on your way to no ulcers. Now, how long have you had these ulcers?"

"Three months."

"What do the doctors want to do?"

"Operate."

"What happened three months ago."

Three months ago he'd invested $3000 with his brother-in-law—one of *those* brother-in-laws—and the investment went to zero.

"Has your brother-in-law got ulcers?"

"No, but it's killing my wife—and it's *her* brother."

"Paul, do me a favor," I said to him. "You're stuck $3000.

You have all these doctors now. An operation will be $750, and I'm sure before it's all through you'll be up to $5200. So when you see your brother-in-law, smile at your brother-in-law, put your arm around him, confuse him—until *he* gets ulcers from his guilt."

The gardener took my advice. I think it at least helped to cure his ulcers.

My own ulcers were discovered when I was thirteen. Real, on-the-ground, wretching, screaming pain was what I had. My mother took me to Beth Israel Hospital. I'll never forget how scared I was. A little kid—you walk into this place looks like a Buck Rogers room, full of grotesque machinery. They make you take all your clothes off while they're standing around in heavy rubber aprons, and then they give you this awful stuff to drink. (In forty years nothing has changed, except the aprons are a little smaller and the barium is now chocolate-flavored. If an X-ray specialist reads this, I ask you please to take a moment to explain to your kid patients why there's no need to be horrified and why he has to be naked while the adults are all so protected.) Anyway, they took a series of tests and told my mother, "There's nothing wrong with him that a good physic [that's homey for laxative] won't cure." With this kind of expert help there is no explanation for the ulcers cooling down for so long except the genius of nature and good luck.

Whatever the reason, I had my ulcers under control— beaten, I figured—until Doris Day triggered them off years later in 1953, when Vernon Duke and I did the score for the movie *April in Paris,* starring Doris Day and Ray Bolger. Vernon was a natural to be involved because he had written the song "April in Paris" with the redoubtable E. Y. Harburg, who almost gave *him* ulcers.

Vernon Duke, *né* Vladimir Dukelsky—truly an incredible

guy. I don't think he could write a bad song. As Vernon Duke
he wrote some of the great popular standards, and as Vladimir
Dukelsky he wrote so-so classical music. I think the only
problem with Vernon Duke–Vladimir Dukelsky was that he
never knew what name to use. When he went to sleep he used
to pray to wake up in the Czarist days in the White Russia
he'd come from. He wore a handkerchief in his jacket sleeve
and a huge carnation in his lapel, one that might even frighten
Johnny Green, that noted carnation aficionado. The walls of
his New York apartment were covered with books everywhere—in the hallways, in the bedroom, in the bathroom. (A
composer of popular songs who read *books*—most unusual,
damn near subversive.) He was, I have to say, the single most
talented composer I ever worked with. Most popular songs
are written in four eight-bar sections with a bridge—a depar-
ture—in between. For instance, when "I'll Walk Alone" goes
to, "I'll always be near you, wherever you are"; that's the
bridge. Vernon Duke had more variations in the bridge than
anyone I ever knew.

I brought him out to Hollywood and finally managed to get
a picture for us to do at Warner Brothers. The moment we
were signed I went over to our office at the studio, which was
inaccessible—Mr. Duke had filled it with flowers. I tried to
dissuade him from his natural compulsions—the hanky, the
carnation, and, now that he was working, a big cigar—because,
as I warned him, one day Jack Warner was going to see him on
the lot and say, "Who's the schmuck who thinks he's me?"

Despite the flowers and cigar smoke we did manage to do
our work, and came the day when we went to Doris Day to
audition the songs for "April in Paris." She expressed delight
and joy over each of them, and I danced away from that
audition. A few days later we were told she'd hated every
note, every word. Frenzy and panic. We started to rewrite, and
I would stake Vernon's reputation, much bigger than mine,

that the rewrites—no matter what Doris Day thought good or bad—were inferior to the originals. And perhaps it was knowing that, and feeling helpless to do anything about it, that helped bring my ulcers back.

A few years later Doris Day would make them bleed. Permit me to approach the moment via some apparently roundabout background. I have produced one movie in my time. It was for Warner Brothers and called *Three Sailors and a Girl*, and it came smack between *Bwana Devil*, the first 3-D (three-dimensional) movie, and Warner's *House of Wax*, the second 3-D movie. You see, *Bwana Devil* was demolishing every other picture, so Jack Warner pulled the brake on the entire studio and retooled. "Stop everything, we're making a 3-D picture!" The same thing must have been happening with Harry Cohn at Columbia, Zanuck at 20th, and the nabobs-in-residence at the moment at MGM. Here's how they finished: Jack Warner was first with *House of Wax*; Harry Cohn was second with a Western; 20th Century-Fox showed with something I frankly forget. And MGM finished dead last with *Kiss Me Kate*—by the time it was ready, they even had to take the 3-D out of it, which tends to reaffirm my thesis about MGM's being famous for taking up what was topical and finishing with it when it was typical.

Jack Warner, though, was an extraordinary man. He had a little black book that showed how each picture was doing. If happy pictures were making money, he made happy pictures. If sad pictures were making money, he made sad pictures. Personally, Jack Warner liked happy endings best. If he could manage it there'd be no hospital scenes in a movie. If a woman had to have a baby, let her have it in a cab. If you were making a picture about Lincoln, it would end with Mrs. Lincoln saying, "How about theater tonight?" Happy endings. Snakes were not allowed in his pictures. Guys with loud ties weren't allowed. If an actor had a blemish on his face he lost his job.

While all this into-3-D-out-of-3-D was happening, I was trying to make another motion picture, not getting anywhere, and facing the judgment day called option time—to be or not to be renewed. Doris Day had by now made it to queen of the Warner Brothers lot, which meant all she had to say was, "Of course Sammy will produce my next picture." The late Steve Trilling, knowing my sentiments, came and begged me, "Sammy, she's the only musical star we've got. Go see her." (Steve Trilling was Jack Warner's assistant and alter ego. For instance, if Jack Warner had a date to play tennis and the forecast was for bad weather, Steve Trilling would cut it out of the newspaper so Jack Warner wouldn't see it. True story. But Steve was a good man and a dear friend.)

So I went to see her on the set. "Doris, could I see you for a moment?"

"Of course." Shining and radiant.

Only twice have I asked someone for a job. Once was Doris Day. The other was David Merrick when he was going to do *Sugar.* He said, "Sam, I'm sorry, I already have a lyric writer —Bob Merrill—it's out of my hands." I said, "I think you're lucky, and I envy you, because you fellows are going to have to be very talented to screw this up." Merrick said, "Don't worry, we're very talented." . . . Which reminds me of the time Samuel Goldwyn asked me to read the script of *The Secret Life of Walter Mitty* by James Thurber and Ken Englund. I read it and believed it the single best screenplay I'd ever read. I told Goldwyn that. He looked at me, smiled, and hit me with what could be his as well as Hollywood's epitaph: "Wait 'til I get through with it."

Those times were laughs. As for Doris Day: "Of course," she said, "are you kidding?" This is to the accompaniment of hugs and embraces. So I went dancing back to Steve Trilling's office, telling myself it's sometimes worthwhile to humble yourself. She was so *warm.*

The moment I entered his office Steve said: "They really don't want you, Sam."

I felt my stomach open up.

One thing about me: I don't outwardly panic. I went to the phone and called Dr. Rex Kennemer and asked if he could meet me at Cedars of Lebanon. I then got in my car and drove to Cedars of Lebanon. When we met there I said, "I think I'm bleeding." He got Dr. Max Rabwin to examine me.

They stood over me. They were going to slice me. I got very frightened, and I did what I always do when I'm in a jam. I called Ed Traubner.

"Ed, they want to take my stomach out—what do I do?"

"You could go to the Mayo Clinic for a further opinion, but why go that far? There's a clinic up in Palo Alto where there are a lot of men from Mayo."

That night Nanette Fabray, Gloria—we were still together at the time—and I got on a *Lark* train from Los Angeles to San Francisco, and the next day I checked in at the clinic. There I met one of the rare human beings in my life, Dr. Albert M. Snell. They say the only trouble with Christianity is there are too few Christians. The late Albert M. Snell was a true Christian in every sense of the word.

I'll never forget him walking into the room. I was reading *The Cruel Sea*, by Nicholas Monserrat, which I found one of the most depressing novels ever. Dr. Snell's first line was, "Did you walk in here?" I said I had. "So forget it. *You'll* decide when and if you're operated on, and right now you don't have to be operated on." It was like taking a hundred anvils off of my stomach. His next line was, "But I do suggest you stop reading that book, or you'll get ulcers." We both laughed, God bless him.

During the next three days he told me that mine was the classic ulcer history; that there was little doubt in his mind that eventually I'd need to be operated on. Everything he said came true, but this time around I once again beat the ulcers and kept them under control for years—until the crisis of my divorce—by keeping myself under his care.

Lying there in that hospital at the time I developed a sense of gratitude toward Doris Day. I realized she'd done me a great service. She'd finally made me realize the time bomb living inside me. She may even have saved my life.

So every time I think of Doris Day, I smile. A little tight maybe, but a smile . . .

Nixon and I got it on the same day of the year he ran for Governor of California. We both got knifed—he by Pat Brown and I by Dr. Mark Rabwin.

When my stomach really kicked up during Gloria's and my try at a second honeymoon in New York I waited only until we got back to the Coast to call Dr. Kennemer, who sent me to Dr. Lindsman to be X-rayed. (Dr. Lindsman has been taking pictures of me since I first went to Hollywood. There was a time when there was more film of my insides than of Phil Silvers' close-up comic facial contortions.)

Dr. Lindsman said, "You're blocking. If I were you, Sammy, I'd be operated on immediately." I said, "Give me those X-rays," and I air-mailed them special to Dr. Ben Greenspan, a friend of mine at Albert Einstein Memorial Hospital in Philadelphia. He called and said, "I would do this right away." I said, "Okay, do you want to do it?" He said, "No, you have some crack hospitals out there. Get yourself a crack surgeon."

I went into Cedars of Lebanon, and the surgeon turned out to be Dr. Mark Rabwin, one of the fellows who had stood over me there when I was bleeding over Doris Day. "When do we do it?" He said Wednesday. I said, "If you let me go to Palm

Springs, I'll come back Wednesday." "I'll do better. Go to Palm Springs and stay there this week and next. Come back a week from Sunday."

I came back on the Sunday; they did all the tests and said the operation would be on Tuesday, which was an election day. Election day, elective operation . . .

Monday night before the event. Enter—how to say?—this effeminate individual to shave me. He lathers up my stomach and is about to descend in his ablutions when I say, "Hold it! This is supposed to be an ulcer operation, not a circumcision." He said, "I'm supposed to shave you everywhere." I said, "I'll take the responsibility for this." Enter next, Dr. Rabwin, who said, "See you in the morning." I said, "See *you* in the morning."

Then I called New York and spoke with my brother-in-law Jules Goldberg, who's married to my sister Florence, my show-business sister. She'll tell you about a show a year before it opens, about a song a year before it's published.

I said to Jules, "Hi, don't get nervous. I'm about to tell you something." Which of course immediately made him nervous. "I'm going to be operated on in the morning." It took about five minutes to calm him down. "It's an elective operation," I said. "I feel strong and it should be okay. But don't tell the girls. How can they help? By worrying? But I want you to know so, just in case something goes wrong, they don't hear it on the radio." I told Jules I'd keep a long-distance line open to Ina, the secretary to NBC vice-president Dave Tebet, another dear friend. "She'll keep you informed, so just relax," I said. And I hung up and I went to sleep.

I had had visions of all the movie and television hospital scenes. Big lights. Being wheeled into the operating amphitheater. Even some musical background. The doctor giving a reassuring smile before they put the chloroform mask or whatever it is over your nose.

Forget it. Next thing I knew it was seven o'clock Tuesday night, November 7, 1962, and four people were standing around me: my wife, Dave Tebet, Ed Traubner, and Jules Goldberg. Playing wise guy, my first question was, "How's Pat Brown doing?" My second, to Jules, was, "Why are you here?" Jules' appropriate response was, "Do you know what your sisters would do to me if I hadn't come out here? I'd rather be in a stream of piranha fish." And the doctor said, "Are you the one who stopped that fellow from shaving you? When they brought you upstairs, it delayed the operation a half-hour." To each his own . . .

In the post-operative period I discovered how vital the everyday functions are: eating, drinking, urination, defecation, and, most important, "breaking wind." For the next five days it seemed my survival depended on my scorecard showing progress or lack of it in the big five. Most important of all, it seemed, and most embarrassing, without question, was this terrible nurse standing over me and saying, "Please, please, pass gas."

I hated her. *Hated.* Somebody almost fired her but I wouldn't let them. I figured my hate for her would help keep me alive.

While I was still in the hospital a further souring in my domestic affairs apparently pushed me into a relapse. Came the doctors, and they saved my life. They stood over me four days and four nights. I literally *felt* I was dying. They had me on intravenous and kept lacing the fluid with what seemed every antibiotic known to man.

The "no visitors" sign was on my door, but one night, around 11:30 P.M., I heard this voice saying, "I know it's late, but I've flown all the way from New York. Please let me see him." And then that damn nurse saying "no." Followed by the other voice, which I recognized now, saying, "I don't want to bother him, I just want to sit in the room." I called out as best

I could to "let him in." She finally did, and he sat there on the other side of the room, crying softly. It was Cye the Shirt-maker.

Two things, I'm convinced, really saved me: the sound of Cye's tears and my hate for that nurse. Love and hate . . .

Cye the shirtmaker . . . In the same building that housed the Warner Brothers Music Company—the RKO Building in Radio City—there was a luxurious men's haberdashery called Maison de Cye that I'd pass a half-dozen times a day.

When "*Bei Mir*" broke big I was taken under the wing of Mack Goldman of WBMC. As a professional manager, his job was to see to it that the songs got to all the singers, bands, and song pluggers. Mack Goldman was an elegant man. Every morning he'd come into the office, take his paper money out of his pocket, toss it to his secretary and say smartly to her, "Take this out and have it laundered," which in those days meant nothing more sinister than going to the bank and exchanging old bills for crisp new ones. Mack always looked as though he had just stepped out of a barber shop.

Now, in my recent estate of prominence due to "*Bei Mir's*" success, Mack Goldman said, "Come with me," and proceeded to walk me into Maison de Cye. "Cye, I've got a live one for you," he said, and started to pick out shirts for me —and shorts and socks and pajamas and ties and handkerchiefs.

I have to tell you that the success of "*Bei Mir*" was not as it might have been portrayed in an old B-movie—a hit! montage: sheet music, money floating down, sheet music, champagne, sheet music, money floating down. Not like that at all. I was getting three-fourths of a cent a copy and couldn't possibly have walked into Cye's on my own. When Mack Goldman got through, the bill—this was 1937—came to $1200! And then Cye said, "That'll be $600, I'm starting a sale tomorrow morning." He let me beat the sale by one whole day. How better to start a friendship? . . .

Cye the Shirtmaker. Cye Kronfeld—a gentleman, and gentle man, with thick curly graying hair and a smile that could only be developed through dealing with the Mack Goldmans of the world. I liked him immediately, and he became like a father to me.

Anytime you visited Cye you were likely to see a spectrum of clients ranging from racketeers to bookmakers to music publishers to a songwriter (me). (When Legs Diamond lay dying, he is supposed to have said, "Bury me in a Cye shirt.")

I would get calls from all over the country from people begging me to intercede with Cye so they could get some shirts. He was pretty casual about long-distance dealing. With him it was always strictly personal. And from all over the globe—Singapore, Bangkok, wherever—people would send their shirts back to Cye for laundering. His laundry, in fact, was his main source of power. He insisted that his shirts be laundered by himself, and when Cye sent them back to you they were like brand new.

One of the proudest moments in my whole life was when my son Steve was bar-mitzvahed at the University Temple near UCLA. As the rabbi took the torah and handed it to my father, who handed it to me, who handed it to Steven, my eye fell on Cye the Shirtmaker and Spencer Tracy sitting side-by-side. I have a hunch Spence arranged it that way so he could ask Cye, "Where the hell are the shirts you promised to send me five years ago?"

Cye was a man of many eccentricities: He was never satisfied with the physical set-up of his plant, so every day he and his assistant would buy timber and make new entranceways, move the cutting tables from front to back, the laundry room from one side to the other, the showroom to the left and the pattern room to the right. You needed to take a piece of string with you to make your way out of the maze.

Cye never picked up a check in all the years I knew him. He also never went to dinner by himself but would wander by the popular eating places, stare in, and eventually a customer hoping to receive an order of shirts and/or get his laundry delivered would ask him in.

Cye never asked a waiter for anything—I guess that insured against it possibly being his check. If Cye wanted a slice of bread he would say to whomever he was sitting with, "Don't you want a slice of bread?" Or butter. Or even water.

He was married and divorced twice. First he was married to a very charming lady, who, on the only occasion I ever met her, told me the story I am about to tell you, and then to Bea Kalmus, the wonderful gal who sang and did one of the first radio talk shows.

Mrs. Cye No. 1, who always remained good friends with Cye, swore that this was why they got divorced:

Cye would never allow the furniture in their home to remain in one place for one full day (just as with his work plant). The living room would be switched into the library and the library into the bedroom. She never knew what she was coming home to. More than once she had opened the front door and, thinking it was the wrong apartment, turned around and left.

The final blow was coming home one day and finding the bedroom furniture in the kitchen. Almost in tears she said, "All right, Cye—this you will have to explain, because our marriage hinges on your answer." He gave her a look, followed by: "How many times have you wanted a glass of milk or a piece of fruit during the night?"

Damon Runyon once did a whole column on Cye, who had gotten into the papers when Judge Samuel Seabury, investigating the rackets, wanted to know how hoodlums without any visible means of support could buy hundreds of thousands of dollars' worth of haberdashery at Cye's. He wanted Cye to open his books to the investigating committee—which would have been a death warrant for Cye, who instead went out of business as Maison de Cye and opened his shirt plant.

A lot of people miss Cye, but nowhere near as much as I miss him. He was there . . .

When I opened my eyes in Cedars of Lebanon and asked, "How's Pat Brown doing?" it was Dave Tebet who said, "He's doing to Nixon what Dr. Mark Rabwin just did to you." I'd thought Dave was back in New York with my brother-in-law Jules, and here they both were, standing over my bed.

I first met David Tebet in 1947 at the first rehearsal of *High Button Shoes*—book by Stephen Longstreet, songs by Jule Styne and Sammy Cahn, and starring Phil Silvers and Nanette Fabray. He was then a theatrical press agent, with Nanette Fabray as his prime client.

Not just a press agent, really. I knew many of those, but Dave worked with the producer of a show from its inception; he let out his publicity release through such prestigious media as the drama pages of *The New York Times* and the then *Herald Tribune;* he would also create the billboards and the billing. His efforts went far beyond merely trying to get you an occasional mention in Walter Winchell or Leonard Lyons or Earl Wilson or Ed Sullivan.

We took to one another at first sight and became lifelong friends. Teb was and remains a man of high principle—not so common in the theater—and high good humor. Phil Silvers was my older chum, but—and no offense, Phil—Tebet was the kind of guy you could talk to once in a while about something besides the price of the fight at the Garden or who was going to pitch tomorrow for the Yankees—two of Phil's chief preoccupations.

I remember his telling Phil to hire himself a powerful press agent because he, Tebet, was going to "steal the show for Fabray." As it turned out, Nanette Fabray sort of stole the show for herself, but the addition of Tebet to her corner helped win her the Tony Award that year. Phil, running in bad luck, won nothing.

High Button Shoes won Tonys for many people—none for Phil Silvers, none for Jule Styne and me. I admit I sometimes wondered what the critics thought Nanette Fabray was singing out there when she stopped the show with "Papa, Won't You Dance With Me?" Come to think of it, if Tebet had said to me what he said to Phil Silvers, I think I would have hired him then and there. Later I did become his client—he's the only press agent I've ever had.

Tebet married "the star he made," and he and Nanette often stayed with us when they vacationed in Hollywood. The marriage ended in divorce (they say the husband is always the last to know; in this case the host and old friend was right behind—it was a real shocker).

Teb also helped make a celebrity of Max Liebman of *Your Show of Shows,* and so he stood very high at NBC. But one day the show's ratings began to slip, and Liebman was out and so was Teb. Showbiz . . . Fortunately, though, Teb was a long-time friend of Emanuel Sacks, right-hand man to the General, which at NBC means General David Sarnoff. In the Mr. Nice Guy department, no one tops Manny Sacks. Once he was operated on for a throat ailment and I wired him: "DEAR MANNY, I HOPE THEY CUT OUT YOUR 'YES.' " It was also said to be a lucky thing Manny wasn't a girl or he'd be on his back all the time.

Manny took Dave Tebet on as his relief pitcher, so to speak, at NBC—and then, to the dismay of all who ever had anything to do with him, Manny Sacks became ill and died. His job went deservedly to Dave Tebet, who as of this writing is celebrating his fifteenth year with NBC. Dave Tebet, who also helped me through my divorce, who, like Cye the Shirtmaker, was there when I was coming out of deep surgery, who has been for me the brother I never had.

High Button Shoes became a big hit and ran two years at the Shubert Theatre. On its first anniversary the curtain went down and went up again to reveal a tremendous buffet catered by Max Asnas, fabled proprietor of the Stage Delicatessen. I'd known Max when he had what was just a little delicatessen at 57th Street and Sixth Avenue and I was struggling and starving along with Saul Chaplin. Max, as I've mentioned, used to stake us to meals. Now, on the stage of the Shubert, he came over to me and—he always sounded like that wonderful funnyman B. S. Pulley—growled in his deep frog voice, "Hello, we bot' made it, didn't we?"

CHAPTER 14

"Come Fly With Me"

Come fly with me!
Let's fly! Let's fly away! . . .

WOMEN, I once upon a naïve time believed, were no mystery to me. I was, in my salad days, the sort of fellow who at times had the chutzpah to propose bed before dinner to a date. I got my face slapped quite a lot—and quite a lot I didn't.

When I married Gloria I went full circle. As I've mentioned, I became a totally committed husband and father—and maybe, as I've also said, I overdid it. Nonetheless, the fact was I was very much out of the "race"—by choice. And now, with us separated, I was abruptly back in again—and *not* by choice.

Still, after near-death I'd decided I'd better get on with the business of living, which seemed to be confronting me as I sat now in a plane carrying me from Los Angeles to New York. She was a very, very attractive stewardess. Sam, I declared to myself, let's see if it's still there. I strolled up to the galley and said to the young lady, "Please don't make a scene, my name is Sammy Cahn, and if you walk off this plane with me when it gets to New York I think I can promise you one of the pleasant evenings of your life. If sex comes up, it will only be because you bring it up, and even then you will need a gun to make me because I don't give in easy—" (Brash, I grant you. And yet not so brash . . . I'd learned long ago not to "lean in" too hard. I'd let the lady know I was a man, and after that she took me to bed or we didn't go. I know this is old-fashioned, but it seemed to me that it usually was a more important decision for the lady than for the man.)

The lovely stewardess stopped me with a smile. "I think I believe you, but I really can't. You see, I think I'm engaged——"

"You *think* you're engaged? Who is he?"

"I can't tell you. I think you know him."

"If I know him you'd better tell me who he is, because then I'll tell you if you're engaged."

After a little more coaxing on my part she told me it was Henry Fonda.

"Henry Fonda! He'll leave you cut and bleeding and for dead and—well, I shouldn't have said that, guess I'm just over-anxious. I'll tell you what, I'll make a deal with you. I hope you get married and it turns out marvelous, but if . . . well, will you call . . ."

She smiled again. (Her name was Shirlee Adams and she *married* Henry Fonda. She is still married to him, and I'm pleased to report we're all friends today—in fact, I told him this story just the other night.)

After about twenty minutes the then unmarried and maybe engaged Shirlee came back to my seat and said, "Sam, there's another stewardess on this plane who's a marvelous person and a dear friend. Would you like to walk *her* off this plane?"

"If she's your friend, she's my guest." (Not so hot, but not so bad for a rusty operator.)

Shirlee's friend's name was Boots. Boots—and, truly, no pun intended—was made for loving, not walking. I've had my romances, but ours was surely one of the most enjoyable and charming, no doubt spiced by the separations and intense renewals that are a built-in part of an airline stewardess' way of life. There's no time for much of anything except making love.

I saw Boots for almost two years, and if American Airlines showed a deficit during that time I think I can now tell them at least one of the reasons. Boots—who was tiny and dark— would walk off each flight and come over to my apartment lugging two enormous shopping bags filled with whatever she could "requisition" from the plane, which was damn near everything except the wings and engines—for instance, a couple hundred of those little packs of cigarettes with only two cigarettes in them; dozens of those tiny sample bottles of booze, more Macadamia nuts than I ever want to see again; those little salt-and-pepper shakers; grosses of silverware; wine glasses; even those little vials you break in case of air- sickness. I even considered redecorating my apartment to resemble the forward lounge of an airliner so all that stuff would seem more at home. Two good years, and a most unhappy sequel—Boots would one day die of cancer. She was a wonderful person. I will not forget her.

Back to living, back on the trail. More than once I asked myself what the hell a man of fifty was doing chasing around like a Lothario of twenty. But chase I did—I felt I had to or perish.

Back to Hollywood . . .

One of my good buddies at the time was, and still is, Denise Minnelli, now Mrs. Prentis Cobb Hale. Denise was, and still is, kind of the social arbiter of the Hollywood scene. She is a Yugoslav with the unique attractiveness of that lineage, and the accent of Garbo. She was then married to one of my favorite men in the world, the remarkably talented Vincente Minnelli, director of such films as *An American in Paris, Meet Me in St. Louis, Gigi,* and *Lust for Life.* If I were the owner of a studio I'd allow only two men to make all my pictures—Vin- cente Minnelli and Billy Wilder.

One day the phone rang, and it was Denise in her charming

accent asking if I would do her the favor of escorting a lovely divorcée to a party Denise was giving at the Bistro for Lynda Johnson and George Hamilton.

"For you, anything or anyone," I said. "I wouldn't even care if she was ugly—" "But," Denise butted in, "she is lovely, and she is staying with friends in Palm Springs. Her name is Mary, and I have told her you would call her."

I placed the call and asked for Mary. A voice came on the phone that still places number one with me in the rankings of liquid Southern-sounding voices.

"Haah," she wafted at me.

"I'm Sammy Cahn. Denise Minnelli asked me to call you and invite you to her party at the Bistro."

"Isn't that the most charmin' thing, and ah'd just adore"— make that "a-doah"—"going with you-all."

I promised to pick her up at the Beverly Hills Hotel, which was conveniently near the Minnellis.

Partly I was back in Hollywood for a film assignment, partly to take possession of the new house I'd had built on North Cañon Drive, diagonally across the street from Kirk and Anne Douglas. One day the Douglases stopped by to see what the new house was like and were shocked to find me living in a state closely resembling a bombed-out Germany. For tax purposes—I confess it—I had to be sleeping there, which I was; the lights had to be on, which they were; there had to be running water, which there was. A couple of slight details were missing—I'm not sure I had a ceiling, and one of the walls was not yet in place. Kirk and Anne said this was ridiculous and suggested I move out of the open air and come in from the cold with them, which I did. (If the I.R.S. is interested, this is to tell them that I was still on Cañon Drive and in my own house all day, but at night I slept in the guest room at the Douglases', which I hope is no crime.)

The next afternoon after the Douglas inspection of my premises, I was talking to Anne and remembered I was to call to see if the lady from Palm Springs had arrived in Beverly Hills. She "sho' " had. I asked if she liked her accommodations. She "sho' " did. Was there anything I could do for her? Well—she smiled through the telephone—she was having sort of a problem . . . "My maid packed two left shoes." I wasn't sure what that meant exactly, but I told her I was with Mrs. Anne Douglas, who had just been chosen one of the ten best-dressed women in the world, and that if anyone could handle such a problem it was Anne Douglas. I introduced the two of them over the phone, and Anne said she had a pair of shoes I could take along to the lady when I picked her up that night. That night, all dressed up in my dinner jacket, I carried a little Gucci shopping bag containing the shoes over to the Beverly Hills Hotel and knocked on the door of the lady's suite. It opened and there she stood, Scarlett O'Hara. From that moment on I tried to do a Rhett Butler, wondering more than once where Clark Gable was when I needed him. She flashed her smile, which in person more than lived up to my image of the telephone version.

"I am from Hertz Rent-a-Shoe, and if you will sit down I would like to try these on you." Lord, how that lady could smile. She sat down, I put the shoes on her feet, she looked down. "You brought me two left shoes." Luckily she couldn't hear Anne, who, when informed, remarked, "What is she, some kind of effen' left-shoe nut?"

I hung up hastily on Anne and said to the Southern belle that with a face like hers there was hardly a chance anyone would look at her feet if she went with *no* shoes—which is what we did, she in a stunning dress long to the floor.

At the Bistro my friends' effusive greetings to me back from the East seemed to delight my Scarlett O'Hara. By around 2 A.M. I had the piano to myself, and given a piano and the right lady and the right moment I can damn near prove a match even for Rhett Butler.

It was a marvelous night. I took the lady back to the door of her hotel suite, shook her hand, told her I hoped that she'd had a nice time and that she would give me a warm endorsement when she spoke to Denise. Then off I went—as, I've said, I never "lean in" on a lady.

She was scheduled to go back to Palm Springs the next day, but instead the phone rang and it was she, saying, "Haah . . ." We chatted and she said she'd had such a good time she'd decided to stay over and would I like to take her to dinner? Would I? Come on, how often does Sammy Cahn from the East Side get to play Rhett Butler for real?

I was going to start leaning in. I took her to Dominick's, the so-called "in" place in Hollywood, a shack that holds around ten tables presided over by Dom, behind a wonder of a bar, Dom's wife Peggy, a wonder of a cook, in the kitchen, and Dom's niece Addie. This night my Scarlett was really glowing.

From then on I really felt like Rhett Butler until she at last had to go back to Palm Springs, and our "Gone with the Wind" story continued by telephone and the mails. I have never seen such tiny handwriting as hers; she would write ten- and twelve-page letters, both sides of the page. We were deep into one of the lovely romances of my life. I still remember all of it, and this is to say a special thank you, Mary. You were just about perfectly cast as Scarlett—maybe too perfectly, because if you hadn't been such a romantic you'd have to have known the best I could do was play at being Rhett. I'm pleased I did it pretty well for a while . . . at least I hope I did. Mostly, I hope you think so . . .

Back on the trail . . .

Dee Hawks and I had always been a case of apparently bad chemistry. On occasion she would look at me coolly and say, "*You're* the great Sammy Cahn," and I would reply not too smartly, "Yes, I'm the great Sammy Cahn and you'll go to your grave wondering why . . ." Neither of us made a damn bit of sense.

Dee had been married to Howard Hawks, the legendary movie director; her sister Eden was married to Groucho Marx. Eden was as nice a person as you would ever want to meet. (This may shake up some people, but I am not a Groucho Marx fan. I mean any man who tickles your palm with his finger while you're shaking hands, accompanying the tickle with his one take—"the leer"—well, I recognize Mr. Marx's talents, but they hardly include qualifying for being one of the nice people I've known.)

Through her marriage to Groucho, Eden naturally came to know Barbara Marx, Zeppo Marx's wife and a member in good standing of the Racquet Club Mafia. After Dee divorced Howard Hawks she was drafted by Eden and Barbara into the Racquet Club, which my then wife Gloria was trying to join, which in turn brought me around now and again. And at such times Dee and I would go at it. I must say, she most always had the best of it.

Years later, divorced, thanks to my four sisters I found myself boxed into accepting the Henry Street Settlement's "Man of the Year" award. Forget false modesty, which I neither claim nor have. I was hesitant about it, though; I usually am the figure behind the scenes at such affairs, writing songs and special material and certainly not being the man. Still, I had once attended the Henry Street Settlement, I used to play the violin there and this was more a night for my sisters than for me.

So it was set. April 28, 1968, at the New York Hilton—what a night and what a dais. Johnny Carson was there, despite an ailing eye; Jack Benny was the master of ceremonies. There were two senators, Jacob Javits and Robert F. Kennedy. Also on hand were Steve Lawrence and Eydie Gormé; Red Buttons; Paul Anka; RCA president Robert Sarnoff and ASCAP president Stanley Adams; Warren Beatty, who really abhors such events but who came because he is like a son to me; and Dave Tebet, who put it all together. Frank Sinatra, as mentioned earlier, was not there.

After all the songs were sung at me and after all the brickbats were tossed in jest, it was my turn. I stood up and with new words to all my own songs I told the story of the life, such as it is, that you're reading about in this book. When I came down from the dais I went among the tables, and seated at one with Pat and Maurice Uchitel was Dee Hawks—surprisingly all warmth and charm. "Sammy, this is one of the most warm and endearing things I've ever experienced." Speak of being caught off guard! I was so conditioned to our old antagonism that I said something wonderful like, "What does a broad like you know about warm and endearing?" Defensive, of course. But hardly an excuse for outrageous bad manners. At least it bothered me as I wandered on from table to table.

Next day I called the gentleman who had escorted Dee and asked him if it would be all right if I called her to apologize. He said sure, and that she was at the Gotham.

I called her and I said, "You must please allow me to talk for one minute, and then I'll be quiet and let you talk, which is something I don't usually do." I fell all over myself apologizing for my boorishness in response to her generosity, and ended up saying I would love to prove my contrition any way she wished.

"You can prove it very easily," said Dee. "Take me to dinner tonight."

She'd picked the one night I was already committed to a dinner party at Le Mistral, a lovely French restaurant in Manhattan, so I said if she didn't mind coming along I would be only too happy to take her there. She said she'd be delighted, and we arranged that I would come by the Gotham at sevenish for a drink and we'd go on to dinner.

This phone call was around 3 P.M. At six o'clock the heavens opened up and it started pouring rain, accompanied by doomsday thunder and lightning peculiar to New York City. I plunged and called for a limousine. Busy signal, busy signal. I went down a whole page of the Yellow Book and must have dialed a finger off. I called friends who had cars, but struck out. I called Dee, who was understanding and said she would wait for me at the Gotham no matter how long it took.

At 6:45 I put on my proper dark blue evening suit, hoisted an umbrella and went downstairs to pray for a cab or a friend or an act of God to get me from 136 East 55th Street at Lexington to the Hotel Gotham at Fifth Avenue and 55th, three (by now oceanic) blocks away. When I got to the lobby the streets were pitch black and the rain was bouncing back up to heaven.

Suddenly a police car pulled up in front of my building, and the doorman started to chat with the two policemen in the car. I ran out to the police car. "Anything wrong?" I asked the officers. "No, nothing," one of them said. "Shows you what you know," I said. "I got to get over to the Hotel Gotham." "So?" "So I wish you'd take me." "You nuts?" "Look," I said, "if I took this umbrella and broke this window, you'd take me in the car, wouldn't you?" "Not to the Gotham." "Exactly, but do I have to break a law to get you to give me a lift?" And so forth. You know what? Finally one of the cops said, "Get in the car, we'll take you to the Gotham."

In the car I told them my name, then coached a little until one of them finally said, "The songwriter?" I told them I was hoping to have dinner with one of the most beautiful women in the world, who wouldn't hardly believe how I had made it through the downpour to her hotel. "I don't know how to thank you fellows," I said, "but if you'll be here when I come down with her, I promise you won't be offended by the sight of her." "We'll see," they said.

With Dee now in her room at the Gotham, the vodka
chilling, she looking ravishing:

"Okay," I said, "Tell me how I got here."

"Submarine?"

"No."

"Rowboat?"

"No."

"I give up."

"Would you believe a police car?"

I told her the story, and she asked if I thought they'd
actually still be there when we went downstairs. "A long-
shot," I said, "but I hope they're there just for the sake of my
finish. If they're there, I have one, if not . . ."

We finished our drink and went downstairs. Nobody there.
I shrugged—can't win them all. Then I heard a siren, and
around the corner from the church across the street came the
police car. They drew up to the hotel, we got in, they took us
to Le Mistral. "Gentlemen, did I lie to you?" . . .

"Sammy," she said, as I dropped her back at the Gotham,
"I've gone out with eligible bachelors from Jim Aubrey to
Cary Grant, and you've done what even Cary Grant could
never do."

Well, considering all the other advantages Cary Grant has
over Sammy Cahn, it seemed only right to have one for our
side. I saw Dee Hawks several times after that, and they, for
me at least, were all delightful. For two people whose chemistry had once seemed so unpromising, we did manage a
happy rearrangement of our personal equation.

And yet, and yet, I was still restless, uneasy. The trail had its
undeniable rewards, but were they the real answer? In my
heart I knew the answer, and I knew I'd better find it soon. . .

CHAPTER 15

"The Second Time Around"

Love is lovelier
The second time around,
Just as wonderful
With both feet on the ground . . .

MORE DISAPPOINTING than *Skyscraper* was *Look to the Lilies*, in 1970, a Broadway musical adapted from the movie *Lilies of the Field*, which had starred Sidney Poitier and been a smash everywhere. The director was Josh Logan, the producers were Edgar Lansbury (Angela's brother), Dick Levine and Joe Beruh. The book was by Leonard Spigelgass, the songs by Styne and Cahn. Sidney Poitier was Al Freeman, Jr. (who'd been so impressive in such shows as James Baldwin's *Blues for Mr. Charlie)*; our Mother Maria, the head nun, was Shirley Booth. Sounds good? A book is only as good as it reads. A show is only as good as it plays up there on the stage. Reputations or lack of them are on the line every time out—which is the terror and the challenge of the business.

My involvement began with, "Would you do a show with Jule Styne and Josh Logan?" Jule, of course. And Josh Logan—the Josh Logan of *South Pacific, Mr. Roberts, Annie Get Your Gun, Picnic*—you couldn't have held me back with a machine gun. Plus that they wanted Sammy Davis, Jr., for the lead.

We proceeded to do a score for Sammy Davis, and we flew

to London to play the score for Sammy Davis; he sang it back to us as we did our thing.

There was, however, one problem—it's terrifying even to tell, but Sammy Davis needed $30,000 a week, he apparently has so many expenses. Which put Sammy Davis out of the picture.

Styne and Logan then came up with Al Freeman, Jr. I had, I admit, reservations from the start; I wanted to hear a record of him. Jule Styne told me to "stop being a Hollywood character. This is an actor," he said. "What good is a show if the *book* doesn't come off? He'll bring it off." I said, "Let the book writer handle the book, I'll handle the songs."

The first day of rehearsals Al Freeman challenged every line. I believe he should have been replaced on the spot. What happened was we stood around while Josh Logan explained every line to his leading actor.

Came opening night. I'd been told that Al Freeman could act. Like I said, it's a new ballgame every time out—and this wasn't one of Mr. Freeman's better outings, I think it's fair to say.

I read the reviews and got sick. I also never dreamed I would do a show without one successful song coming out of it. *Look to the Lilies* was what I believe is known as a humbling experience. I hoped I'd had my quota.

There was one song from the show—"I, Yes, Me! That's Who!"—that I'm convinced will someday have its day. The show, like the movie, was in a sense a love story between a Mother Superior and an itinerant black man. The challenge was to write an appropriate love song for them. The black man has built the nuns a little church in the sands of New Mexico. And then he decides to leave, and the nuns come to the Mother Superior and ask, "How can we exist without him?"

I *finally* came up with an answer, putting it into a ballad between the principals:

I, for one, will face one day as though I never met $\begin{cases} him. \\ her. \end{cases}$

I, for one, will find a way, some quick way to forget $\begin{cases} him. \\ her. \end{cases}$

I, for one, won't miss $\begin{cases} him. \\ her. \end{cases}$ *my life through;*

I, yes, me! That's who!
I, yes, me! That's who!

I guess I'm especially proud of that song.

I got one unexpected and beautiful dividend out of *Look to the Lilies.* When I came to New York to work on it I was going on fifty-seven years of age and at least in my subconscious had begun seriously to feel that it was time to stop fooling around, to get off the trail again and for good.

There was one person, a divorcée in California with two young sons, that I was almost convinced should be the lady. Almost.

While in New York I was invited to the opening of a movie that was a musical version of *Goodbye, Mr. Chips,* followed by a dinner party at the Tavern-on-the-Green. I needed somebody to take to the dinner and the movie, and asked for a suggestion from Vicki Levin, wife of Broadway producer Herman Levin. Vickie said, "I know the perfect girl, but she won't go out with you." I said, "You know me—I'll talk her into going out with me." Vicki said, "No, she doesn't take to transients."

Sufficiently and shrewdly provoked and programmed, I got the telephone number out of Vicki, and I called. The voice on the other end said, "Sammy!" I was perplexed. The voice said, "Don't you know who you're calling?" Silence. "No, you don't know."

It turned out I'd actually met her twice. She was Tita Curtis, a friend of Vicki Levin's. Originally Tita Basile, she'd been divorced from Paul Curtis of the American Mime Theater.

The opening of *Goodbye, Mr. Chips* was a big-deal event at the Palace, complete with a bus to the Tavern-on-the-Green. Jule Styne had a limousine, and I used to say, "Jule, would you do me a favor? You're on 72nd Street; would you stop at 71st and pick me up?" I was proceeding according to pattern now. I said, "Jule, will you pick up my date Tita?" When Tita opened her door and saw Jule and the limousine she was a bit shocked—which I guess is what I was hoping for. Us little guys, I'd found out long ago, can generally use an edge.

She was absolutely a stunner, the hit of the party and the evening. Tita is statuesque and dark—Italian Calabrese dark. She has warmth and elegance that are enhanced by charm, grace and wit. I'm not sure when I decided, but I suspect it was on first seeing Tita, that she was the person I'd always wanted; and everyone who knows both Tita and me agrees that she is the perfect woman for someone like me.

At that time she was working for dress designer Donald Brooks, and I later learned that the main topic in her office that day had been, What should Tita wear? Whatever it was, it was perfect. I took her home at two-thirty in the morning and shook her hand, expecting never to see her again.

This was in November of 1969. I was still constantly in touch with the other divorced lady. One day there was a call from Tita Curtis. She was giving a party and wanted me to come. "Should I bring someone?" She laughed and said, "Oh, there'll be lots of attractive girls around." Since there were to be a lot of attractive girls, I brought along my good friend Benoit Dreyfus.

I'd been working on an album of my songs. A box of these albums had arrived, and I thought I might as well bring along one of them as a little Christmas gift. I went to the party, had a good time, and then Dreyfus and I left to check out Le Mistral and El Morocco. Once more, I didn't expect to see Tita again.

Next morning at ten-thirty, a phone call. It was Tita and she said she'd been playing the album for three hours, laughing and crying, never before realizing how many songs I'd written. She started to *discuss* my songs with me. She talked to me about lines in my songs that she particularly liked, found meanings that I didn't know were there . . . From that moment I knew I would say to her, "What are you doing tonight?" When I did, she said, "Oh, I'm staying home, I'll wash my hair." I said, "You've got to eat, don't you?"

And from that day to this we've not been apart, except for the three days before the opening of *Look to the Lilies*.

There was still, though, this other divorced lady in California, who was coming in for the opening. She did, and finally I realized I was not going to marry her. I would invent excuses to get away from her to phone Tita. I knew, then, that Tita, who is my junior by twenty-five years, was the lady I wanted to marry.

I proposed to Tita while driving back from a visit to Nancy Sinatra in Palm Springs—Nancy Sinatra, the matchmaker of my first marriage. We were married August 2, 1970, and went to Lake Tahoe for our honeymoon. On stage with the show there was Danny Thomas, who'd been on stage at the Martinique during my first honeymoon, twenty-five years earlier. Back to "go," for a second chance I never thought I'd be lucky enough to have.

CHAPTER 16

"Call Me Irresponsible"

Call me irresponsible, call me unreliable,
Throw in undependable too
Do my foolish alibis bore you?
Well, I'm not too clever, I just adore you . . .
I'm irresponsibly mad for you.

I GUESS I've met just about all the great performers in show business from the time I was ten years old. Talk about vivid memories. . . .

When I was a young boy Louis Armstrong was already a legend. All these rumors that he was not allowed in the country, that he was a junkie, that he'd married a *white* (gulp) woman. Louis Armstrong? There was no Louis Armstrong. He was a trumpet and a voice you heard on a record in the middle of the night. I would listen and listen to those records.

One day Connie Immerman of the Cotton Club—also famous for Immerman's hot chocolates—said he wanted to introduce me to Louis Armstrong. Connie took me to the Cotton Club, and when I walked in and saw Louis I just gaped.

The first thing Armstrong said to me was, "When were you born?" I said June 18. He whipped out this book he had and flipped through the pages to that date. He turned the book around and showed me the names of other people—famous people—who'd been born on June 18. I hoped some of it would rub off on me.

I found out Louis was terribly weak at memorizing lyrics. His wife would place lyrics all over the house—in his socks, in his shoes, any place he couldn't miss and so at least would have to *look* at them a lot.

At the Cotton Club most of the songs were written to help work out a piece of business in a show. They had a little boy for an act and needed a way of getting him into the show. I had the idea of a shoeshine boy coming forward through the tables—which is how "Shoe Shine Boy" got written. I wrote a number for Sister Rebecca Tharpe, "I Bring You Religion on a Mule." They hired a little white mule. She came riding in on it. Two days later Connie Immerman said to me, "You and your ideas!" I said, "Isn't the song stopping the show?" Connie said, "Sure it's stopping the show. Everybody's quitting. Somebody found out the mule is getting more than the chorus girls." I've never suggested an animal act since.

I became close to Louis Armstrong. One night we covered ten different joints in Harlem, and each place somebody was doing Louis Armstrong. In the tenth and last one it was a really terrible imitation. I said, "Louis, why are we here? This man just tries to do everything you do." Louis said, "He may do somep'n I don't do."

I learned that Armstrong's solos never varied, and I asked him why. He said, "Is it good?" I said yes. "So?" No argument.

Once I saw Fats Waller at a rehearsal with a quart of gin on the piano. "That's a funny way to run a rehearsal," I primly said. He answered just fine: "Hey, I get four arrangements to a quart."

Louis Armstrong, Fats Waller. Can you top them. . . ?

The resident Hungarian at MGM was Joe Pasternak. He called me one day to come over and meet composer Nicholas Brodszky. Brodszky had patent-leather hair and the kind of shape that, if you pushed him over, he'd roll back up—which is good if you are going to compose.

On the piano he had a printed sheet of music—not a hand-written manuscript, but printed. No chance of changing a note with this man! It was titled, "Love Theme for Mario Lanza." Could I write the words for it? they asked.

I started to work, and what gradually came out was:

Be my love, for no one else can end this yearning,
This need that you and you alone create . . .

Now if you've only heard Mr. Lanza on a record or a tape or in a movie, you've never heard him at all, because no mechanical reproduction could capture the startling brilliance of that voice. It scared the hell out of you. I believe he had a soft pedal and a loud pedal in his throat. The lyric of "Be My Love!" had to be pre-tested before it could be sung out of that incredible voicebox, and while I was writing it I convinced Brodszky, who'd had some operatic training, to sing back every word. But when the time came to sing the song to Lanza, you know who did the singing. You know who literally can't keep his mouth shut when it comes to selling–singing his own material.

Chutzpah! Real chutzpah! Cahn singing to Lanza! Happily he already knew the melody and accepted the lyrics from me.

I wish we could have Mario Lanza with us today.

The first time I ever sang to Bing Crosby he said, "You're pretty good." I said, to keep up the image, "Pretty good? I'm the best!" "What about Mack Gordon?" Mack Gordon was a legendary lyricist. A massive man. He weighed about two hundred and fifty pounds.

"Mack Gordon? He's disqualified," I said. "He really *sings*."

When Mack Gordon and the wonderful Harry Warren auditioned for Zanuck he'd throw in an entire trombone chorus, out of his own throat. He was finally banned from singing his songs to Zanuck, who explained his action in terms of self-defense: "That sonofabitch could sell me any-thing."

Scene: the steam room of the Sands Hotel in Las Vegas, one of the literally hottest so-called "in" places in show business. At one time most every male star had a special bathrobe in the steam room with a title on the back that denoted the owner. Frank Sinatra's, for example, read, "The Pope"; Vic Da-mone's, "The Singer"; mine, "The Nervous Jew."

The phone rang. This voice said, "Mr. Cahn?"

"Yes."

"This is Paul Anka."

"I don't believe it's Paul Anka, but if it is, what do you want with *me*?"

"Mr. Cahn——"

"Please stop calling me 'Mr. Cahn,' because I'm not going to call you 'Mr. Anka.' "

"Oh no, I'm Paul. You're Mr. Cahn."

"Is this a gag? What do you want with me?"

"I know you write songs for all the big stars. Would you write a special song for me?"

"For you? Why would I write a special song for you? You're a songwriter."

"I can't write what you write," said the voice that I finally was beginning to believe was Paul Anka's. "Would you please?"

"Well," I said, "if you're Paul Anka, I'd be damn pleased to write whatever you want, whenever you want."

He said that what with Bobby Darin, Tommy Sands, and Frankie Avalon all having recently gotten married, he wanted a song that would portray him as the last of the single singers.

"Fine," I said. "When do you want it?"

"In May."

"In *May*? Why call me in January about a song in May? Call me a week before you need it."

He said he would do that, and I left the steam room and went into Jack Entratter's office, my office away from home —Entratter is the president of the Sands—and wrote two lyrics for Paul Anka, whom I'd never met, but whose talents I admired.

I.

[to the tune of "That Old Gang of Mine"]
Not a singer left in nightclubs,
That's a pretty certain sign
That wedding bells are breaking up
That old gang of mine.

II.

[tune obvious]
I'm not *getting married in the morning,*
Ding, dong, the bells ain't going to chime.
Frankie and Tommy
Both must be balmy,
I won't *be at the church on time.*

I put these two lyrics away and forgot about them.
Some months later the phone rang.
"Mr. Cahn? This is Paul Anka and——"
"Stop calling me Mr. Cahn."

I asked Anka where he was, and he said the Beverly Hilton, right around the corner. I said I'd be over. I dug out those lyrics and went to the Beverly Hilton and walked into the room to meet Paul Anka for the first time. With him was his manager at that time, Irving Feld, who later left Anka to take on the presidency of Ringling Brothers–Barnum & Bailey. (I wonder which he thinks more complex, Paul Anka or the five rings and the elephants.)

I sat down and handed Paul the lyrics. He looked them óver and said, "When did you write these?" "Just before I came over here." (Well, a white lie at worst.)

After I'd left, Irving Feld called me and asked what they owed me. I told them nothing, that I didn't do special material for a living. I did it for friends. I still do, and I still love it.

Paul and I have since become close special friends. Personally and professionally, Paul Anka has style. When he walks out on any stage he brings with him the highest, most carefully honed yet somehow natural-sounding expertise. His orchestrations, his musicians, his sound equipment and technicians—all impeccable. He once asked me to sit in on a rehearsal at Steinway Hall of some new "charts," meaning arrangements. He had hired *twenty-four* top sidemen for the occasion. Not even Sinatra, not even Crosby, not anyone shows quite such involvement.

Tita and I often go along with Paul in his travels for the sheer pleasure of his company. The last of the single singers—Canadian by birth, by the way—married a beautiful girl named Anne, and today they have four daughters—Alicia, Alexandra, Amanda, and Anthea. They are sitting on top of the world, right where they belong.

Some people have suspected me of writing some of Paul's lyrics. This is to tell them they're wrong, including the song "My Way." It is true, though, that Paul Anka and I are now writing songs together, by long-distance phone or via cassette. We've recently been signed to do a movie musical about Hans Christian Andersen—based on the actual life of the man, not his fairy tales. And Paul and I recently had our first song published, "Let Me Try Again," written at the behest of Frank Sinatra, who has recorded it.

I suppose in a sense Paul Anka is a son I never had, a son I

*Friars Club party honoring Sammy Cahn, Sid Caesar, Jimmy Dur-
ante, Groucho Marx, Leo Durocher, Art Linkletter and Milton Berle.
(NBC Photo: Frank Carroll)*

*Who is telling off Gregory Peck and Mrs. Peck? Who else but Sammy
Cahn! Tita and all are dressed for the famous Share Charity Western
affair! (Photo: Jules Davis)*

One of the happiest nights of my life! At age sixty, my Tita and Paul Anka arranged a "sixty hours for sixty years" party at Caesar's Palace in Las Vegas. Milton Berle MC'd; Cary Grant made an ASCAP presentation; Paul presented my honorary diploma from Seward Park High School and Johnny Carson presented a plaque from Mayor John Lindsay. An incredible night! (Photo: Las Vegas News Bureau)

Standing before a cake which must have taken at least sixty years to bake are left to right: Mel Tormé, Jack Jones, Cary Grant, Don Abrams, Finger-Lickin' Cahn, Happy Tita, Jack Carter, Happy Anka hiding Anne Anka, Milton Berle, Danny Thomas and Wayne Newton. June 18th 1973; Caesar's Palace! (Photo: Las Vegas News Bureau)

Chaplin, Kanin, Berle, Silvers and Cahn. (Photo: Allan J. Studley, Hollywood)

I've never been prouder of any success (even my own) than I am of Liza's. The little neighbor on Mapleton Drive fulfilled our wildest dreams. (Photo: Tim Boxer)

Doesn't it figure that I am the only one in this picture who needs an identifying badge? The man on the phone is of course, George Barrie, the chief executive officer of Fabergé-Brut, as well as the composer of the songs for "Touch of Class." I think the gray haired man with the glasses is Cary Grant.

wanted to work and share with. I hope my own son isn't offended, but there it is, the truth. None of us gets everything he wants, especially, it seems, in his family. You do what you can and learn to accept joy where you find it. I found Paul Anka.

One night in the Palo Alto Hospital, where I'd gone for one of my periodic check-ups with Dr. Albert Snell:

The phone rang. It was Lillian Schary Small, my agent, telling me Paramount wanted Van Heusen and me to do a picture for Fred Astaire. Fred Astaire! For years I'd thought it would be a peak for me to write for Fred Astaire, who doesn't especially sing . . . he does much more than sing.

I nearly fell out of bed, but I hung on long enough to say, "I want that job no matter how much we have to pay them." Lillian said, "Don't be silly. *They* want *you*. But there's a problem." I said, "There can be no problem, because I must do this picture." Lillian said, "You're under contract to MGM for a Mario Lanza picture, remember?"

"Well," I said, "isn't a fella named Dory Schary related to you? And doesn't he run MGM? And doesn't he adore you, his favorite sister?" Result was they let me do the Astaire picture while still doing the Lanza picture—the first time I know about when a songwriter was working at two studios simultaneously. Daytime I'd be at MGM with Nicholas Brodszky in the Lanza idiom, nighttime with Jimmy Van Heusen in the Astaire idiom. My heart and I couldn't wait for twilight, when I could run, not walk, to fulfill my longtime ambition to write for Fred Astaire.

The Astaire picture, produced by Robert Emmet Dolan with a script by the Ephrons, Henry and Phoebe (parents of the clever writer Nora), was about the father of the old movie star Corinne Griffith. The character was supposed to be a bit of a drunk and the film to be titled *Papa's Delicate Condition.* (It turned out the father was never called a drunk and the picture should have been called *Papa's Delicatessen.*)

I'd go to Van Heusen's house and read the script, which seemed to have the word "irresponsible" popping up throughout—this "irresponsible" character, this "irresponsible" man. When Van Heusen went to the piano and noodled out the tune of "Call Me Irresponsible" as we know it now, it all seemed to fall into place, and about one o'clock in the morning we had our song.

I said,"We must play it for Astaire." Van Heusen had a profound aversion to auditioning a song. I, on the other hand, live especially for the sort of moment of truth when you walk into the bullring and pitch your song at them—*at* them, not to them. I couldn't gush my boyhood dreams about writing for Astaire to Van Heusen, so I just said, "Look, I think this song is the heart of the motion picture and one of the best I've written and I would like to sing it for Mr. Astaire. Besides, if I'm wrong about this one, either we or Astaire are wrong for this picture."

The best I could do was to get Van Heusen to rehearse it for two hours the next day at the studio. He rehearsed it and rehearsed it to the point of nausea, as far as he was concerned. Once he made a mistake at the piano and burst out with a string of Anglo-Saxon words, of which the first letters of each (FSCP) were his call letters as a pilot. Really. I told him, "If you do this again it's the end of our collaboration. Just please keep it to yourself if you blow one. If you make a mistake I won't tell, so don't you tell." (I only hope, Jim, that when you read this you'll understand now why I was so up-tight and anxious to play for Fred Astaire.)

At the end of the two hours we went to see Robert Emmet Dolan and Fred Astaire. Jimmy went to the piano with, as usual, his back to the scene. I took my stance, first telling Mr. Astaire that the song came out of a scene in which Papa has done some completely irresponsible things, like buying a circus for his little girl, and has to explain to his wife, who's in bed with her hair in curlers and her lips pressed tight. So he haltingly, desperately starts to sing: "Call me irresponsible, call me unreliable, throw in undependable too . . ." (You'll notice there are some five-syllable words there, by a guy from a one-syllable neighborhood.)

When we got through the first half of the song Astaire said, "Stop . . ." I thought Van Heusen would have a heart attack at the piano over this apparent disaster I'd pushed him into, but before he went into cardiac arrest Astaire said, "That's one of the best songs I've ever heard." I said, "That's one of the best *half*-songs you ever heard, and I believe it's the weaker half."

When we finished Astaire beamed his applause and said, "You know why you two got this job, don't you?" No, we said, we didn't. "Because Johnny Mercer wasn't available." I took it then and now as great praise.

We wrote four or five more songs for the picture, most important of which was "Walking Happy." It came about because we had to write a song about a drunk. Van Heusen and I stayed up until two in the morning, trying every which way to write a good song for a drunk. Finally I turned to him and said, "How would you describe the walk of a drunk? Stumbling? Sloppy? Without cohesion?" We then physically explored every conceivable kind of walk. I acted them out—I must have walked thirty miles that night and was in shock from fatigue when I came home. We had our song when we finally decided a drunk walks "happy":

> There's the kind of walk you walk
> When the world's un-done you,
> There's the kind of walk you walk
> When you're walking proud.

There's the kind of walk you walk
When the neighbors shun you,
There's the kind of walk you walk
That attracts a crowd.

There's the kind of walk you walk
When somebody loves you;
That's very much like walking on a cloud.

Good fortune's found you, Chappie,
And your life's a happy Valentine,
When you're walking happy
Don't the bloomin' world seem fine!

As much as I enjoyed doing "Call Me Irresponsible" for Astaire, the anticipation of playing "Walking Happy" for him was even greater.

When we arrived, he said, "You're not going to tell me you've finished a better song than 'Call Me Irresponsible.' " I honestly if immodestly said, "We've just written the best Astaire song ever written, and I know all the Astaire songs from Gershwin to Berlin to Cole Porter." We played him "Walking Happy" and he said, "You're right."

It wasn't to be, though. The good Lord gives, and the good Lord takes . . . I never had the fulfillment of seeing Fred Astaire doing one of my songs. He was called away to a prior commitment for MGM, and that was that. The magic powers of Lillian Schary Small could work only so far. The picture was abandoned.

It wasn't until seven years later that I picked up the *Hollywood Reporter* and read that Martin Rackin, a buddy who was then in charge of production at Paramount, had signed Jackie Gleason to play Jack Griffith in *Papa's Delicate Condition*. I leaped to the phone. "Is it true you're going to make *Papa's*

Delicate Condition?" "Sure is." "How'd you come to get Gleason for it?" "Well, who would you cast to play a heavy
drinker—Billy Graham?"

I reminded Marty of the songs Van Heusen and I had
written seven years before. He said, "There aren't going to be
songs in this picture." I said, "Have you heard the songs?"
"No." "Wait'll I get there."

So seven years later Van Heusen and I were again on our
way to audition our songs for *Papa's Delicate Condition*, this
time for Marty Rackin and Jack Rose, the new producers of
this movie. En route Van Heusen and I decided that since they
didn't want *any* songs, we couldn't do five, so we'd only do
two—"Walking Happy" and "Call Me Irresponsible."

Now, goaded by the frustration of seven years, I leaned in
and we did "Walking Happy." They adored it. "It's in," they
said. "That's the weak song," I said, and really leaned in to
wallop them with "Call Me Irresponsible."

Jack Rose said: "Not in my picture." Me, shouting: "What
did you say?" Jack Rose: "I can't see the character singing such
a self-pitying song." To which I replied, "Spare me, please,
your character analysis. This song has been on the shelf for
seven years. Damn near every singer from Frank Sinatra to
Tony Bennett to Billy Eckstine to Peggy Lee has been waiting
to sing it. It could win an Oscar. Marty," I said to Rackin,
"you're the head of the studio. Would you cut that song out of
the picture?" He didn't answer, and as Van Heusen and I
walked away we were sure it was destined to lie on the shelf
forever.

A week later the phone rang. It was Jack Rose in New York.
"We just played it for Jackie Gleason, but there's a prob-
lem——" "What do you mean *you* played it for Jackie Gleason?
I audition my songs." The temperature was rising. Rose said:
"*Wait* . . . he wants it in the picture, but he wants it in thirty-
five times." Temperature subsiding . . .

So they made the picture. At the first sneak preview they got the feeling that "Walking Happy," the first song in the film, "slowed the action." Well, I never knew a first song that *didn't* slow the action. Never mind, "Walking Happy" was taken out of *Papa's Delicate Condition*. They also tried to get "Call Me Irresponsible" out—but no way. "Walking Happy" was returned to Van Heusen and myself as a property, and a lot of people started recording "Call Me Irresponsible." The picture, though, still hadn't been released.

The Academy of Motion Picture Arts and Sciences is a local guild, with offices on Melrose Avenue at the corner of Doheny Drive. It consists of every craft in pictures, with a board of governors and approximately 4000 members divided into their respective categories: actors, directors, photographers, scriptwriters, songwriters, editors, etc. Any picture that plays in the Los Angeles area for one week in any part of the calendar year is eligible to be nominated for that year's award—the same for any person or part of any picture. I went to Marty Rackin to ask him to "please, please release the picture for at least a week." Marty explained that "the New York office"—it's always the New York office—"says the picture can't be released until next year." I was about to renounce my New York citizenship . . .

The number 13 seems pervasive in my scheme of things. While I give no credibility to such superstitions (I keep telling myself), I was, nevertheless, born in 1913; the first lot I built a home on was Lot 13; the address was 175—the digits add up to 13—Mapleton Drive, which is 13 letters. And the Academy Awards in the year 1963 fell on April 13.

During the preceeding year the singer Jack Jones had come to me and asked would I help with his act at the Living Room nightclub in New York. I looked at the list of the top forty songs, noted there wasn't a ballad among them and said,

"Why don't you do 'Call Me Irresponsible'?" He put it in his act and recorded it in his beautiful voice, and it became a hit and a candidate for the Oscar, the film having at last opened in that year.

Also between Awards nights, I'd been sweating out the year of the interlocutory decree for my divorce. Ed Traubner had told me a week before that my wife was going to court to pick up the divorce on the thirteenth, which was my reason for deciding not to be in town for the Awards. Instead I hid out in Las Vegas at the Sands Hotel with my friends Carl Cohen and Jack Entratter. On Sunday evening the phone rang, and it was Mr. Lionel Newman, head of the music department of 20th-Fox, the same Lionel Newman who gave Jimmy Van Heusen crash courses in salty language. George Cukor was going to direct *Let's Make Love,* starring Marilyn Monroe and Yves Montand, and they wanted Van Heusen and me to come in on Monday morning to do the songs for her. I asked him please to let me pass but he says, "No way, we'll *never* be able to get her here again."

I sneaked back into Los Angeles on Monday, and we did the songs for Marilyn Monroe. I made my way to the Beverly Comstock, where I'd taken rooms while sweating out the divorce. No one knew I was there except Ed Traubner, who called at eleven o'clock to say, "You've just been divorced," and again at three to announce, "We've just sold the house."

I am not a coward, but I just couldn't see myself sitting at the Academy Awards having lost a marriage in the morning, a house in the afternoon, and the Oscar that evening.

There were three songs in the race that year: "More," "Charade," and "Call Me Irresponsible." The way I handicapped them, "More" was the horse to beat, "Call Me Irresponsible" could surprise, "Charade" would show or place. "More" was a gigantic international hit, but I didn't feel any great shakes in its lyric content (though I *could* have been prejudiced). It had been the theme music for the movie *Mondo Cane;* the melody caught on and they added a lyric—not strictly kosher in terms of a song written for a motion picture.

I had decided it would be nice if my daughter Laurie would accompany Van Heusen to the Awards. She had asked me what she should say if by some happy chance our song won. "Say, 'I'd like to thank you in the name of my father, Sammy Cahn, who should have been here but call him irresponsible.' " She said, "Gee, Daddy, I don't want to make a joke." "Well, just say, 'Thank you for my father.' " Then Van Heusen asked, "What'll I say?" "Why don't you say: 'Thank you for my father too.' "

So the stage was set—me hiding out and watching on the TV at the Beverly Comstock, Van Heusen and my daughter at the Pantages Theatre. Suddenly the phone rang. It was Van Heusen. "Where the hell are you?" "In a phone booth with a flask, that's where I am." "Look, Jimmy," I said, "go back and sit down because this song could surprise you."

And he did go back and sit down. And when the fellow opened the envelope, I sat there and cried while Laurie said, "Thank you for my father," and laughed when Van Heusen thanked *his* father, Arthur Babcock. And then the phone really started ringing . . .

It was, of course, hugely gratifying to have "Call Me Irresponsible" win the Academy Award—especially after so many disappointments with it. And yet I'd be lying if I denied I never quite got over the let-down of not having it performed by Fred Astaire. Maybe some other time . . . some other song. He's worth waiting for.

CHAPTER 17

"I'll Walk Alone"

I'll walk alone
Because to tell you the truth I'll be lonely,
I don't mind being lonely,
When my heart tells me you
Are lonely too . . .

MACK GOLDMAN, head of Warner's music publishing company and also noted for his thin lips, used to take me around in the 1930s to hear all the hot bands. Our stops included the Lincoln—now Royal Manhattan—Hotel, where Artie Shaw was king.

I've just told about some of the warm good memories of my life among the greats. To play it straight before the finale, I think I should balance things out with my private saga of Artie Shaw—which started sweet and went to sour. Artie Shaw, head man in the can't-win-them-all department . . .

Shaw and I immediately took to each other—at least I thought he took to me and I know I took to him. Why not? I was a young kid in my twenties, struggling like hell to stay alive and get going in the business. I had yet to have a hit—it was even before *"Bei Mir Bist Du Schön."* Artie Shaw had more than arrived. He was beautiful. He stood tall. He had his hair. He and his magic clarinet were Sir Galahad with a lance. Musically, he is still considered to have been far ahead of his time: in 1936 he led an octet that included two trumpets. Later it was successfully augmented with a string quartet, making him the first to use a string quartet in jazz music. He was also the first to bring in a harpsichord, and he hired Billie Holiday in a day when the arts were still totally segregated.

One day in 1939—I was twenty-six—Shaw casually called to say, "You want to go to Cuba?" I was young and single and with no ties of any kind. I said: "Sure." We got on an Eastern Airlines plane and flew down toward Cuba for the weekend.

I'd never been on a plane before. It was a twin-engine propeller job, long before the age of jets, and it was the worst plane ride I've ever taken. I also didn't even know you could get sick from flying.

Suddenly I saw Mr. Shaw turn a shade of green and shortly thereafter depart rapidly from his seat for the john. When he came back I leaped up and did my number—a double.

The plane flew about 300 feet above the ground all the way to Miami, where we were to transfer to another plane to Havana. It was an ordeal I can still shudder over. For the rest of that flight I tried to keep my insides more or less where they belonged and chatted about my buddy Ed Traubner. He immediately told me had a *better* friend than I had—a drummer name of Ace Hudkins.

We arrived in Miami, got off the plane and, sure enough, there was Ace Hudkins, waiting, as if to confirm Shaw's characterization of him as most faithful friend. We flew on to Havana, where we took a marvelous suite at the Nacional Hotel. In all my life I think I've had the most fun when hanging out with musicians. Their wit is their own; their lifestyle is their own. For three days musician Artie Shaw and I had a great time.

The first day we went to Paradise Beach for lunch on a beautiful terrace. They put something peculiar to eat before us (remember, I had had ulcers since a tender age), which helped me persuade Shaw to take the rest of our meals at the hotel.

It was a magic place to me: You'd ring for room service, and in would come two captains to take the order. Half an hour later the door would open and in would come a parade of at least six men, pushing tables laden with food—two whole honeydews sitting in a tureen of ice; steaks, potatoes; a tremendous tureen of vegetable soup with whole ears of corn floating in it.

Shaw told me that Ace Hudkins was going to work for him. What kind of job? Valet! Some job for a best friend . . .

As I said, I hadn't yet had my first hit, *"Bei Mir Bist Du Schön,"* and I told Artie of my difficulties with my mother, who didn't understand what I was trying to do. Artie said, "You must never worry about your mother." "What do you mean?" He said that many times he'd tried to leave his own mother, on which occasions she'd scream at him, "By the time you get downstairs my body will be in the street!" Finally he upped and left her anyway. I said: "What happened?" He said: "When I got downstairs she wasn't there." . . .

The one hitch to our three days in paradise was my ulcer, which was kicking up badly—no doubt over all that sudden rich good eating and living. I was in wretched, retching pain. I'd already discovered, though, that if you're in trouble anywhere in the world and you're somehow associated with a motion-picture company, you go to the phone and call the local representative of that company. So in fifteen minutes I got through to the Warner Brothers man in Havana, who was very nice and came right around with a nice Cuban doctor.

Meanwhile and during all this, Mr. Shaw has discovered the pleasures of the poems of Ogden Nash and Samuel Hoffenstein. I was waiting for the doctor and moaning in pain while my friend was reclined across the room reading Ogden Nash and Samuel Hoffenstein and laughing like hell.

"They're two of *my* favorites too," I said, "but if you were dying I think I'd at least be reading Tolstoy or something." Which line threw Artie into even more exuberant laughter. So when the Cuban doctor came in and looked me over and said to nobody in general, "This man is in pain," I said to the doctor, gesturing with my thumb at Artie, "Don't tell me, tell him."

I asked the doctor for enough pain-killers to get back to the States. If it was necessary, I decided I didn't want to be operated on in Cuba . . . they not only at the time weren't too much with sophisticated anesthetics there, they hadn't even invented Castro. As you can see, this was quite a long time ago.

We flew back to the States, and the plane was met by an ambulance. Shaw watched me be taken from the plane and put in the ambulance, which took me to Manhattan General Hospital, at 16th Street and Second Avenue, where I was treated. Mr. Shaw didn't call, didn't come to see me; I never heard from him. That should have given me another clue, along with his friend for a valet. In fact I did decide then not to have anything more to do with Mr. Artie Shaw. And I might have stuck to my guns if Mack Goldman hadn't straightened me out. "You got it all wrong," he explained. "He's not supposed to call you, you're supposed to call him. Even if you're dying, call and ask him how *he* feels. Because he plugs the song." So I went back to being friendly with Mr. Shaw—please remember, I was young and innocent—and traveled all over with him on one-nighters, riding on the bus with the band that was playing to *thousands* of people (in the days, also please remember, before television).

I again stopped running with him because I couldn't afford it. I was picking up all the checks. I won't say Artie was cheap, but he was a little careful. He was the sort to cut his own hair, and I suspect would have pulled his own teeth if he could have managed it painlessly. He also had a lawyer–manager named Andrew Weinberger, who came to me and said, "Sammy, please stay with him—you're good for him. Pick up the checks and we'll reimburse you."

Fair enough, I thought (I was still very young), and went back with Artie, who now thought I'd suddenly become one of the great sports in the world. He'd look at the tips I'd leave and say, "What're you doing? You're not rich." I'd say, "Don't worry about it, Artie." Big deal . . .

Artie liked to buy himself watches—he called them "my medals." Once in Atlantic City he passed a jewelry store where a watch in the window caught his eye. But it looked like a girl's wristwatch. He went in and asked, "Is that a girl's wristwatch?" Yes, it was. "Okay," said Artie, "put a larger strap on it."

He hated the public, hated the band members. I think the real reason Andy Weinberger wanted me to travel with Shaw was that with me he smiled now and then.

So now Artie Shaw and I were still close. Everything he could do to drive people crazy, he'd do it. In the middle of a one-nighter he'd decide he didn't want to play any more, he wasn't feeling well. It was in the days when an Artie Shaw could draw 5000 people for a one-nighter, and the promoter would beg him to continue. Artie'd say no. "Well, play every other set." "Okay." So they'd make an announcement: "Ladies and gentlemen, Mr. Artie Shaw is indisposed. He wasn't to appear here at all tonight, but being the truly great performer he is, he's on-hand with a doctor who has consented that he play every other set." Thereafter, at every other set, Shaw and I would walk out on stage. I was the doctor; I'd get a bigger hand then he would.

One day when I wasn't with the Shaw band Artie called to

say, "I'm passing through New York on my way from Philadelphia to Boston, and you've got to meet me, I've got to talk
with you." I asked him why.

"I've fallen in love."

"You in love? I can see you in love, with *you*."

He got angry and insisted he had just left the first girl he'd
ever really been in love with.

"Who?"

It was Betty Grable, who was in Philadelphia in the out-
of-town tryouts of *Du Barry Was a Lady*, co-starring Bert Lahr.
Artie was now on the way to play at the Ritz Hotel in Boston,
and I went along.

He's in love, he's in love, he's in love, but he had to wait a
year because Betty Grable was married to Jackie Coogan. (It's
curious—he took away the girls from former kid stars. He took
Betty Grable away from Jackie Coogan. He took Ava Gardner
away from Mickey Rooney. That was his style.) I said, "You
wait a year? I won't hold my breath."

Du Barry came to New York in December, and Artie was
back from Boston. He, Betty and I were much like people out
of a Gene Kelly movie, dancing down the streets of Fifth
Avenue at night after her show, shouting and laughing. And
these two people were *so* much in love. Finally Artie got a call
to go out to Hollywood to do a picture for MGM.

During all this time my friend Phil Silvers had been signed
personally by Louis B. Mayer to go to California to be in
movies at MGM. I told Artie, "Don't worry about a thing. The
minute you hit the Coast you'll be taken in hand by Phil
Silvers, and you'll be fine. And I'll be here with Betty, and
she'll be fine."

Every night at eight I'd go to the 46th Street Theatre to talk
with Betty and listen to her read these letters from Artie, the
most *marvelous* letters in the world. He'd met that one girl in

the world, darling Betty, for whom he'd give up everything
else. And so on. Also, he and Phil are getting along famously,
because Phil fancied himself a clarinet player.

One night I was in Betty's dressing room and she was
reading another of those beautiful letters from Artie, so
beautiful you couldn't stand it. When I walked out onto the
street the newsboys were hawking the headline: "Read all
about it! Artie Shaw marries Lana Turner!" Lana Turner was
in the same picture with Artie, *Dancing Co-ed*. She was a year
out of high school. He married her on their first date.

He'd used his line, about, if he could *only* meet *that* girl, he'd
chuck everything and go off to an island . . . Most any lady
would laugh in your face or mine, right? But this was *the* Artie
Shaw saying it, and this was Lana Turner, saying, "I'm that
girl. Let's go." Phil Silvers was in the car with them, and he
later told me the story of how on their first date they were
flying to Las Vegas and Phil figured this fellow was crazy,
which frightened Phil, who already was terrified because he
didn't fly. Phil drove them to the airport to fly off to Las Vegas
to get married on their first date. He drove back.

After that, I couldn't go back to the 46th Street Theatre to
see Betty Grable.

A little later I went out to the Coast and saw Artie Shaw and
Lana Turner in their house on Summit Ridge Drive (he at one
time even made a record, "Summit Ridge Drive"). There was
a pool table in the house, and my Hester Street training came
back to help me *kill* Artie at the game. One day we were
playing and the butler—which incidentally wasn't his friend
Ace Hudkins any more because his friend Ace Hudkins
couldn't take any more—came in to where we were playing
and said, "There's a telephone call for you, Mr. Cahn." I
turned away from the table. Then, realizing I didn't want to
take the call, turned back to see Artie Shaw pocketing the ball

with his hand. He laughed, I laughed. He had to beat you one way or another. I guess if I'd listened to Mack Goldman I'd have let Artie beat me every time.

I never met a woman in my life who could comb her hair in as many ways as many times a day as Lana Turner. She also wore the sheerest of blouses, and I confess to a certain amount of staring. "What are you staring at?" she'd say. "You know," I'd say.

They were married in February of 1940 and divorced in September of 1940. She'd call him and call him and call him—and the more she called, the harder he was to get. Once she called him when he was in San Francisco and told him she wanted to be made love to by telephone. He told her, "If you just have a cup of tea you'll be all right." Passion among the stars . . .

Also curious—I was close in a different way to both Artie Shaw and Frank Sinatra, and Ava Gardner ended up with both of them. Artie plucked Ava Gardner, Lana Turner and Betty Grable when all three of these ladies were at their full power and fame—an impressive feat. Yet in a sense all these beautiful women seemed to be the same woman. They pursued *him*—why, I'm not certain, but I think the fact that he was unobtainable, couldn't be reached, had much to do with it. If Frank Sinatra had been able to treat Ava Gardner the way Artie Shaw did, he might have held her. He couldn't, though, which is all right, too. Like the fellow said, we all run the way we're gaited.

Artie later married Betty Kern, and they stayed in the home of her father, Jerome Kern. Artie would also tell Jerome Kern what was wrong with his songs—try and top *that* for chutzpah. Well, this next nearly does: One night he was going to a dinner party at which a fellow guest was to be Sinclair Lewis. I said, "Artie, will you try to remember what he says? I at least want the vicarious experience." The next day Artie said, "Well, he was dull. I had to do all the talking . . ."

Way back when he was playing at the lovely old Ritz Hotel in Boston and was so in love with Betty Grable, he and I went to a matinee of *George White's Scandals*, complete with thirty-two—count them, thirty-two—girls in the chorus. Artie nudged me. "Look at the body on that girl." "What body on what girl?" I said, because it was like looking at a windowful of diamonds. Which diamond?

He pointed her out to me—second row, fourth girl in. He was right, a really *beautiful* girl. Two years later he said to me, "Do you know the girl that Sid is running around with?" It was her, a girl named Frances—no last name necessary. I tried one last time. "Look, Artie, do me a favor and pass this one. I happen to know Sid's left his wife and children for her." (Sid was Sid Slate of the very funny Slate Brothers.)

"Let's see what she has to say," says Artie.

"What's so important about it?"

"Don't you remember the *George White's Scandals*—second row, fourth girl in?"

He took her away from Sid, who came to me and I told him, "No matter how much she's hurt you, he'll hurt her more."

A few months later Mr. Shaw flew to Burbank Airport—and there was this same girl, Frances. He walked right past her as if she weren't there. It happened just like I told Sid it would . . .

I was on the scene the night Artie Shaw quit his band at the Pennsylvania Hotel, around Christmas of 1939. His income at this Depression time was about a quarter of a million dollars a year, but he'd been writing articles attacking jitterbug dancing and had been making noises about quitting.

Andy Weinberger asked me please to go upstairs and talk to him. "You're the only one who can talk to him." I went upstairs to Artie's room and I talked to him: "Artie, you know it's not just quitting a band. It's quitting sixteen people and their wives, children, mothers, fathers, lovers, friends. You just can't do this. Artie Shaw is a million-dollar industry—"

"I can do it."

"Please don't do this."

"I'm doing it."

"Don't you owe anything to these guys?"

"I owe them nothing."

Which could be his epitaph: "I owe them nothing." I should have known the fellow who'd risk not beating his mother to the street wouldn't be moved by such prosaic persuasion. I went downstairs and told Andy Weinberger: "He's quitting." I've seen a few men get drunk in my time, but that night I saw Andy Weinberger take six doubles, down them—wham!—and get bombed more thoroughly than anybody I've ever seen since.

Artie next took off to Spain, where he stayed for many years and where the living was easy, cheap and well-ordered under Franco.

I haven't talked with Artie Shaw for a very long time now. I see him on occasional television talk shows, and I find it difficult to believe my eyes. I never thought much about it before, but looking at him now I'm pretty much convinced that eventually what you are is what you come to look like. A miser gets to look like a miser, a cunning man like a cunning man, a saint like a saint. Artie Shaw was once one of the handsomest men who ever lived. Now he looks like what he is.

I read his book, *The Trouble with Cinderella*, and threw it against the wall, which he doubtless will do with this book if he should happen to read it. I'm neither equipped to give, nor especially interested in trying, an amateur piece of Freudian analysis about what made Artie run. To belabor the obvious would be cheap. For deeper explanations, I refer you to others more knowledgeable. My approach, as you might expect, is more showbiz. What follows could apply to many other people in show business; I'm sure they will know who they are:

It takes the form of a science-fiction movie to be called *The Empty Man*. It opens in an operating room where a surgeon is checking out the patient's vital organs—heart, lungs, liver, kidneys—and the electronic console keeps registering *perfect, perfect, perfect*. The surgeon opens up the patient, and our shot from beneath shows all attendant faces looking down. Incredulity: the surgeon runs his hands through the patient's chest cavity, his abdomen . . . and finds nothing there. Nothing at all. The Empty Man.

CHAPTER 18

"You're a Lucky Guy"

You're a lucky guy
When you consider, the highest bidder
Can't buy the gleam in your eye,
You're a lucky guy!

I HAVE LEARNED not to question where good luck comes from
—especially since mine has come from so many strange, unexpected places. One of my oldest and dearest friends in the
whole world is Stan Krell, until recently, in my opinion, the
single greatest percussionist alive. Hal Hastings, the conductor who helmed so many of the great Hal Prince shows,
surely agreed: he wouldn't let a curtain go up unless he knew
he had Krell at the drums.

I've known Stan at least forty years, since we played together in tiny bands, and for forty years he has been a Rock of
Gibraltar to me.

Stan, as a young drummer in the pit, looked up at the stage
one day and fell madly in love with one of the greatest lovelies
that ever danced in a Broadway musical. Her name was Sis
and they were married and have lived the happy life ever
since. I know it's not supposed to happen—especially with
entertainers—but for Stan and Sis it has.

Sis Krell gave up dancing and made a happy home for
Stanley. She raised two lovely daughters. She taught them to

be young ladies. Krell spent all his evenings in the musical pits, and during the day he spread his expertise among the young drumming students who were lucky enough to get him to teach them. Life was beautiful!

In the meantime I had made it to the West Coast, life was beginning to be beautiful for me; each time Stan and I met it was usually when I was unpacking upon arrival in New York or packing when I was ready to leave.

Years later I was in Hollywood, and things were no longer going so well for me. I had just come off writing, to Jimmy Van Heusen's music, what I thought was one of the most challenging lyrics, "Thoroughly Modern Millie." Even the powers at Universal Pictures agreed that the song added millions of dollars to the box office. After that Van Heusen and I figured we'd be a little in demand. On the contrary. We were not called for *any* assignment. Matter of fact, as a team we have not written anything for hire since that time.

Four Oscars, the only Emmy, and waiting again for that damn phone to ring. It never does. Why? One can't be sure, I admit it's easy to get a little crazy when things aren't breaking right and there doesn't seem a good or even rational explanation for them, but I do feel it's fair to lay out a couple of theories and, as they say, if the shoe fits . . .

There is an absence of the work of people like Van Heusen, Warren, Fain, Evans and Livingston from the music people hear in the movies today—music fairly enriched, I guess anybody would agree, by their talents. And it is a fact that such absence makes losers of us all—the public and the professionals. I could, as I said, be crackers on this point, but it does strike me that the good and admittedly talented gentlemen who write the background scores for films seem to have displaced most of the so-called name songwriters, especially those associated with Hollywood and movies in the past (and let's remember "name" songwriters got to be names because a good many millions of people liked what they wrote. Pride, not apologies are in order for that). Background scorers have tended, I think, to envy the men who wrote the songs—envied them their ASCAP earnings, their royalties, the rest. No doubt they have had some justification, and they deserve redress of whatever real grievances they may have. But Van Heusen, Warren, Fain . . . ?

They say everybody dies, and, as I suggested, I was beginning to think it had happened to me sitting up by the phone. And when finally it did ring again—a request for lyrics for the SHARE Benefit; Dean Martin needs to sing something for the Golfing Association; Frank Sinatra is going into Caesar's Palace . . . But no single tingle from a single studio about an assignment. Instead, one day, it was Stan Krell on the phone: "Sam, I have an important decision to make. Suddenly the other night while I'm drumming in the pit of *Cabaret*, a head comes over the rim and it's George Barrie, an old pal from my danceband days. He handed me his card: 'George Barrie, Chief Executive Officer, Fabergé–Brut,' the perfume outfit. He insisted I come to see him. I went to his office and he said he wants me to come work for him. What should I do?" I yelled: "You will tell your chum Hal Hastings to find another drummer." I continued with the argument that his wife had spent all those years at home alone raising their wonderful girls, and now *she* deserved a break. He talked it over with Sis, who reluctantly—woman's intuition?—agreed. So Stan Krell gave up the musical pits for the nine-to-five at Fabergé–Brut.

His first day on the job, when five o'clock came around and Stan walked into George Barrie's office to tell him good-night, George Barrie said, "Where are you going?" pressed a button and the wall to his left slid away to reveal a complete music room—including drums and pianos and bass fiddles and organs and vibes. "How about we jam a little before you go home?" George said to Stan. "Jam a little" ran into the early morning hours, and after four or five nights in a row of this I spoke to Sis Krell, whose intuitive early reluctance was correct. She said, "Sam, that didn't really work out to a nine-to-five job, did it? He might as well be back in the pits with Hal Hastings." Of course, it eventually eased off and Stan did get home and the move worked out to be marvelous for him and Sis and George. Stan is now one of the most successful men in the perfume business—and enjoying himself. Besides, as he might say, with his current product he never has to worry about a performer or fellow musician smelling up the place with third-rate music. His world *always* smells good.

Stan's good fortune linked up directly to mine. One day into our home on Cañon Drive, Tita's and mine, came Stan Krell with George Barrie, who turned out to be gregarious and friendly. Shortly thereafter we were on his jet to New York, which like his office is musically equipped to the nines. Barrie, who likes to play the piano even more than I do—wrong, *nobody* likes to play the piano more than I do—sat doodling some bits of melody. One of them was attractive enough for me to ask what he called it. He said he didn't call it anything. "I think you ought to title your work and record it on cassettes so you can keep track of what you're writing." He said he would. A bit later Krell said, "You know Sam, if you would write a lyric for one of George's tunes, he'd just damn well die!" I said, "Let him send me a tune and its title and I'll write a lyric, and let's see if he dies." Some weeks later a cassette arrived. It was titled "The Happy Hooker," which will teach me to tell people to title their own tunes.

Still, title aside, it was a most contagious melody and agreeably suited to a faintly more elegant title, "Touch of Class." Once I decided on the title, it practically wrote itself.

What he has is pure pizz-zazz
Plus a touch of class!
It's all there, that savoir faire
Plus a touch of class!
He walks in and grins that grin
And they all fall en masse
Got to be the total he
Plus a touch of class! . . .

It was a kick for me to send it back to George Barrie, who was delighted with it and immediately started to send back other cassettes and other melodies. Some doubt that George Barrie of Fabergé–Brut actually wrote the melodies I wrote the lyrics for; this is to tell them I've kept all the original cassettes bearing the original melodies. Barrie may be chief executive officer of a successful fragrance company, and president of a promising entertainment-producing company, but deep under he's still a musician, a man who'd rather sit around the piano with chums than most anything else. Along with my association with Barrie as lyricist to his composer, I also along with Cary Grant, am a consultant for Brut Productions. I'm sure I write better than I consult, but it's a fair and working relationship. One I like and value.

Sammy Cahn, out of Hollywood, is now anchored in New York. And this time I made it back into the Hollywood scene, into the Academy Award race ("Touch of Class" was a nominee), not with a member of the Composers' and Lyricists' Guild of America but with a member of Local 802 of the New York Musicians union. A touch of class.

I was sixty when I started this book, and now that I'm near the end of it I'm going on sixty-one. It is a Wednesday morning here in New York, a cloudy, gray and threatening day. I'm sitting here wondering what effect the weather will have on the box office at the Golden Theatre on Broadway, where Sammy Cahn is starring in *Words and Music*, the story of the life of Sammy Cahn in his own words and music, aided by a small but very gifted cast of three singers and one pianist.

I never used to think of weather in connection with the theater, but now I realize *everything* has an effect on the theater. It is either a week before Lent or the week after Lent or it *is* the week of Lent. . . .

When I finish typing this I will start to work on the lyrics for the birthday party the Friars Club is giving me—all the lyrics to be sung to me by some friends. Nothing flattering, mind you. Just stuff like:

> *Of the Cahns we'll name, which will hist'ry blame,*
> *Genghis? Ali? Or Sammy?*

When I finish the lyrics for the Friars bash I'll finish editing this book. (*I Should Care: The Sammy Cahn Story*, by Sammy Cahn. Figures.) Then I'll try to get over to the Fabergé–Brut office on Sixth Avenue. After some hours there I'll wander over to the Golden. Wednesday is matinee day. Come two o'clock the door to my dressing room will open and they'll announce: "Half hour!" Which means that in thirty minutes I must be in place to walk out on the stage. Can you imagine that Sammy Cahn at the age of sixty-one is starring in his own story on Broadway? It is an incredible Cinderella story—at least to me—and I surely the most improbable Cinderella. We've had amazing reviews, are about to give our one-hundred-fiftieth performance, and have never done a show without the audience standing and calling out at least a few "bravos" at the end. But the big reward is when old chums, chums of a lifetime, come backstage. And then I start to remember . . .

If I am sixty-one, Milton Berle is sixty-six, because he was on stage in a flash act at the age of fifteen when I went to my first vaudeville show at the age of ten. From that moment almost fifty-one years ago up until the time I took the stage in *Words and Music,* I have harbored a Walter Mitty desire to perform, working it out of my system by the way I deliver my songs when I'm selling them. If, as the Broadway critics most kindly agreed, I am a performer, I here and now confess to them that I have been rehearsing for fifty-one years.

Whatever I do on stage myself is and must be a reflection of all the talents I have seen and known. I'll never forget Ruby Zwerling, the orchestra leader at Loew's Delancey, telling me that I must bring food enough to spend an entire day at the theater, because one of the single great performers of all time, James Barton, would be appearing.

I've said I've seen them all in my time, but if there were such a thing as a decathalon for performing, James Barton would take the honors and leave the field far behind him. He could sing better than any singer, could dance better than any dancer. I never heard a better monologist, never saw a better mime. You name it, Barton did it better.

I am sure that now and again, up on stage, I am borrowing from Barton, and from all of the vaudeville greats from Harry Lauder to Jimmy Savo, God bless him, to Joe Frisco to Kramer-and-Boyle to Smith-and-Dale to Burns-and-Allen to Jack Benny to Frank Fay and Jackie Osterman and Richie Craig. The familiar names you will of course identify, but the Ostermans and Craigs were also prominent among the men who triggered the "ham in Sam" that's at long last finding fulfillment at the Golden Theatre.

And it was actually Jackie Osterman at the Academy of Music on 14th Street who inspired my songwriting career. I went to the opening show, and there was Osterman being as funny as anyone could be. In the middle of the act he took a change of pace and said he'd like to sing a song he'd written. It was a fascinating thing for me to be actually looking at a songwriter—in person. In those days I'd already begun making some ribald rhymes for the edification of the guys in our little band, the Pals of Harmony, never thinking anything of it. But listening to Jackie Osterman do a rather lovely ballad and then walking home from the Academy of Music, I began to frame a song in my head. By the time I reached home I had actually written a lyric—and a lyric-writer's tune. (A lyric-writer's tune is a da-da-da melody of no or little distinction.) The song was a piece of idiocy called "Like Niagara Falls, I'm Falling for You—Baby!" But if, as Confucius or Chairman Mao or somebody said, a journey of a thousand miles starts with the first step, that was the first step.

Despite my brief and distant nightmare experience in Philadelphia with *Glad to See Ya!* it had never, ever occurred to me that the day would happen when I would take the stage in a real show, not for an instant. Then one day in 1972 the phone rang—everything, as I've said, begins with a phone call. It was publicist Sid Garfield of CBS, another old friend, to say that Maurice Levine of the 92nd Street YM-YWHA would be calling to ask me to be one of the participants for a series at the Y called "Lyrics and Lyricists." These would be one-man or -woman evenings by such songwriting giants as Dorothy Fields, Alan Jay Lerner, E. Y. "Yip" Harburg. I quickly consented—it was a chance to "get on," and mainly I wanted to tell two stories, the story of *"Bei Mir Bist Du Schön"* and the story of "Three Coins in the Fountain." Well, I got on, but because of the length of all my stories I had to cut and cut, and when I finally got on I never did tell the two stories. Nonetheless, it apparently was a successful evening.

It resulted in Maurice Levine's asking if he could see to it that I be produced on-Broadway. Then off-Broadway. Then off-off-Broadway. Finally the idea just petered out.

Meanwhile I had been asked to do *Coming of Age*, a short

musical narrative of the American Revolution as seen through the eyes of a fourteen-year-old boy. It was based on *The Crystal Cornerstone*, by Lorna Beers, a book published by Harper & Row, which firm now wanted to send it out as a show to high schools.

I wrote it with Lan O'Kun, a young composer–lyricist. We felt each other out, worked compatibly and it turned out to be a labor of love. When completed, it came to the attention of quite a few people. Everybody loved it in 1972—if we could hold it until 1976 for the Bicentennial . . .

Still meanwhile, toward the end of 1973, I was called to the offices of the Maximus Music Company by my good friends Frank Military and Jay Morganstern because Broadway producer Alexander H. Cohen is himself looking for a property for the Bicentennial. When Lan O'Kun and I got to the Maximus office, I sat down in a corner, and Lan went to the piano and played and sang. I could detect all through the audition overtones of surprise from Alex Cohen, his eyes seeming to look at me in the corner and say, "Why not you?"

At the end I said, "Alex, do you mind if I sing one song?" "Mind? I've been waiting here an hour to hear you sing." So I stood up and, as you know is my wont, leaned in and sang "Growing Up," one of the songs of *Coming of Age*. Alex appeared impressed. "Have you ever thought of doing a one-man show?" "Thought of? I *did* a one-man show at the Y." As a matter of fact Harvey Granat, who was to become associate producer of *Words and Music*, had caught it that evening at the Y and, as I later learned, had been impressed.

Alex said, "Could I hear it?" "Yes, you can, it's on tape. I'll send you the cassette." The next day I sent the cassette to his house and—

In most every other instance when I'd sent somebody this cassette there'd been at least some telegrams back to me, some reaction . . . From Alex Cohen, total silence. It was ego-

deflating, I tell you. I said to myself, I guess this is the difference between 92nd Street (where the Y is) and 44th Street
(where Cohen has his office).

Two weeks later the phone rang. Alex Cohen: "Sammy, we
must have breakfast together." I said, "We don't need to have
breakfast for you to turn me down." He said, "Don't antici-
pate." "Okay," I said, "where?" He said the St. Regis Hotel. I
didn't know they had a coffee shop at the St. Regis.

I walked into the dining room of the St. Regis and up to
Alex Cohen, and he said, "You are opening on Broadway." I
sighed a big sigh and said, "Alex, I'm very pleased, but you've
got to tell me one thing. Where were you for two weeks?" "I
was in Boston for two weeks with a show called *Good Evening*—the revue by Peter Cook and Dudley Moore. It's a big
hit, and now I'm ready for you. I promised my wife Hildy a
few nights ago that we must sit down and listen to your
cassette. I thought we'd just have a drink, listen a bit and go to
dinner. Well, we never went to dinner. Your show is en-
chanting. The next day I took the cassette to the office and
played it for all the staff. I told them, 'This is going to run an
hour and fifty minutes. If any of you want to leave, then leave.
I won't mind. I just want to know why you left or why you
stayed.' And I'm here to tell you, Sammy, that not one of the
office staff left and at the end they gave you a standing ovation. That's why you're opening on Broadway. But you have
to understand, Sammy, this will mean eight times a week at
the Golden Theatre, week in and week out." I said, "I understand and I'll be there." For a person like me who mostly has
been on the move, such a promise was not an easy thing. "I'll
have my manager Ed Traubner call you. There's no need to
say more." We shook hands and I left.

When Ed Traubner called me the next day, after he'd talked
on the phone with Alex Cohen, he said, "You know why
Cohen is so excited about this? He was assistant to David

Wolper back in 1944 when you went on that time in *Glad to See Ya!* [produced by Wolper] in Philadelphia." It's true, and I have the program to prove it.

Tita and I went back to California, and now she was starting to share with me the thrill of preparing to go on Broadway. She decided the first thing I should do was take off some girth. She didn't want me to bounce on stage like a little fat man. I was up to 167 pounds, when my fighting weight is' 155. Luckily I refused. It turned out I need that girth—I lost nearly fourteen pounds working out under those lights on stage. What a way to lose (weight) and win—the best of both worlds, for sure.

I let Alex Cohen put the whole show together, insisting only that I must have Richard Leonard at the piano, the same Richard Leonard as in the performance at the Y. All my life I've had the good fortune of having fine pianistic collaborators, men who play so beautifully, which affects me like the lure of the muse. It just flows out of me when a fella plays prettily; I can write lyrics by the day, the week, the year. To this day Saul Chaplin is one of the great, great pianists, and if he plays behind you, you go. Ditto for Jule Styne. Ditto James Van Heusen. Right into the tradition of all those men, along came Richard Leonard at the age of thirty-eight, introduced to me by Maurice Levine of the Y. Richard is the single most incredible accompanying pianist I've ever met. In *Words and Music* neither Richard nor I ever do the same show twice; we play off one another, keep trying to please one another. As a matter of fact I left the choice of most of the cast to Richard, who also made all the vocal arrangements.

Tita and I arrived back in New York on April 4, 1974. On Sunday, April 7, everybody came together for the first rehearsal at the Golden Theatre. On the eleventh, at four o'clock, we did the first dress rehearsal—which meant the scenery was in, the lighting was in. Afterward we all assembled in my dressing room, where I felt Mr. Cohen and director Jerry Adler were treating me like I was Alfred Drake and Robert Preston, all in one.

"We have to discuss notes, cuts, and changes," they said. "I don't know what you mean." "Well, we think the show should run without an intermission, so we'll have to take fifteen minutes out." I said: "They're out." "Which fifteen minutes?" "I'm not sure, but you'll have it." "One more thing," said Alex Cohen, "and then you can go home. We think that for projection of your voice you'll have to wear a Vega mike."

I don't know who invented the Vega chest microphone, but whoever this gentleman is I send him my blessings and my greetings. Every night at 7:30, Joey Monaco, the electrician for *Words and Music,* comes into my dressing room at the Golden and puts me into my Vega contraption (well, Alfred Drake I'm not). There's a special little harness Lonnie the wardrobe master made for me, and from it the mike hangs down my neck while a wire goes down past my navel and makes a left turn to the hip, where there's a pouch in which the Vega transmitter sits. The aerial runs down my leg. By God and by Vega, we project, and the voicebox stays intact.

Came the afternoon of Good Friday, April 12, we did the second dress rehearsal, this time with fifteen minutes out. That night we did the first preview. I have vivid impressions of Tita trying to hide her anxieties for me. Came the moment where I stand backstage, just prior to making my entrance. I listened to all the machinery of backstage functioning and Murray Gitlin, the stage manager, saying into a telephone: "Take the house to half. Joey, turn on the Vega. House out. Hit one." At "hit one" the light for my entrance went on, and Bill James, the assistant stage manager, put his hand on my shoulder and pressed it. I walked out and did the show as I had dreamed I would do it.

There's a deceptively casual opening line—"I'm so pleased you're here"—intended to have the effect of "Come into my living room." Then I say, "I'm so pleased Richard Leonard's here." And then I'm on stage for around twenty-one consecutive minutes.

They bravoed—heavenly noise—at the final curtain that night, Friday. Saturday we did a matinee—same, thank God, reaction. Saturday night, same. That night at eleven o'clock after the show Alex Cohen walked up to me and kissed me. I said, "What's *that* for?" He said, "Just because." I know that no one kisses me just because, and a few minutes later Alex Cohen told the cast that from here on out they could relax. Seems he made a practice of allowing the critics to come to previews. Enough had already come so that the worst was behind us. I said to myself, "Aha, that kiss, I hope, was for one of the critics."

Sunday matinée I sort of floated through the final preview, but when I came off and started up the stairs to my dressing room—the single hardest part of this entire venture, because I'm on stage almost two hours and then have to climb a flight of stairs—well, this Sunday for the first time I felt a twinge of self-pity. What am I doing here? Why am I climbing these stairs? How did I get into this?

I was about to get really obnoxious when there was a tap on my shoulder. Alex Cohen again, and again he kissed me on the cheek. I said, "Alex, we've got to stop meeting like this. What's *that* kiss for?" "That kiss," said Alex, "is because Clive Barnes"—the drama critic of *The New York Times*—"just danced out of here looking very uncritically delighted."

We were dark Monday, no show. Tita and I spent a kind of relaxed day and evening. That night in bed, after we turned out the light, we began to play out this little charade we've been playing ever since. "Tita, what's happening to us?" "Sam, you're opening on Broadway." "I know, but how and why?" "How and why notwithstanding, you are opening on Broadway." And then we held hands and just giggled.

I usually get up at 7 A.M. when the fellow says, "Good morning, this is the *Today* show," and I say to the TV, "How are you? My name is Sammy Cahn." On Tuesday, April 16, 1974, the morning of opening night for *Words and Music,* I slept a bit later than usual. Tita, who is understandably proud of our New York apartment, had laid on my favorite breakfast—fresh fruit, grilled cheese and ham on English muffin and her special coffee. Around 2 P.M. of O-day I went to the theater and stayed there, leaving Tita the most unrewarding job: seeing to it that all our friends, including last-minute arrivals from wherever, were taken care of with house seats—and all in the second row. By the way, a house seat is *not* an "on-the-house" seat; it's a guaranteed choice seat held out by the management or actors, but every seat must be paid for.

That night at seven-thirty Bill James announced, "Half-hour," and the ritual began. Joey Monaco came in to put me into my Vega harness. I put my undershirt over the Vega mike, and my dinner jacket over the underwear, the dinner jacket of a tuxedo created by Mario at the request of my friends Pat and Morris Uchitel.

At 7:15 Bill James announces: "Fifteen minutes." At eight he announces: "Places." And at 8:05, with Bill James pressing my shoulder, I head for the stage. At this point I realize I could have done any one of four awful things: 1) Said to myself, Are you crazy? 2) Started to cry. 3) Fainted. 4) Run out of the theater. For reasons I don't understand at all, I did none of them. I went on stage before a standing-room-only audience of some 800 people. The show, incredibly, played with the same result as that first time at the Y. At the end there were even the standing ovations—and *not,* you wise guys, counting my four sisters and their husbands, whom I had manacled to their seats.

Backstage was flowers, friends, booze, and then we all went

over to Sardi's. I guess I've had more than my share of high points in my life—like the birth of my firstborn, the birth of my secondborn, winning of Academy Awards—but nothing quite catches the exhilaration of walking into Sardi's, the show-business restaurant of the world on 44th Street in the heart of the theater district, and having the whole place stand up and applaud. Ham? You bet . . . . I want Tita to know how proud I was of her at that moment.

We went up to the Belasco Room, a private banquet space above Sardi's proper, where a special buffet had been set out and the walls were decorated with TV sets. At ten-thirty someone yelled for quiet, and the first television reviewer came on, Stewart Klein of Channel 5. When he got to ". . . one of the most delightful shows of the year . . . pure pleasure . . . beautiful"—well, you get the picture. It had all taken shape from Sunday the seventh to Tuesday the sixteenth.

Again we were asked to be quiet, and Alex Cohen said we were going to listen to the Clive Barnes review in *The Times* as read to us over the phone. I repeat with no apologies some excerpts from it. Apologies . . . hell, I was so damn proud. So grateful . . .

> Mr. Cahn pretends to be a lyricist . . . . But don't be fooled. Inside every song writer . . . there is a performer trying to get either in or out . . . . [Sammy Cahn] is undeniably one of the most successful, memorable and happy lyric writers of the last 40 years. His second claim to fame is even more interesting. He is probably the best bad singer in the world . . . As a singer he has so much style that if God had made him Frank Sinatra, then the world would have seen something.

At that point I started to cry, and Tita put her arms around me and helped me cry a little. It was so wonderful to see the happiness radiating from my wife, my sisters, all my friends. Tita and I still go to bed every night and hold hands and giggle and go through our routine of . . . "Tita, what's happening to us?" "Sam, you're opening on Broadway . . ."

I know that some people are frightened because they feel America is in crisis. I ask them all to sleep well, because if Sammy Cahn at age sixty-one is starring on Broadway, having received such reviews, then America is at least still a place of truly golden opportunity.

I have a confession to make. When the "deal" was being made for me to do the show for Alex Cohen and Harvey Granat, they of course haggled and negotiated. Now I can safely tell Messrs. Cohen and Granat that I would have paid them anything for the opportunity. Of course they'll have to take my word for it.

I'm often asked if I live my lyrics. Well, I'm certainly living one of them—"The Second Time Around." I'm married to that beautiful girl Tita—who loves music and lyrics as much as I do, loves me and loves to come to the Golden not just to watch the stage but to watch the audience. She says for her it's the best part of the show, which I mean to take up with her some time. I don't think I'll get too far, though. Partisan and loving booster, friend and ally she may be, but she's murder on the stuffed shirt. I offer in evidence the parody sung by her at my Friars Club sixty-first birthday party. Pretty humbling stuff, and she sang it with as much relish as style and wit. You know the tune . . .

A fine romance,
My friends, this is.
I'm now known as the star's missus.

His conversation now tends to just embarrass—
He only quotes from Clive Barnes and Leonard Harris.

But when his ego begins climbin'
I just quote from dear John—Simon

And that's when he goes into his spastic dance
Gives me that famous glance
I haven't got a chance!

A fine romance,
My friends, this is.
There's no time now for mere kisses.

Romantic'ly I'm not now at all beholden
His only matinees now are at the—Golden

And if ever we do—do it
He wants me now to—re—view it,
And there's no understudy to fill his pants
I haven't got a chance—
This is a fine—a less than divine—
This is a fine romance!

If this keeps up then this dago
May just move to, say,—Oswego
In such a place there'd sure be no sycophants
For Sammy to entrance

This is a fine
Too bad it's mine
This a fine romance.

Words by Sammy Cahn. Sentiment heartily sung by adoring but no-nonsense wife.

In no B-movie has it ever happened that the star breaks a leg, the understudy goes on, the understudy breaks her ankle and somebody says—"Send the songwriter on!" It could never happen, but it did eight times a week at the Golden Theatre on Broadway.

... Makes Strong Men Whimper and Women Faint

I DIDN'T APPRENTICE at Cordon Bleu, but I can and do claim some expertise in preparing two rather unusual dishes that I like making for my closest friends. I also enjoy passing these recipes on to them and take the liberty of doing the same for you here. (After all, you deserve a bonus if you've been kind enough to stay with my story to the end.) I hope the recipes below sort of help top it off for you when you make and enjoy them. I guess after songwriting and performing, I love most to play chef and host for loved ones—which now definitely includes you.

The first is a Teflon version of the ancient *matzoth brei*, which, when translated, is simply fried matzoth with egg. The other is my Hawaiian Chicken—a delicacy I was introduced to by a true gourmet, Ray Heindorf, who was also a fine pianist, conductor, arranger and composer.

Matzoth Brei

1 sheet of unsalted *matzoth*
1 egg
Salt and pepper

Have a Teflon pan warming on the stove. Break the *matzoth* into an eight-ounce measuring cup and pour hot water over the pieces. Let them soak—not too long, though; the *matzoth* should be a bit firm. Next pour the *matzoth* pieces onto a clean dishcloth. Break the egg into the measuring cup and beat briskly. Now squeeze the water out of the *matzoth* and combine it with the beaten egg. Mix thoroughly. Add salt and pepper to taste.

Pour the mixture into the frying pan, cover and let brown *slowly*—approximately seven minutes for each side. Please, remember to keep the heat low to prevent burning.

Matzoth brei can be served with sour cream, jam or perhaps just salt and pepper (my own preference). Double or triple or even quadruple the recipe for the number of people you plan to serve. And as we say in our tribe: *Es gezunter hayt!*

Hawaiian Chicken Barbecue

1½ cups peanut oil
½ cup dark brown sugar
4 or 5 cloves
¼ cup soysauce
¼ cup white vinegar
Honey to sweeten
Sweet white sauterne
A three-pound broiler, quartered

To prepare the marinade simply combine the first six ingredients in order listed in a blender and mix thoroughly. Then place the quartered chicken in a bowl, cover with marinade until completely immersed, and allow to stand in a cool place for at least six hours. Turn the chicken pieces frequently enough to insure maximum absorption of the marinade.

It is terribly important that the fire be a *slow* one. Because of the ingredients in the marinade, the chicken will quickly blacken and burn if the flame is not carefully controlled. Allow enough time for the fire to burn down before placing the first batch (bone side down) on the fire. To cook the chicken to golden perfection takes between forty-five minutes and one hour.

The final showmanly touch is the spray of a fine white sweet sauterne wine which is applied just as the chicken is served. It is best applied with an old empty and clean Windex spray bottle—and just enough to cover the chicken with a delicate mist.

This recipe will serve two and can be doubled, tripled and quadrupled to accommodate any number of guests.

Enjoy!

Lyrics

Bei Mir Bist Du Schön
(Means That You're Grand)

Verse:
Of all the girls I've known, and I've known some,
Until I first met you I was lone-some,
And when you came in sight, dear, my heart grew light
And this old world seemed new to me,

You're really swell I have to admit, you
deserve expressions that really fit you,
And so I've racked my brain, hoping to explain all the things that you do to me;

Chorus:
"*Bei Mir Bist Du Schön*," Please let me explain
"*Bei Mir Bist Du Schön*" means that you're grand,
"*Bei Mir Bist Du Schön*" Again I'll explain
Boy: It means you're the fairest in the land
Girl: It means that my heart's at your command,

I could say "*Bella, Bella*," even say "*Voonderbar*,"
Each language only helps me tell you how grand you are,
I've tried to explain, "*Bei Mir Bist Du Schön*,"
So, kiss me and say you understand.

Rhythm Is Our Business

Chorus:
Rhythm is our bus'ness, rhythm is what we sell.
Rhythm is our bus'ness, bus'ness sure is swell.

If you're feeling blue, rhythm's what you need,
If you've got rhythm you're sure to succeed;

Rhythm is our bus'ness, rhythm is what we sell.

Patter:
He's the drummer man in the band.
When he does tricks with sticks,
The boys in the band all play "hot licks."

He plays saxophone in the band.
When he runs up and down the scale,
He's sure to get you "hot" without fail.

He plays on the bass in the band.
When he slaps on all those strings,
Happiness to you, that's what he brings.

He's the trumpet man in the band.
He's the boy who "hit 'em high";
He makes you think that he's in the sky.

(It Will Have To Do)
Until the Real Thing Comes Along

Verse:
I've tried to explain that you are my Heaven on earth.
Still I've tried in vain,
Since words can't explain my love and its worth.
This much I know is true,
There'll never be another you.

I've read all the plays from Shakespeare to Eugene O'Neill.
To find just one phrase that conveys the way that I feel.
I met with no success;
I'm strictly on my own I guess.
And so,

Chorus:
That's why I'd work for you, I'd slave for you,
I'd be a beggar or a knave for you,
If thathisn't love,
It will have to do
Until the real thing comes along.

I'd gladly move the earth for you,
To prove my love, dear, and it's worth for you,
If that isn't love,
It will have to do
Until the real thing comes along.

With all the words, dear, at my command,
I just can't make you understand.
I'll always love you, darling, come what may.
My heart is yours, what more can I say?

I'd cry for you, I'd tear the stars down
From the sky for you,
If that isn't love,
It will have to do,
Until the real thing comes along.

Please Be Kind

Verse:
Somehow the thrill I feel is new,
I must confess,
I never loved 'til I loved you,
Or did you guess?

Chorus:
This is my first affair,
So, please be kind.
Handle my heart with care,
Oh please be kind.

This is all so grand,
My dreams are on parade,
If you'll just understand,
They'll never, never fade.

So tell me your love's sincere,
Oh, please be kind.
Tell me I needn't fear,
Oh, please be kind.

'Cause if you leave me, dear,
I know my heart will lose its mind.
If you love me,
Please be kind.

You're a Lucky Guy

Chorus:
You're a lucky guy
When you consider the highest bidder
Can't buy the gleam in your eye
You're a lucky guy!

Thank your lucky star
You've got a honey, who wants no money
She'll take you just as you are,
Thank your lucky star!

Hey fella, say fella, open up your eyes
It's fated, you rated, you must realize

You're a lucky guy
You're just beginning, so take your inning
And let your troubles go fry
No one can deny—you're a lucky guy!

Saturday Night
(Is the Loneliest Night in the Week)

Verse:
When the phone starts ringing
I just let it ring.
I just don't feel like going out
Or doing anything.

Chorus:
Saturday night is the loneliest night in the week,
'Cause that's the night
That my sweetie and I used to dance cheek to cheek.

I don't mind Sunday night at all
'Cause that's the night friends come to call.
And Monday to Friday go fast
And another week is past,
But Saturday night is the loneliest night in the week,

I sing the song that I sang before
For the mem'ries I usually seek.
Until I hear you at the door
Until you're in my arms once more
Saturday night is the loneliest night in the week.

I Should Care

Verse:
I know I should pity me,
But I don't because, you see,
I have loved and learned
And as far as I'm concerned;

Chorus:
I should care,
I should go around weeping.
I should care,
I should go without sleeping.

Strangely enough I sleep well
'Cept for a dream or two,
But then, I count my sheep well.
Funny how sheep can lull you to sleep.

So, I should care,
I should let it upset me.
I should care,
But it just doesn't get me.

Maybe I won't find
Someone as lovely as you,
But I should care
And I do.

Guess I'll Hang My Tears Out to Dry

Verse:
The torch I carry is handsome;
It's worth its heartache in ransom.
And when the twilight steals,
I know how the lady in the harbor feels.

Chorus:
When I want rain,
I get sunny weather;
I'm just as blue as the sky.
Since love is gone,
Can't pull myself together.
Guess I'll hang my tears out to dry.

Friends ask me out,
I tell them I'm busy,
Must get a new alibi.
I stay home,
And ask myself where is he/she
Guess I'll hang my tears out to dry.

Dry little tear drops,
My little tear drops,
Hanging on a string of dreams.
Fly little mem'ries,
My little mem'ries,
Remind him/her of our crazy schemes.

Somebody said just forget about him/her
I gave that treatment a try;
Strangely enough, I got along without him/her
Then one day he/she passed me right by,
Oh well, I guess I'll hang my tears out to dry.

I'll Walk Alone

Verse:
They call, no date,
I promised you I'd wait.
I want them all to know
I'm strictly single-o.

The longing will grow the slightest bit less.
And there will be moments, yes!
When it disappears!
I'll bet I forget her completely,
In about a hundred years!

Chorus:
I'll walk alone
Because, to tell the truth,
I'll be lonely.
I don't mind being lonely
When my heart tells me you are lonely too.

I'll walk alone,
They'll ask me why
And I'll tell them I'd rather;
There are dreams I must gather,
Dreams we fashioned the night
You held me tight.

I'll always be near you, wherever you are,
Each night in ev'ry prayer.
If you call I'll hear you,
No matter how far;
Just close your eyes and I'll be there.

Please walk alone
And send your love and kisses to guide me.
'Til you're walking beside me,
I'll walk alone.

It's Been a Long, Long Time

Verse:
Never thought that you would be
Standing here so close to me.
There's so much I feel that I should say
But words can wait until some other day.

Chorus:
Just kiss me once,
Then kiss me twice,
Then kiss me once again,
It's been a long, long time.

Haven't felt like this, my dear,
Since can't remember when,
It's been a long, long time.
You'll never know how many dreams I dreamed about you
Or just how empty they all seemed without you.

So, kiss me once,
Then kiss me twice,
Then kiss me once again,
It's been a long, long time.

Day by Day

Chorus:
Day by day I'm falling more in love with you
And day by day my love seems to grow,
There isn't any end to my devotion,
It's deeper, dear, by far than any ocean

I find that day by day—you're making all my dreams come true,
So come what may I want you to know
I'm yours alone and I'm in love to stay,
As we go through the years, day by day—day by day

Let It Snow! Let It Snow! Let It Snow!

Verse:
The snowman in the yard is frozen hard;
He's a sorry sight to see,
If he had a brain he'd complain,
Bet he wishes he were me.

Chorus:
Oh! the weather outside is frightful
But the fire is so delightful
And since we've no place to go,
Let it snow! let it snow! let it snow!

It doesn't show signs of stopping
And I brought some corn for popping;
The lights are turned way down low.
Let it snow! let it snow! let it snow!

When we finally kiss good-night,
How I'll hate going out in the storm!
But if you really hold me tight
All the way home I'll be warm.

The fire is slowly dying
And, my dear, we're still good-byeing,
But as long as you love me so,
Let it snow! let it snow! let it snow!

Five Minutes More

Verse:
Dear, this evening seemed to go so awfully fast.
We had so much fun and now you're home at last.
I looked forward to a kiss or two at the garden gate,
But you gave me just one peck and insisted it was late.

Chorus:
Give me five minutes more,
Only five minutes more,
Let me stay,
Let me stay in your arms.

Here am I begging for
Only five minutes more,
Only five minutes more of your charms.

All week long I dreamed about our Saturday date.
Don't you know that Sunday morning you can sleep late?

Give me five minutes more,
Only five minutes more,
Let me stay,
Let me stay in your arms.

Time After Time

Verse:
What good are words I say to you?
They can't convey to you what's in my heart.
If you could hear instead
The things I've left unsaid!

Chorus:
Time after time
I tell myself
That I'm so lucky to be loving you,
So lucky to be the one you run to see
In the evening when the day is through.

I only know what I know,
The passing years will show
You've kept my love so young, so new.
And time after time you'll hear me say
That I'm so lucky to be loving you.

It's Magic

Verse:
I've heard about Houdini and the rest of them
And I'd put you up against the best of them.
As far as I'm concerned, you're the tops,
And you don't resort to props;

Things I used to think were inconceivable,
You've got a way of making them believable.
And upon a night like this
I'm afraid you just can't miss.

Chorus:
You sigh, the song begins,
You speak and I hear violins
It's magic.

The stars desert the skies
And rush to nestle in your eyes,
It's magic.

Without a golden wand or mystic charms
Fantastic things begin when I am in your arms.
When we walk hand in hand
The world becomes a wonderland,
It's magic.

How else can I explain those rainbows when there is no rain,
It's magic.
Why do I tell myself
These things that happen are all really true
When in my heart I know the magic is my love for you.

Be My Love

Chorus:
Be my love,
For no one else can end this yearning;
This need that you and you alone create.

Just fill my arms
The way you've filled my dreams,
The dreams that you inspire
With ev'ry sweet desire.

Be my love,
And with your kisses set me burning;
One kiss is all I need to seal my fate,

And hand in hand,
We'll find love's promised land.
There'll be no one but you, for me eternally.
If you will be my love.

Because You're Mine

Chorus:
Because you're mine the brightest star I see
Looks down, my love, and envys me
Because you're mine
Because you're mine
Because you're mine.

The breeze that hurries by
Becomes a melody and why?
Because you're mine,
Because you're mine,
Because you're mine.

I only know for as long as I may live,
I'll only live for the kiss that you alone may give
Me. And when we kiss that isn't thunder, dear,
It's only my poor heart you hear,
And it's applause,
Because you're mine!
Because you're mine!

Teach Me Tonight

Chorus:
Did you say, "I've got a lot to learn"?
Well, don't think I'm trying not to learn,
Since this is the perfect spot to learn,
Teach me tonight.

Starting with the "A, B, C" of it,
Right down to the "X, Y, Z" of it.
Help me solve the mystery of it,
Teach me tonight.

The sky's a blackboard high above you.
If a shooting star goes by
I'll use that star to write I love you,
A thousand times across the sky.

One thing isn't very clear, my love,
Should the teacher stand so near, my love?
Graduation's almost here, my love,
Teach me tonight.

Three Coins in the Fountain

Chorus:
Three coins in the fountain,
Each one seeking happiness,
Thrown by three hopeful lovers,
Which one will the fountain bless?

Three hearts in the fountain,
Each heart longing for its home,
There they lie in the fountain
Somewhere in the heart of Rome.

Which one will the fountain bless?
Which one will the fountain bless?

Three coins in the fountain,
Through the ripples how they shine
Just one wish will be granted,
One heart will wear a valentine.
Make it mine!
Make it mine!
Make it mine!

Look to Your Heart

Chorus:
Look to your heart,
When there are words to say
And never leave your love unspoken.

Day by day,
We go our thoughtless way
And only when we pray,
Do we remember those we love.

Too late we find,
A word that's warm and kind,
Is more than just a passing token,

Speak your love,
To those who seek your love,
Look to your heart,
Your heart will know what to say,
Look to your heart, today.

Love Is the Tender Trap

Chorus:
You see a pair of laughing eyes
And suddenly you're sighing sighs,
You're thinking nothing's wrong,
You string along, boy, then snap!
Those eyes, those sighs,
They're part of the tender trap!

You're hand in hand under the trees
And soon there's music in the breeze,
You're acting kind of smart,
Until your heart just goes whap!
Those trees, that breeze,
They're part of the tender trap!

Some starry night,
When her/his kisses make you tingle,
She'll/he'll hold you tight
And you'll hate yourself for being single.

And all at once it seems so nice,
The folks are throwing shoes and rice,
You hurry to a spot
That's just a dot on the map!

You wonder how it all came about,
It's too late now, there's no getting out
You fell in love,
And love is the tender trap!

Love and Marriage

Chorus:
Love and marriage, love and marriage,
Go together like a horse and carriage,
This I tell ya, brother,
Ya can't have one without the other.

Love and marriage, love and marriage,
It's an institute you can't disparage,
Ask the local gentry
And they will say it's element'ry.

Try, try, try to separate them,
It's an illusion,
Try, try, try
And you will only come to this conclusion.

Love and marriage, love and marriage,
Go together like a horse and carriage,
Dad was told by mother,
You can't have one,
You can't have none,
You can't have one without the other!

All the Way

Chorus:
When somebody loves you,
It's no good unless he loves you
All the way.

Happy to be near you,
When you need someone to cheer you
All the way.

Taller than the tallest tree is,
That's how it's got to feel;
Deeper than the deep blue sea is,
That's how deep it goes,
If it's real.

When somebody needs you,
It's no good unless he needs you
All the way.

Through the good or lean years
And for all the in-between years,
Come what may.

Who knows where the road will lead us?
Only a fool would say,
But if you let me love you,
It's for sure I'm gonna love you
All the way,
All the way.

Come Fly With Me

Verse:
When dad and mother discovered one another,
They dreamed of the day
When they would love and honor and obey.

All during all their modest spooning,
They'd blush and speak of honeymooning.
And if your memory recalls,
They spoke of Niagara Falls.

But today, my darling, today,
When you meet the one you love
You say:

Chorus:
Come fly with me!
Let's fly!
Let's fly away!

If you can use some exotic booze,
There's a bar in far Bombay,

Come fly with me!
Let's fly!
Let's fly away!

Come fly with me!
Let's float down to Peru!
In Llama Land there's a one-man band
And he'll toot his flute for you,

Come fly with me!
Let's take off in the blue!
Up there! Where the air is rarefied,
We'll just glide, starry-eyed.

Up there!
I'll be holding you so near,
You may hear angels cheer,
'Cause we're together.

Weatherwise, it's such a lovely day!
Just say the words
And we'll beat the birds
Down to Acapulco Bay.

It's perfect
For a flying honeymoon, they say,

Come fly with me!
Let's fly!
Let's fly away!
Come away!

High Hopes

Verse:
Next time you're found
With your chin on the ground,
There's a lot to be learned,
So look around.

Chorus:
Just what makes that little ol' ant
Think he'll move that rubber tree plant;
Anyone knows an ant can't
Move a rubber tree plant.

But he's got high hopes,
He's got high hopes;
He's got high apple pie in the sky hopes.
So any time you're gettin' low,
'Stead of lettin' go,
Just remember that ant.
Oops! There goes another rubber tree plant!
Oops! There goes another rubber tree plant!

Verse:
When troubles call
And your back's to the wall,
There's a lot to be learned,
That wall could fall.

Once there was a silly old ram,
Thought he'd punch a hole in a dam;
No one could make that ram scram,
He kept buttin' that dam.

'Cause he had high hopes,
He had high hopes;
He had high apple pie in the sky hopes.
So any time you're feelin' bad,
'Stead of feelin' sad,

Just remember that ram.
Oops! There goes a billion-kilowatt dam!
Oops! There goes a billion-kilowatt dam!

Chorus:
So keep your high hopes,
Keep your high hopes;
Keep those high apple pie in the sky hopes.
A problem's just a toy balloon,
They'll be bursting soon,
They're just bound to go "Pop!"
Oops! There goes another problem, kerplop!
Oops! There goes another problem, kerplop!
Kerplop!

The Second Time Around

Chorus:
Love is lovelier the second time around,
Just as wonderful with both feet on the ground.

It's that second time you hear your love song sung,
Makes you think perhaps that love like youth is wasted on the young.

Love's more comfortable the second time you fall,
Like a friendly home the second time you call.

Who can say what led us to this miracle we found?
There are those who'll bet love comes but once, and yet—
I'm, oh, so glad we met the second time around.

Call Me Irresponsible

Verse:
Seems I'm always making resolutions.
Like ev'ry night for me is New Year's Eve.
Things they chisel on those institutions;
The lofty thoughts I never quite achieve.
Each time I'm taking bows 'cause ev'rything went well
Things go awry, and there am I saying I meant well.

Chorus:
Call me irresponsible,
Call me unreliable,
Throw in undependable too.

Do my foolish alibis bore you?
Well, I'm not too clever.
I just adore you.

Call me unpredictable,
Tell me I'm impractical,
Rainbows I'm inclined to pursue.

Call me irresponsible,
Yes, I'm unreliable,
But it's undeniably true,
I'm irresponsibly mad for you!

(Chicago Is)
My Kind of Town

Verse:
Don't ever, ever ask me what Chicago is,
Unless you've got an hour or two or three.
'Cause I need time to tell you what Chicago is,
All the things Chicago is to me.
Gee! It's—

Chorus:
My kind of town, Chicago is
My kind of town, Chicago is

My kind of people, too,
People who smile at you
And each time I roam,
Chicago is calling me home,

Chicago is one town that won't let you down,
It's my kind of town!

The Wrigley Building, Chicago is—
The Windy City, Chicago is—
The Union Stockyards, Chicago is—
Comiskey Ballpark, Chicago is—
One town that won't let you down,
It's my kind of town!

Thoroughly Modern Millie

Verse:
There are those, I suppose
Think we're mad—heaven knows
The world has gone to rack and to ruin,
What we think is chic, unique, and quite adorable
They think is odd, and Sodom and Gomorrable—but the fact is

Chorus:
Everything today is thoroughly modern
(Check your personality)
Everything today makes yesterday slow
(Better face reality)

It's not insanity, says *Vanity Fair*
In fact it's stylish to raise your skirts
And bob your hair—

In a rumble seat the world is so cozy
(If the boy is kissable)
And that tango dance they wouldn't allow
(Now is quite permissible)

Good-bye, good goody girl,
I'm changing and how,
So beat the drums 'cause here comes
Thoroughly modern Millie now!

Lyrics

I've Heard That Song Before

Verse:
Music helps me to remember,
It helps remind me of things behind me.
Though I'm better off forgetting,
I try in vain each time I hear that strain:

Chorus:
It seems to me I've heard that song before;
It's from an old familiar score,
I know it well, that melody,
It's funny how a theme recalls a favorite dream,
A dream that brought you so close to me.

I know each word because I've heard that song before,
The lyric said "Forever more."
Forevermore's a memory.
Please let them play it again,
And I'll remember when I heard that song before.

Songography

1933	*"Bei Mir Bist Du Schön"*
1933	"Shake Your Head From Side to Side"
1935	"Rhythm In My Nursery Rhymes"
1935	"Rhythm Is Our Business"
1936	"Until The Real Thing Comes Along"
1936	"Shoe Shine Boy"
1938	"Please Be Kind"
1939	"You're A Lucky Guy"
1942	"I've Heard That Song Before"
1943	"Vict'ry Polka"
1944	"As Long As There's Music"
1944	"The Charm of You"
1944	"Come Out, Come Out, Wherever You Are"
1944	"Guess I'll Hang My Tears Out To Dry"
1944	"I Fall In Love Too Easily"
1944	"I Should Care"
1944	"I'll Walk Alone"
1944	"Poor Little Rhode Island"
1944	"Saturday Night Is the Loneliest Night In the Week"
1944	"Some Other Time"
1944	"There Goes That Song Again"
1944	"What Makes the Sunset?"

1945	"Day By Day"
1945	"I'm Glad I Waited For You"
1945	"It's Been A Long, Long Time"
1945	"Let It Snow! Let It Snow! Let It Snow!"
1946	"Five Minutes More"
1946	"The Things We Did Last Summer"
1947	"Can't You Just See Yourself"
1947	"I Believe"
1947	"Papa, Won't You Dance With Me?"
1947	"Time After Time"
1947	"You're My Girl"
1948	"It's Magic"
1948	"It's You Or No One"
1948	"Put 'Em In A Box, Tie 'Em With A Ribbon"
1949	"Be My Love"
1950	"Wonder Why"
1951	"Second Star To The Right"
1952	"Because You're Mine"
1952	"Good Little Girls Go To Heaven"
1953	"Face To Face"
1953	"Teach Me Tonight"
1954	"Autumn In Rome"
1954	"The Christmas Waltz"
1954	"I'll Never Stop Loving You"
1954	"Three Coins In The Fountain"
1955	"The Impatient Years"
1955	"Look To Your Heart"
1955	"Love And Marriage"
1955	"The Tender Trap"
1956	"Hey! Jealous Lover"
1957	"All The Way"
1957	"I Still Get Jealous"
1958	"Come Fly With Me"
1958	"It's Nice To Go Trav'ling"

1958	"Only The Lonely"
1958	"To Love And Be Loved"
1958	"All My Tomorrows"
1959	"The Best of Everything"
1959	"Come Dance With Me"
1959	"High Hopes"
1959	"The Last Dance"
1959	"Pocket Full of Miracles"
1960	"The Second Time Around"
1962	"Call Me Irresponsible"
1962	"Walking Happy"
1964	"My Kind of Town"
1964	"Where Love Has Gone"
1965	"Everybody Has The Right To Be Wrong"
1965	"I'll Only Miss Her When I Think Of Her"
1965	"Opposites"
1967	"Thoroughly Modern Millie"
1973	"All That Love Went To Waste"
1973	"Let Me Try Again"
1973	"Touch of Class"

Index

Abbott, George, 116, 157
Academy Awards. *See* Awards
Ace, Goodman, 43
Adams, Shirlee, 208
Adams, Stanley, 214
Adler, Polly, 123, 160
Agnew, Spiro, 145
Akst, Harry, 86
"All the Way" (song), 25, 134, 138
Alton, Robert, 173
Anchors Aweigh (film), 134, 147
Andrews Sisters, 65–66
Anka, Paul, 213, 226–228, 235
Apollo Theater, 63–64
April in Paris (film), 192
Armstrong, Louis, 223–224
Asnas, Max, 205
Astaire, Fred, 235–238
Awards,
    Academy
        "All the Way," 138
        "Call Me Irresponsible," 167, 241–242
        "High Hopes," 188
        "Love and Marriage," 138
        "Three Coins in the Fountain," 53, 146, 175
    Emmy, 157
    Gold Records, 169
    Henry Street Settlement "Man of the Year," 146, 213
Axler, Joseph, 13
Axler, Mel, 13

Babcock, Edward Chester. *See* Van Heusen, Jimmy
Barrie, George, 258–259
Barton, Ben, 119
Barton, Eileen, 119
Barton, James, 261
Barnes, Clive, 267, 269
Basile, Andrea, 14
Basile, Frances, 14

Basile, Salvatore, 29
Basile, Tita. *See* Cahn, Tita
Bayer, Irma, 14
Bayer, Justine, 14
"Be My Love" (Song), 225
Beatty, Warren, 214
Beckman, Al, 55
Beckman and Pransky, 55–56
"Bei Mir Bist Du Schön" (song), 23, 63–71, 97, 200
Benny, Jack, 152, 213
Berkeley, Busby, 104, 105, 106, 109
Berle, Milton, 25, 111, 182
Bernardi, Herschel, 182
Bernstein, Mrs. Sam, 14, 21, 22
Beruh, Joe, 217
Blank's, Shimele (music store), 65
Blau, Victor, 51
Bloomingdale, Al, 114
Boesky, Ivan, 13
Boesky, Seema, 13
Bogart, Humphrey, 182
Bolger, Ray, 192
Bolton, Guy, 103
Booth, Shirley, 217
Boston Opera House, 115
Brewster, Pat, 10
Brigant Hotel (Atlantic City), 28
Brodszky, Nicholas, 153, 224–225
Brut Productions, 259
Burke, Johnny, 150, 151, 160
Buttons, Red, 213
Buzzell, Eddie, 76–77

Cahn and Chaplin, 37
Cahn, Gloria, 120–123, 181–190
Cahn, Laurie, 124, 159, 181, 184, 242
Cahn, Steven, 123, 181, 184, 201
Cahn, Tita, 13, 14, 220–221, 267–268, 270
Caldwell, Helen Lee, 14
"Call Me Irresponsible" (song), 138, 167, 236–242

Campbell, Flo, 37
Capitol Records, 176
Capra, Frank, 157
Carson, Jack, 101
Carson, Johnny, 213
Cerf, Bennett, 146
Chaplin, Saul (Kaplan), 32, 34, 36–37, 52–53, 70, 73–74
    "I'm a Musical Magical Man," 48, 50–51
    "Please Be Kind," 46–47, 49
    "Rhythm Is Our Business," 35, 43
    Rookies on Parade, 52
"Christmas Waltz, The" (song), 138–139
Coe, Fred, 154
Cohen, Abraham, 18, 21, 22, 23, 32, 33, 113–114
Cohen, Mrs. Abraham (Elka), 21–22, 23, 29, 32, 34, 113
Cohen, Albert J., 52
Cohen, Alexander H., 13, 263–265
Cohen, Evelyn. *See* Greenberg, Mrs. Abe
Cohen, Florence. *See* Goldberg, Mrs. Jules
Cohen, Pearl. *See* Zodi, Mrs. Joe
Cohen, Sadye. *See* Bernstein, Mrs. Sam
Cohen's (restaurant), 22
Cohn, Harry, 73, 76–91
Cohn, Joan Perry, 80, 82, 90
Columbia Pictures Corporation, 10, 73–81, 88–89, 170
Coming of Age (show), 262–263
Cowan, Josette, 13
Cowan, Warren, 13
Crane, Harry, 100
Crawford Music Company, 81
Crosby, Bing, 167
Crosby, Bob, 52
Curtis, Tita. *See* Cahn, Tita
Curtiz, Michael, 98–100

Davis, Eddie (actor), 104–105, 108
Davis, Eddie (playwright), 105, 115
Davis, Sammy, Jr., 217–218
Day (and Night) in the Life of Harry Cohn, A, 82–88
"Day by Day" (song), 172
Day, Doris, 10, 99–101, 192–195, 197
Dean, Barney, 160, 167
De Castro Sisters, 176
Decca Records, 10, 35, 43–44, 65, 176
Delson, Abner, 120–122
Delson, Audrey, 121, 124–127
Delson, Gloria. *See* Cahn, Gloria
Delson, Sydelle, 120–122
de Paul, Gene, 176–177

Dorsey, Jimmy, 130
Dorsey, Tommy, 64–65, 129–131, 172
Douglas, Anne, 210
Douglas, Kirk, 210
Dreyfus, Benoit, 13, 14, 221
Duke, Vernon, 192–193
Dukelsky, Vladimir. *See* Duke, Vernon

Ellis, Seger, 43–44
Emmy Award, 157
Entratter, Jack, 227
Ephron, Henry, 235
Ephron Phoebe, 235
Epstein, Dasha, 13
Epstein, Henry, 13
Epstein, Julius J., 98
Epstein, Philip G., 98
Evans Hotel (Catskills), 37, 43, 55
"Ev'rybody Has the Right to be Wrong at Least Once" (song), 179

Fabergé-Brut, 257–259
Fabray, Nanette, 203–204
Feld, Irving, 227–228
Feuer, Cy, 74, 178
Fine, Donald, 10
"Fine Romance, A" (song), 270–271
Fisher Theatre (Detroit), 178
Fitzgerald, Ella, 44–45
"Five Minutes More" (song), 97
Fonda, Henry, 208
Forbstein, Leo, 49
Forrest, Helen, 76
Foy, Eddie, Jr., 111, 113, 115
Freeman, Al, Jr., 217–218
Friars Club, 260, 270
Friedman, Harry, 76, 88, 90

Gaiety Burlesque (theater), 56
Gaiety Music Shop, 70
Gannon, Kim, 75
Gardner, Ava, 95, 250
Garfield, Sid, 262
Garland, Judy, 83, 99, 100, 182
Gehman, Richard, 29
Giannini, A. P., 182
Glad to See Ya! (show), 103–117
Gleason, Jackie, 167
Goldberg, Jules, 23
Goldberg, Mrs. Jules, 14, 21
Golden Theatre, 9, 14, 146, 260, 265
Goldman, Mack, 46–47, 200, 243, 246
Goldwyn, Mrs. Frances, 90

Goldwyn, Samuel, 90, 195
Gordon, Bert, 37
Gordon, Mack, 225
Gormé, Eydie, 213
Gottlieb, Alex, 98
Gould, Mrs. Harry, 13
Grable, Betty, 248–249
Granat, Harvey, 14, 263
Gray, Glen, 130, 170
Greenberg, Mrs. Abe, 14, 21
Griffith, Robert, 154, 157
"Growing Up" (song), 263

"Haute Couture" (song), 179
Harris, Julie, 178–179
Hale, Mrs. Prentis Cobb. *See* Minnelli, Denise
Harvey, Laurence, 90
Hawks, Dee, 212, 214–216
Heindorf, Ray, 10
Henry Street Settlement, 146, 213
Hitson, Harry & Co., 13, 14
High Buttons Shoes (show), 117, 123, 124, 203–205
"High Hopes" (song), 138, 187–188
Hole in the Head (film), 188
Howard, Cy, 114–115
Hughes, Howard, 98
Hunter, Ross, 168
Hutton, Betty, 99–101
Hutton, Marion, 99, 101

"I Bring You Religion on a Mule" (song), 224
"I Should Care" (song), 171–172
"I, Yes, Me! That's Who!" (song), 218
"If You Should Leave" (song), 44–45
"I'll Walk Alone" (song), 97
"I'm a Musical Magical Man" (song), 48, 50–51
Immerman, Connie, 223–224
"Impatient Years, The" (song), 155
"It's Been a Long, Long Time" (song), 97–98
"It's Magic" (song), 101
Iturbi, José, 83, 85
"I've Heard that Song Before" (song), 74, 80, 90, 98, 132, 171

Jacobs, Jacob, 69, 70–71
Jaffee, Henry, 155
James, Harry, 75
Javits, Jacob, 213
Jolson, Al, 83
Jones, Jack, 241

Journey Back to Oz (film), 182
Joy, Georgie, 35
Judd and Brown (publishers), 33

Kahn, Gus, 36
Kahn, Mike, 23
Kalmus, Bea, 202
Kammen, J. and J., 68–71
Kanin, Garson, 59–61
Kaplan, Saul. *See* Chaplin, Saul
Kapp, Dave, 65
Kapp, Jack, 10, 43–44, 65–66
Katz, Benny, 70
Kaye, Danny, 90
Kelly, Gene, 83
Kelly, Tom, 95
Kennedy, John F., 187–189
Kennedy, Robert F., 213
Kennedy, Rose, 145
The Kid from Brooklyn (film), 90
Kilgallen, Dorothy, 179
Kingston, Al, 52, 73
Kipness, Joe, 123
Kirk, Andy, 44, 130
Knight, June, 104, 110
Koch, Howard, 140
Koster, Henry, 173
Krell, Sis, 255, 258
Krell, Stan, 255–256, 257
Kronfeld, Cye, 200–203
Kyser, Kay, 88

Lahr, Bert, 111
Lansbury, Edgar, 217
Lanza, Mario, 153, 225
Lawford, Pat, 145
Lawrence, Steve, 213
Leeds Music Publishing Company, 33
Leon and Eddie's (night club), 104
Leonard, Jack E., 182
Leonard, Richard, 265
"Let Me Try Again" (song), 228
Lettermen, The, 172
Levin, Vicki, 219–220
Levine, Dick, 217
Levy, Alfred, 99, 100
Levy, Lou, 22, 23, 24, 32–34, 63–67
Lewis, Ted, 49–51
Liebman, Max, 204
Lilly, Doris, 123
Linkletter, Art, 182
Loesser, Frank, 96
Loew's Delancey (theater), 25
Logan, Josh, 217–218

Longstreet, Stephen, 203
Look to the Lilies (show), 177, 217–219
"Love and Marriage" (song), 138, 152–153
Luft, Sid, 182
Lunceford, Jimmy, 35, 44, 130
Lynde, Paul, 182

McCauley, John, 111
McGuire, Don, 100
Mack, Austin, 46
Mack, Roy, 46, 48
"Man of the Year." *See* Awards
Mann, Delbert, 154, 156
Mansfield, Irving, 13
Marchiz, Duke, 124, 127
Martin, Dean, 176
Martin, Ernest H., 74, 178
Marx, Groucho, 213
Maximus Music Company, 263
Mayer, Louis B., 60
Mayo, Virginia, 90
Merman, Ethel, 182
Merrick, David, 195
Meth, Max, 108–109
Metro-Goldwyn-Mayer, 51–52, 60, 134, 170, 235
Meyerson, Harry, 120
Miggs, Frankie, 16–17, 28, 29
Migliano, Frankie. *See* Miggs, Frankie
Military, Frank, 263
Mills Brothers, 44
Mills, Irving, 35
Minnelli, Denise, 209–210
Minnelli, Liza, 182
Minnelli, Vincente, 209
Minsky, Harold, 56
Monroe, Marilyn, 173, 241
Morganstern, Jay, 263
Morris and Campbell, 37
Morris, Joe, 37–43
Morris Music Company, Edwin H., 97–98
Music Corporation of America (MCA), 33, 76, 134
Music Publishers' Holding Corporation (MPHC), 45
"My Kind of Town" (song), 158

National Broadcasting Company, 154, 204
Neidorf, Mike, 170
Newman, Lionel, 174–175, 241
Newman, Paul, 155
Norvo, Red, 130

Oakie, Jack, 111
O'Kun, Lan, 263
Osterman, Jackie, 261–262
Our Town (show), 152–153

Pals of Harmony, 28, 29, 30, 36, 37
"Papa, Won't You Dance With Me" (song), 204
Papa's Delicate Condition (show), 235–240
Paramount Pictures, 235
Pasternak, Joe, 224
Peltz, Bobby, 13
Peltz, Lauren, 13
Phil Spitalny All Girl Orchestra, 96
Piantadosi, Arthur, 34–35
Pickman, Milton, 49, 50, 51
Pine, Arthur, 9
Pink Tights (show), 173, 175
"Please Be Kind" (song), 46–47, 49
"Pocketful of Miracles" (song), 157, 158–159
Pransky, Johnny, 56
Price, George, 48
Prince, Harold, 157
Prince, Mrs. Harold, 43
Proser, Monte, 123

Quinn, Anthony, 100

Rackin, Martin, 238–239, 240
Rackmil, Milton, 44
Radio Aces, 49
Ragland, Rags, 56, 58, 83
Rat Pack, The (book), 29
Raye, Martha, 123
Remick Music Company, 160
Republic Pictures, 52, 96
Reynolds, Debbie, 47–48
"Rhythm Is Our Business" (song), 35, 36, 43, 59
Riddle, Nelson, 156
Riss, Alice. *See* Cohen, Mrs. Abraham
RKO, 60, 98
RKO 28th Street (theater), 25
Robin and the Seven Hoods (film), 139, 158
Robin, Leo, 99
Rockwell, Tom, 44
Rockwell-O'Keefe Agency, 43–44, 170
Romance on the High Seas (film), 10, 98–99, 101
Rookies on Parade (film), 52
Rose, Jack, 239
Rosselli, John, 13, 14
Rush, Barbara, 139

Sacks, Emanuel, 204
Saint, Eva Marie, 155
Sandler and Young, 46
Sanicola, Hank, 100, 119, 141
Santly-Joy Music Company, 35
Saphier, Jimmy, 99
Sardi's (restaurant), 269
Sarnoff, David, 204
Sarnoff, Robert, 213
Sax, Sam, 45
Say One for Me (film), 47
Schary, Dore, 235
Schwartz, Ethel, 43, 52–53
Schwartz, Stephen, 158
Secunda, Sholem, 69, 70–71
Seward Park Junior High, 24
"Shake Your Head from Side to Side" (song), 33, 34
Shaw, Artie, 243–253
Shaw, David, 155
Shelley, David, 111
"Shoe Shine Boy" (song), 49, 224
Shubert Theatre (Philadelphia), 106, 110
Siegel, Sol C., 173, 174, 175
Silberstein, Ben, 13
Silvers, Harry, 79–80
Silvers, Phil, 9, 37–43, 52, 83–87, 103–104, 203–204, 248–249
Sinatra, Frank, 83, 95, 119, 129–134, 138–147, 153–156, 174–175, 187–189, 250
Sinatra, Nancy, 119, 221
Skyscraper (show), 177, 178
Small, Lillian Schary, 134, 138, 235
Star! (film), 52
Starr, Herman, 45, 48
Stein, Julius. *See* Styne, Jule
Stoloff, Elsa, 10, 73, 74, 76, 89
Stoloff, Morris, 10, 52, 73, 74, 76, 89
Stone, Peter, 178
Stordahl, Axel, 43, 86, 95, 123, 131, 171
Styne, Ethel, 96
Styne, Jule, 9, 79, 80–84, 88–90, 95–97, 121, 177
  "Christmas Waltz, The," 138–139
  "Five Minutes More," 97
  Glad to See Ya!, 103–117
  High Button Shoes, 123–124, 177, 203–204
  "I'll Walk Alone," 97
  "It's Been a Long, Long Time," 97–98
  "It's Magic," 101
  "I've Heard That Song Before," 74–75, 90, 132
  Look to the Lilies, 177, 217
  Pink Tights, 173, 175

Romance on the High Seas, 98–101
  "Three Coins in the Fountain," 173–175
  Two Tickets to Broadway, 98
Styne, Norton, 96
Styne, Stanley, 96, 100
Southern, Georgia, 59
Spigelglass, Leonard, 217
Spitzer, Henry, 98
Spivak, Charlie, 46
Sullivan, Barry, 100
Susann, Jacqueline, 13–14
Swooners, The, 100

Tallmer, Jerry, 10
Tananbaum, Marty, 184
Taps, Jonie, 81–82
"Teach Me Tonight" (song), 176
Tebet, Dave, 198, 203–204, 214
"Tender Trap, The" (song), 149–152
Tharpe, Sister Rebecca, 224
Thomas, Danny, 182
Thompson, Bill, 105
"Thoroughly Modern Millie" (song), 168–169, 256
"Three Coins in the Fountain" (song), 25, 146, 173–175
Three Sailors and a Girl (film), 194
Time magazine, 97
Tom, Dick, and Harry (film), 60–61
"Touch of Class" (song), 258–259
Tracy, Spencer, 201
Traubner, Edward, 14, 29, 30–32, 61–62, 97, 116, 176, 185, 264, 265
Trilling, Steve, 195
Turner, Lana, 249–250
Twentieth-Century Fox, 96, 173, 175
Two Tickets to Broadway (film), 98

Uchitel, Morris, 10, 13, 14, 214
Uchitel, Pat, 10, 13, 214
Ungehauer, Stanley, 27–28
United Dressed Beef Corporation, 22, 26–28, 31

Van Heusen, Jimmy, 140, 159–160, 167–168, 170, 241–242
  "All the Way," 134, 138
  "Call Me Irresponsible," 235–240
  "Christmas Waltz, The," 138–139
  "Haute Couture," 179
  "High Hopes," 187
  Our Town, 152–157

Papa's Delicate Condition, 235–240
"Pocketful of Miracles," 157–159
Skyscraper, 177
Star!, 52
"Tender Trap", 149–152
"Thoroughly Modern Millie," 168–169, 256
Walking Happy, 177, 237–238
Velez, Lupe, 104
Vitaphone Studios, 45, 48

Walking Happy (show), 177, 237–238
Waller, Fats, 224
Walters, Charles, 152
Warner Brothers, 10, 45, 49, 98, 153, 193, 194
Warner Brothers Music Company, 70
Warner, Jack, 98, 194–195
Wasserman, Lew, 134
Weinberger, Andy, 251–252
Weiss, Sam, 75, 98

Weitman, Robert, 170
Weston, Paul, 171
Wilde, Cornell, 85
Wilder, Billy, 209
Wilder, Thornton, 154–155, 156, 157
Williams, William B., 176
Withers, Jane, 104
Wolper, David, 103, 264–265
Words and Music (show), 9, 13, 14, 146, 260–271
Wyman, Gene, 189–190

YM-YWHA, 262–264
Young, Ralph, 46

Zanuck, Darryl, 174, 225–226
Zodi, Mrs. Joe, 14, 21
Zwerling, Ruby, 25